NATIVE TITLE

SECRECY BREEDS CORRUPTION

"Think for yourself."
prentice hall

CONFLICTS OR INTEREST
BREED CORRUPTION
ANYTHING THAT CLOUDS PROPER

Prentice Hall's *Basic Ethics in Action* series in normative and applied ethics is a major new undertaking edited by Michael Boylan, Professor of Philosophy at Marymount University. The series includes both wide-ranging anthologies as well as brief texts that focus on a particular theme or topic within one of four areas of applied ethics. These areas include Business Ethics, Environmental Ethics, Medical Ethics, and Social and Political Philosophy.

EXERCISE
OR
JUDGMENT

AVOIDANCE
DISCLOSURE

Anchor volume
Michael Boylan, *Basic Ethics*, 2000

Business Ethics

Michael Boylan, ed., *Business Ethics*, 2001

James Donahue, *Ethics for the Professionals*, forthcoming

Dale Jacquette, *Journalistic Ethics*, forthcoming

Murphy, Laczniak, Bowie and Klein, *Ethical Marketing*, 2005

Edward Spence, *Advertising Ethics*, 2005

Environmental Ethics

Michael Boylan, ed., *Environmental Ethics*, 2001

J. Baird Callicott and Michael Nelson, *American Indian Environmental Ethics: An Ojibwa Case Study*, 2004

Lisa H. Newton, *Ethics and Sustainability*, 2003

Mary Anne Warren, *Ethics and Animals*, forthcoming

Medical Ethics

Michael Boylan, ed., *Medical Ethics*, 2000

Michael Boylan and Kevin Brown, *Genetic Engineering*, 2002

Rosemarie Tong, *New Perspectives in Healthcare Ethics*, 2003

Social and Political Philosophy

R. Paul Churchill, *Human Rights and Global Diversity*, forthcoming

Seumas Miller, Peter Roberts, and Edward Spence, *Corruption and Anti-Corruption: An Applied Philosophical Approach*, 2005

Deryck Beyleveld, *Informed Consent*, forthcoming

" TRUTH " NOT IN
THE IN

D1564327

Please contact Michael Boylan (michael.boylan@.
Hall's Philosophy & Religion Editor to propose authoring a title for this series!

MORAL RIGHTS: LIFE, LIBERTY, PROPERTY

CATEGORICAL IMPERATIVE —
   ACT IN CONSONANCE w/ UNIVERSAL LAW

CORRUPTION
   SELF GAIN
   ABROGATION OF DUTIES
   CORRUPT CULTURES (EG LOYALTY)

FIVE LEVELS OF HARM
   1. SELF
   2. FAMILY
   3. PROFESSION
   4. ORGANIZATION (2)
   5. SOCIETY

RATIONALIZATIONS
   1. NOBLE CAUSE
   2. TRANSCULTURAL

GRAND SYSTEMIC
   CORPORATIONS
   GOVTS
   RELIGION
   CRIME

CORRUPTION
INCOMPETENCE
BAD BUSINESS JUDGEMENT

MUST RETHINK
GOVERNANCE
TOP TO BOTTOM
   — MECHANISMS
   — PRACTICES
   — REGULATIONS
   — ETHICS
   — OBLIGATIONS
   — ENDS

Corruption and Anti-Corruption

An Applied Philosophical Approach

SEUMAS MILLER,
PETER ROBERTS
and
EDWARD SPENCE

Centre for Applied Philosophy and
Public Ethics, Charles Sturt University and
the Australian National University

PEARSON
Prentice
Hall

Upper Saddle River, New Jersey 07458

[Handwritten annotations:]

ETHICS PAYS IN ULTIMATE WELL-BEING OF ALL.

BAD FOR JOB DESIGN WITH LESS TOTAL POWER FOR CEO

JOB DESIGN FOR REGULATORY OVERSIGHT

ORGANIZATIONS MAY HAVE A CULTURE BUT THEY DO NOT HAVE MENTAL OR MORAL STATES — IT IS THE INDIVIDUALS, INDIVIDUALS & COLLECTIVELY WHO HOLD THE MORAL AUTHORITY & RESPONS.

EMPOWER ALL EMPLOYEES IN ORDER TO ACHIEVE COLLECTIVE RESP.

Handwritten annotations (top):

PREVENTIVE (PROACTIVE)
1. PROMOTING ETHICAL BEHAVIOR
2. CORPORATE GOVERNANCE PROCEDURES
3. TRANSPARENCY

Library of Congress Cataloging-in-Publication Data

Miller, Seumas.
    Corruption and anti-corruption : an applied philosophical approach / Seumas Miller, Edward Spence, Peter Roberts.
      p. cm. — (Basic ethics in action)
    Includes bibliographical references and index.
    ISBN 0-13-061795-4
    1. Ethical problems. 2. Corruption. 3. Moral conditions. 4. Justice. 5. Applied ethics.
I. Spence, Edward, 1949– II. Roberts, Peter, 1947– III. Title. IV. Series.
BJ1031.M55 2005
174'.4—dc22
                                        2004002505

Handwritten annotations (middle):

CODIFICATION OF MORAL CODE

RELATIVISM PASSIVE
1. LINEAR
2. SECRECY MAKES HARD
3. INVESTIGATIONS POORLY RESOURCED
4. GLOBALIZATION & ICT EXPAND OPTIONS
COMPLEX & RAPIDLY CHANGING

VP, Editorial Director: Charlyce Jones-Owens
Senior Acquisitions Editor: Ross Miller
Assistant Editor: Wendy Yurash
Editorial Assistant: Carla Worner
Director of Marketing: Beth Mejia
Marketing Manager: Kara Kindstrom
Marketing Assistant: Jennifer Lang
Production Liaison: Fran Russello
Manufacturing Buyer: Christina Helder
Cover Design: Bruce Kenselaar
Project Management: Karen Berry/Pine Tree Composition, Inc.
Composition: Interactive Composition Corporation
Printer/Binder: Courier Companies, Inc.
Cover Printer: Coral Graphics

Copyright © 2005 by Pearson Education, Inc., Upper Saddle River, New Jersey 07458.
Pearson Prentice Hall. All rights reserved. Printed in the United States of America.
This publication is protected by Copyright and permission should be obtained from the
publisher prior to any prohibited reproduction, storage in a retrieval system, or transmission
in any form or by any means, electronic, mechanical, photocopying, recording, or likewise.
For information regarding permission(s), write to: Rights and Permissions Department.

Pearson Prentice Hall™ is a trademark of Pearson Education, Inc.
Pearson® is a registered trademark of Pearson plc
Prentice Hall® is a registered trademark of Pearson Education, Inc.

Pearson Education LTD., London
Pearson Education Australia PTY, Limited
Pearson Education Singapore, Pte. Ltd
Pearson Education North Asia Ltd
Pearson Education Canada, Ltd

Pearson Educación de Mexico, S.A. de C.V.
Pearson Education–Japan
Pearson Education Malaysia, Pte. Ltd
Pearson Education, Upper Saddle River, NJ

10 9 8 7 6 5 4 3 2 1
ISBN 0-13-061795-4

Contents

ANTI-CORRUPTION ORGANIZATIONS
NEEDS CODE
LIST OF INFRACTIONS & PUNISH.

THE OPPOSITE OR INTEGRITY
IS DEVIANCE.

MUST BE ABLE TO
TRACK & UNDERSTAND
COMPLEX TRANSACTIONS
IN GLOBAL ELECTRONIC
SYSTEM

WHISTLEBLOWING
DEFINED

(1) INTERNAL MEMBER
(2) NON-TRIVIAL WRONGS
(3) GOES PUBLIC
(4) RISKING REPRISAL

CULTURE OF ETHICAL
RESISTANCE
VITAL THAT ALL UNDERSTAND
HOW TO REPORT WRONGS

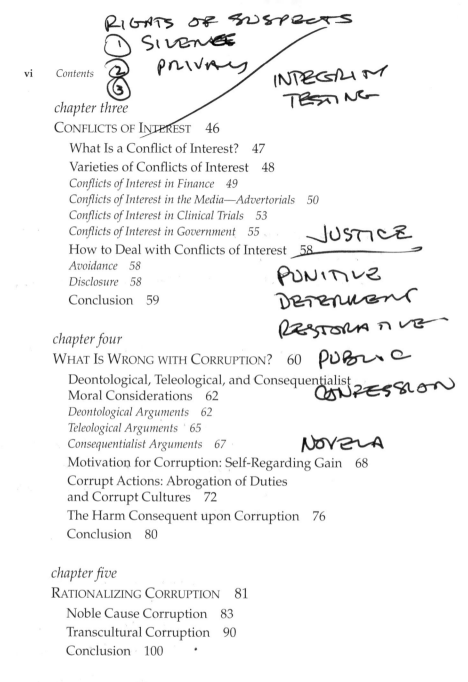

chapter three

CONFLICTS OF INTEREST   46

chapter four

WHAT IS WRONG WITH CORRUPTION?   60

chapter five

RATIONALIZING CORRUPTION   81

chapter six

CORPORATE CORRUPTION AND COLLECTIVE
MORAL RESPONSIBILITY   101

Foreword

This welcome book makes a signal contribution to the corruption (and anti-corruption) literature. As such, it will undoubtedly greatly strengthen the determination and focus of those throughout the globe who are confronting corruption on a daily basis and who are working for change—nongovernmental organizations no less than those in the public and the private sectors. Written in a straightforward and readable style, it addresses a general audience, and is the more powerful for its absence of intellectual conceit.

The ethics approach adopted here demonstrates what too many economists and others have been overly slow to realize. Certainly, institutions need to be right-sized and well designed, and laws, rules, and practices need to be clear and well-thought-out. But any attempt to counter corruption that simply takes a stick to the problem—or even a stick and a carrot—will not get anyone very far unless the approach also carries with it a strong emphasis on people, their personal ethics, and the ethics of the places where they work.

The three authors lead us through a series of illuminating case studies, approaching everything from a position of applied philosophy—from what is wrong with corruption per se, whistleblowers, and the ethical responsibility of corporate bodies to the rights of the accused, effective forms of punishment, and "noble cause corruption." By so doing, we come to see salient aspects of corruption and anti-corruption through the lens of the ethicist, so enriching our understanding even as it challenges some of our instinctive assumptions.

To start with, the authors demolish the ad hoc working definitions of corruption used by the World Bank and others. Corruption, they argue persuasively, is not limited to "the abuse of entrusted power for private benefit"—a restricted definition that led some to claim that there was "no corruption" in the Enron affair because no "bribes" had been paid. The authors make out the case for a "moral" approach to the struggle against corruption, and in doing so challenge those efforts being made today that are based solely on appeals to self-interest.

As the analysis shows, our understanding of corruption has suffered as a result of being captured by economists and from their obsession with transactions—"It takes two to tango. . . ." Yet, in reality, as the authors demonstrate, even a single parent can treat his or her child "corruptly" when, as a parent, he or she directs the child to provide sexual favors to businessmen for money. Developing coherent understandings of corruption is very much more than debates about economics, transactions, and the equations that economists develop in their attempts to capture the phenomenon. Using the "parent" analogy, we are led to understand that there is no need for more than one person to be involved for an action to be characterised as being "corrupt," nor is there any need for benefits to flow. Remove these elements and most of the equations of the economists are confounded.

Nonetheless, as a matter of practicality if not of applied philosophy, the limited "definition" has proved to be a useful way in which the reform-minded can map out the ground for a battle against corruption that does not at the same time dissipate energy and resources by tilting at every windmill in a highly imperfect world.

At the same time, however, many of these reformers have been discomfitted by the knowledge that the great bulk of people see corruption as being something much more than just bribery, nepotism, and abuse of official decision-making powers. They see it as a highly immoral activity. This is not to say that all forms of immoral activity are forms of corruption; far from it. Genocide, for example, is a profound moral wrong; but it is not corruption per se. Nevertheless, the notion of corruption is wider than has often been recognised. For example, many view the abuse by industrialized countries of their diplomatic, economic, and military power as prime examples of the corruption of international discourse, and yet their actions, too, would fall outside the working definition of the World Bank. Given this, the authors would no doubt wish to question President George W. Bush as to just who and what he had in mind when on January 12, 2004, he issued a proclamation banning the entry into the United States of all those involved in "corruption," but only to prevent entry into the country of people who have committed, participated in, or benefitted from corruption conducted while performing public functions.

The analysis of <u>a hierarchy of rights</u>, and of conflicting moral obligations, also demonstrates the vacuous nature of many claims that there can be
"good" corruption; the classic instance, often quoted in the corruption literature, being that of the person who bribes a Nazi guard in order to escape from
a concentration camp. Quite apart from the fact that the Nazi regime had no
morally-legitimate basis for its existence (its institutions were beyond re-
demption and were incapable of being corrupted further), any purported
"duty" not to bribe an official of such a morally-bankrupt regime would
clearly be overridden by the claim to be defending the inalienable right to life.

Similarly, it may have been a corrupt act for General Franco to accept
the tempting sums tendered by Churchill to keep Spain out of the 1939–45
War. But could anyone suggest that the British Prime Minister was "corrupt"
in effectively limiting the scope of the war in this way? Or that payment
reportedly made to Iraqi officers to induce them not to fight in the second
(2003) Gulf War were "bribes" when the effect was undoubtedly to save
many lives on both sides—not to mention those of civilians (leaving aside the
ethics of the attack on the country itself)?

The "applied philosophy" approach also helps us deal with other worry-
ing features of the anti-corruption agenda. For example, the case of the parent
who "bribes" a teacher in order to have his or her child taught in school. The
child has a right to an education that is recognized internationally. The parent
has a moral duty towards the child. Provided the payment is not of a nature
that impinges on the rights of other children to be taught (e.g., gives the
parent's child an unjustified preference over another child to that other child's
detriment), the transaction can only be described as involving a corrupt
teacher—not a corrupt transaction between two consenting parties. A lawyer
would characterize it as extortion. Viewed in this way, the villain of the piece
is plainly the teacher not the parent; and there is little, if anything, to be gained
by appealing to the parent to desist. Strategies must be directed at the teacher
and the <u>environment</u> in which the teacher is functioning rather than at
"raising the awareness" of the parent.

Similarly, the "bribe" paid to a voter by a candidate is only a corrupt act
on the part of the voter if he or she allows the payment to influence him or
her in voting in favor of the candidate. In an ideal world, of course, the offer
of a bribe should be a strong disincentive for the voter to cast his or her vote
for a corrupt candidate, even though the voter might feel justified in taking
the money in order to defend his or her right of privacy and to a secret ballot.
The voter is entitled to take the money, provided only that he or she is not
influenced in ways favorable to the bribing candidate.

The discussion of former President Clinton and his initial denials of
improprieties with Monica Lewinsky—and whether these can be justified
in terms of a defense of his right to privacy—is particularly intriguing (even
if it sets aside the question of an arguably corrupt abuse of the relationship
between a senior office-holder and a young intern). On the other hand, the

deliberate charging of inflated airfares to clients by PricewaterhouseCoopers in the United States so that the partners could pocket the benefits of the firm's bulk air travel purchases would clearly fall within the authors' definition of being a corrupt practice (an outrage only revealed after the book had gone to press).

The question of "shame" is highlighted as a key factor in inducing ethical conduct. Indeed, it is how society in general—and individuals in the immediate vicinity—react to corrupt individuals once they are exposed that is potentially the most powerful deterrent of all. However, this is a factor under challenge in a world obsessed with "celebrities," and prepared, for example, to pay substantial "speaking fees" to convicted criminals such as Nick Leeson, in order to hear from the horse's mouth, as it were, how he managed to bankrupt one of the world's oldest established banks. Where is the shame? Press reports on Leeson's return to Britain after serving his jail term in Singapore suggested that although there were moves at his exclusive Surrey golf club to expel him, the motion found insufficient support amongst its members.

It is not so very long ago that a major New York fraudster was reportedly given a party by his victims when he emerged from prison, so desperate were they to show their admiration for him. Here, even the victims of a con man did not demonstrate any sense of outrage towards the person who swindled them. It is beyond the scope of the present undertaking, but a serious examination of societies' schizophrenic view of the corrupt is well overdue.

The text here is rooted largely in the Western democracies, with only occasional references to the developing world and countries in transition. It is no less useful for this, as it demonstrates how the Western democracies progressed to where they are today, and it illustrates the sad reality that the struggle to contain corruption is, quite literally, a never-ending one. Readers in the developing world and in countries in transition will, I am sure, derive significant insights applicable to their own situations, and, in doing so, their abilities to deal with their own problems will be significantly enhanced.

For example, the approach may provide an analytical tool for incoming administrations to deal with the past, where a country, such as Kenya, is attempting to undergo a rapid transition from a corrupt regime to one that is democratically elected and accountable. By looking at the position of public servants working within the flawed ethical environment of a former regime it becomes compelling to justify amnesties for those whose actions cannot be shown to have negatively and significantly impacted on the rights of fellow citizens.

This would not absolve the corrupt judge or the "grand corruption" of senior politicians, as these would fail the "no harm" test. It would, however, absolve the mass of the public servants who were seriously underpaid in the expectation of being able to make up the deficits through extracting small bribes from their "customers."

In short, this is a book that, by examining corruption from the perspective of applied philosophy, helps all those with an interest in understanding a little more deeply one of the worst phenomena of the age in which we live and one which will help to provide answers for some of our most pressing questions.

Jeremy Pope
TIRI (the governance-access-learning network)
London
January, 2004

Preface

This is a book about *corruption*, and also about *anti-corruption*. The first half of the book concerns itself with the nature, causes, and moral implications of corruption, and the second half with the means for combating corruption.

Moreover, this is a study in *applied philosophy*. As such, the book does not restrict itself to one form of corruption, such as economic corruption. Rather, it considers many forms of corruption including ones that are not economic in substance or in motivation. Consider an academic who plagiarizes her colleagues' work in order to become famous, or a sadist who abuses his political authority by mistreating subordinates because he derives pleasure from doing so.

Being an applied philosophical study, the book deals with practical issues, for example, how to combat bribery, but it does so on the assumption that prior philosophical work is required if those practical issues are to be satisfactorily resolved. Thus, we need to understand the nature of noble cause corruption, including its differences from other common or garden forms of corruption, if it is to be satisfactorily treated. Moreover, since it is applied philosophy, there is a need to take into account *empirical* work, for example, on the causes of specific forms of corruption.

Contrary to what is sometimes said and thought, corruption is at bottom a species of moral wrongdoing or of unethical behavior. It is not simply, or necessarily, a species of unlawful activity. Here it is important to stress that law and morality are not the same thing. Therefore, our starting point in this book is that corruption is a species of immorality. In Chapter 1, we provide a *conceptual analysis of corruption,* thus understood. We also offer a number of taxonomies of corruption, for example, organized, systemic, and grand corruption.

In Chapter 2, we consider three general *conditions that are conducive to corruption:* the nature of the moral environment, absence of accountability mechanisms, and lack of transparency. Each of these general conditions has a number of specific forms, for example, the moral environment might be one in which there are great inequalities of power. In this chapter, we also consider a number of different socioeconomic contexts in which corruption might exist. Here we make use of two case studies, one drawn from Colombia during the time of Pablo Escobar, the other from the Enron scandal.

In Chapter 3, we consider a specific condition conducive to corruption, namely, *conflicts of interest.* We explore a variety of different conflicts of interest, for example, the Keating Five in the political arena, and conflicts of interest in the media, the corporate sector, and clinical trials.

Chapter 4 concerns itself with addressing the question "What is wrong with corruption?" We distinguish between what is morally wrong with corruption per se, for example, it undermines a legitimate institutional process, and what might be wrong with the action at the core of a corrupt action, for example, telling a lie (that, say, undermines a judicial process). We also discuss deontological, teleological, and consequentialist arguments against different forms of corruption and do so in the context of some specific case studies, for example, Watergate.

In Chapter 5, we identify a number of different *rationalizations* used to justify corrupt actions, and we analyze two of these in detail, namely rationalizations arising out of noble cause corruption (doing evil for the sake of good) and transcultural interaction. Case studies used include the "Dirty Harry" scenario in policing, and the Lockheed and Bhopal scandals.

The second half of the book comprises Chapters 6 through 10. In Chapter 6, our concern is with the locus of moral responsibility for combating corruption. In order to focus our discussion, we consider corporate corruption in organizational settings. We describe some of the more notable corporate scandals and periods of corporate corruption, and we provide a detailed analysis of the key concept of *collective moral responsibility.* Also, we apply this notion to the modern business corporation.

In Chapter 7, we examine institutional accountability systems in relation to corruption, and specifically anti-corruption systems. We provide discussions of reactive anti-corruption systems, as well as of preventive anti-corruption systems. We argue for what we term *holistic anti-corruption systems.* Our discussion ranges over both the private and the public sector. One particular issue we look at is corruption control in the context of developments in public sector administration.

Chapter 8 concerns itself with a specific anti-corruption issue, namely, *whistleblowing.* We provide an analysis of whistleblowing, including an account of the relationship between whistleblowing and corruption. Also, we discuss some of the features of institutional systems for protecting whistleblowers and handling their complaints. Case studies used here include that of Daniel Ellsberg in the United States and Mal Colston in Australia.

In Chapters 9 and 10, we shift our attention to those who are corrupt or who are suspected of being corrupt.

Chapter 9 concerns itself with the *rights of suspects* in the context of anti-corruption systems, including corruption prevention, investigation of corruption, and prosecution for corruption. The particular rights that we examine in detail are the right to silence, the right to privacy, and the right not to be entrapped. Some of the case studies used here are the Starr investigation of Clinton and Lewinsky, and ABSCAM.

In Chapter 10, we examine the issue of corruption and punishment. We discuss the standard theoretical justifications for punishment, for example, retribution, deterrence, and rehabilitation. We offer a detailed argument in favor of a particular *restorative justice* model, but we emphasize that our model is pluralist in that it has retributive and deterrence dimensions, in addition to its purely restorative justice elements.

The following articles or books authored by Seumas Miller contain earlier versions of material published in this book. Thanks to the editors and publishers involved.

"Corporate Crime, the Excesses of the 1980's and Collective Responsibility" *Australian Journal of Corporate Law* 5 no. 2 1995.

"Corruption and Anti-corruption in the Profession of Policing" *Professional Ethics* 6 nos. 3 & 4 1998.

"Social Norms, Corruption and Transcultural Interaction" *Theoria* 92 1998.

"Restorative Justice: Retribution, Confession and Shame." In *Restorative Justice: From Philosophy to Practice,* edited by H. Strang and J. Braithwaite. Aldershot: Ashgate, 2000.

Social Action: A Teleological Account. Cambridge University Press, 2001.

"Collective Responsibility" *Public Affairs Quarterly* 15 no. 1 2001.

The following article authored by Ed Spence contains an earlier version of material published in this book. Thanks to the editor involved.

"The Ethics of Clinical Trials: To Inform or Not Inform? That is the Questions" *Professional Ethics* 6 nos. 3 & 4 1998.

The authors would like to thank the following reviewers and commentators: Robert Sutherland, Cornell College; Stephen D. Morris, University of South Alabama; Beth Rosenson, University of Florida; Mark Alfino, Gonzaga University; Barbara S. Andrew, William Paterson University of New Jersey; Andrew Alexandra, University of Melbourne; Michael Boylan,

Marymount University; Dean Cocking, Charles Sturt University; Steve Matthews, Charles Sturt University; Barbara Henderson-Smith; and Barbara Nunn, Charles Sturt University. Ed Spence would like to thank the Centre for Applied Philosophy and Public Ethics, Charles Sturt University, and the Practical Ethics Center, University of Montana, for providing congenial research environments during the period in which this book was written. Thanks finally to Ewen Miller for proofreading and for preparing the index.

Seumas Miller
Peter Roberts
Edward Spence
Centre for Applied Philosophy
  and Public Ethics
Charles Sturt University

chapter one

Corruption:
A Conceptual Analysis

In this chapter, we

- Distinguish some of the diverse forms of corruption, for example, economic corruption, political corruption.
- Provide a conceptual analysis of corruption.
- Offer a taxonomy of corruption types, for example, organized corruption, grand corruption.

DIVERSITY OF CORRUPTION

Corruption is exemplified by a diverse array of phenomena. Here are some paradigmatic cases of corruption: A national leader channels public monies into a personal bank account. A political party secures a majority vote by arranging for ballot boxes to be stuffed with false voting papers. A businessperson bribes public officials in order to win lucrative tenders. A crime syndicate launders money through a legitimate business outlet that it controls. A journalist provides unwarranted favorable comment about the banking sector in return for financial rewards from that sector. Another journalist consistently provides unwarranted unfavorable comment about a political party in order to influence the electorate against that party. A police officer fabricates evidence in order to secure convictions. A number of doctors close ranks and refuse to testify against a colleague who they know has been negligent in relation to an unsuccessful surgical operation leading to loss of life. A student provides sexual favors to her teacher in exchange for good grades. An actor provides sexual favors to film directors in exchange for securing acting roles. A respected researcher's success relies on plagiarizing the work of others. A public official in charge of allocating community housing to needy citizens unfairly discriminates against a minority group he despises. A manager promotes only those who ingratiate themselves to her. A sports trainer provides the athletes he trains with banned substances in order to enhance their performance.

This is a long list of quite diverse examples of corruption, and it could easily be extended much further. But let us consider some of the elements of corruption that are here in evidence. Many of the examples involve unlawful activities. But some do not, and many of the examples are not necessarily unlawful. It might not be unlawful for consenting adults who happen to be (respectively) an actor and a film director to have sex. It might not be unlawful for a journalist to consistently provide unwarranted unfavorable comment about a political party. Nor was it unlawful for the Sydney-based talkback radio host and commentator John Laws to receive cash for comment. In 1999, Laws and some Australian bankers struck a deal whereby he was to be paid to refrain from pejorative criticism of the banking sector. Indeed, prior to 1977, it was not unlawful for U.S. companies to offer bribes to secure foreign contracts. So corruption is not necessarily unlawful. That is the case because corruption is not at bottom simply a matter of law. Rather, it is fundamentally a matter of morality; and law and morality are not the same thing, although they are intertwined in various ways.

In claiming that corruption is fundamentally a matter of morality, we are making an objective claim, a claim in relation to which we can provide justificatory reasons. We are not simply expressing some emotional state or indulging in "moralising." Moral judgments, including judgments in relation to corruption, can be and often are based on objective evidence, and made with certainty or near certainty. Consider the claim that the Rwandan genocide was morally wrong. The truth-supporting reasons for this claim include empirical evidence—such as the dead, mutilated bodies of tens of thousands of men, women, and children—and moral claims—such as that it is morally wrong to kill innocent people. No rational, morally sentient person doubts the truth of such moral judgments.

We know that corruption exists. Accordingly, the making of implicit or explicit moral or ethical claims in relation to corruption is conceptually inevitable. Consider the argument that certain forms of corruption, such as bribing administrative officials to expedite transactions, are a good thing—and not merely a preferred way of doing things—by virtue of their contribution to economic growth. This argument in turn presupposes that economic growth is a good thing, or perhaps that the preference or desire satisfaction of consumers is a good thing. The latter is an ethico-normative claim. Indeed, it is an ethico-normative claim, the truth of which is required for the soundness of the reasoning in the argument in question. If it is not true that economic growth is a good thing, then it is questionable whether we ought to pursue economic growth. And if economic growth is not a good thing, then the argument for tolerating bribery is completely undermined. Our aim here is not to dispute that economic growth is a good thing; no doubt typically, though not invariably, it is a good thing. Rather, we are drawing attention to the conceptual inevitability of ethico-normative assumptions and judgments in reasoning about corruption, including economic reasoning.

Again, consider the claim that corrupt judges who enable guilty Mafia bosses to go free ought to be punished; or the claim that police fabricating evidence against suspects is corruption and ought not to be tolerated; or the more general claim that the guilty, but not the innocent, ought to suffer punishment. Claims such as these are unavoidable—indeed, are presupposed— by entire legal systems. And they are presupposed by policy-makers seeking to combat corruption and to identify those who are corrupt. Yet such claims are moral claims. Indeed, they are objectively true, more or less universally accepted, moral claims.

Naturally, not all laws are morally good, and not all morally good or morally bad practices are (respectively) condoned or condemned by laws. Thus, the racially discriminatory laws in apartheid South Africa or in Nazi Germany were morally bad. Again, it is morally good for parents to be kind to their children, but there is no law to this effect.

So law and morality are not the same thing; and neither are illegality and corruption. That said, many laws can and ought to track moral principles, including anti-corruption principles. Thus, murder is morally wrong, rape is morally wrong, and fraud is morally wrong. For that reason, these activities are unlawful. Serious kinds of moral wrongdoing, including serious forms of corruption, are unlawful; or, if they are not, then they almost certainly ought to be.

There is a further distinction to be made in relation to morality and corruption. Corrupt actions are immoral actions; but not all immoral actions are corrupt actions, since corruption is only one species of immorality. Consider an otherwise gentle husband who in a fit of anger strikes his adulterous wife and kills her. The husband has committed an act that is morally wrong; he has killed his wife. But his action is not necessarily an act of corruption. An important general distinction in this regard is that between human rights violations and corruption. Genocide is a profound moral wrong, but it is not corruption. This is not to say that there is not an important relationship between human rights violations and corruption; on the contrary, there is often a close and mutually reinforcing nexus between the two.[1] Consider the endemic corruption and large-scale human rights abuse that have taken place under authoritarian regimes such as those of Idi Amin in Uganda, and Suharto in Indonesia. And there is increasing empirical evidence of an admittedly complex causal connection between corruption and the infringement of subsistence rights; there is evidence, that is, of a causal relation between corruption and poverty— corruption causes poverty. Indeed, sometimes an act of human rights violation might also be an act of corruption. Thus, wrongfully and unlawfully incarcerating one's political opponent is a human rights violation, but it is also a corruption of the political process. The relationship between human rights violations and corruption is something that we address in Chapter 4.

The notion of a corrupt action presupposes the prior notion of an uncorrupted and morally legitimate process, role, or institution, or perhaps of an uncorrupted and morally worthy person. That is, the act of corruption brings about, or contributes to bringing about, a corrupt condition of something or someone, and the two principal objects of corruption are institutions and persons.[2] Let us refer to the corruption of institutions as institutional corruption and to the corruption of the moral character of persons as personal corruption. Our primary focus in this book is with institutional corruption. However, it goes without saying that since institutions are composed of persons, institutional corruption and personal corruption are interdependent. Specifically, institutional roles are occupied by persons, so that the corruption of a person as an institutional role occupant is institutional corruption.

The condition of corruption exists only relative to (1) an uncorrupted condition, which condition is (2) that of being a morally legitimate process, role, or institution, or that of being a morally worthy person. Consider the uncorrupted judicial process. It consists of the presentation of objective evidence that has been gathered lawfully, of testimony in court being presented truthfully, of the rights of the accused being respected, and so on. This otherwise morally legitimate judicial process is corrupted if one or more of its constitutive actions are not performed in accordance with the process as it is rightly intended to be. Thus, to present fabricated evidence, to lie on oath, and so on, are all potentially corrupt actions. Now consider the uncorrupted tendering process. It consists of a fair, competitive process—a morally legitimate process—whereby the tender is awarded to the person or organization that will do the job well and at the lowest price. This tendering process is corrupted if the job is awarded, not on the basis of merit, but on the basis of a bribe, or if one of the tenderers is given inside knowledge of the price being offered by the others. So an action is corrupt by virtue of the *effects* it has; specifically, it corrupts something or someone. In short, corruption is a *causal* concept.

Moreover, the corrupt condition of the person or thing corrupted exists only relative to some moral standard(s) that is definitional of the uncorrupted condition of that thing or person. The moral standards in question might be minimum moral standards, or they might be ideal moral standards. Corruption in a tendering process is a failure to comply with minimum moral standards enshrined in laws or regulations. On the other hand, gradual loss of innocence might be a process of corruption relative to an ideal moral state. In short, corruption is a *moral* concept (albeit, in the sense of being a species of *im*morality).

An immoral act is not necessarily a corrupt act. Consider the immoral act of killing or assaulting someone. Obviously a person who is killed or beaten up (assaulted) is not necessarily corrupted, although they are necessarily damaged.

Moreover, the act of killing or assault does not necessarily corrupt the perpetrator. Perhaps the killer is a psychopath born without a moral sense and possessed of little or no capacity to control the acts of killing. So the killer has not undergone, and cannot undergo, any moral change; and therefore cannot undergo a process of corruption. Or perhaps the person who commits a wrongful killing does so just once, has an acceptable excuse, and suffers remorse. Revulsion at one's act of killing might cause such a person to embark on a life of moral rectitude. If so, the person has not been corrupted as a result of the wrongful act. Furthermore, murder is not a corrupt form of some uncorrupted activity of killing people, since killing people is in general morally undesirable. Nor is beating up someone, say, in order to steal the person's money, a corrupt form of some uncorrupted activity of beating up people.

The notion of a corrupt official or other role occupant exists only relative to some notion of what an uncorrupted occupant of that morally legitimate role consists of. The notion of an academic has at its core the moral ideal, or at least, the morally legitimate role, of an independent truth-seeker who works in accordance with accepted principles of reason and evidence, who publishes in his or her own name only work that he or she has actually done, and so on. So an academic motivated by a desire for academic status who intentionally falsifies his or her experimental results or plagiarizes the work of others is corrupt relative to the ideal or morally legitimate role of an uncorrupted academic.

On the other hand, a person occupying an academic position who paid no heed whatsoever to the truth or to principles of reasoning and evidence and who made no pretense of so doing would at some point cease to be an academic of any sort, corrupt or otherwise. The property of being corrupt qualifies an existing process or person or thing that has an uncorrupted, and therefore morally worthy, or at least morally legitimate, form. If the process of corruption proceeds far enough, then we no longer have a corrupt official or corruption of an institutional process or institution; we cease to have a person who can properly be described as, say, a judge, or a process that can properly be described as, say, a judicial process—as opposed to proceedings in a kangaroo court. Like a coin that has been bent and defaced beyond recognition, it is no longer a coin; rather, it is a piece of scrap metal that can no longer be exchanged for goods.

In our view, a corrupt action is a one-off action, or an element of a pattern of actions, that contributes to the despoiling of the moral character of a person, and/or to the undermining of a morally legitimate institutional process, role, or condition.[3]

Notice that a person can perform actions that have a corrupting effect on himself or herself. Typically, acts of corruption have a side effect in relation to the corruptor. They not only corrupt the person and/or institutional process that they are intended to corrupt; they also corrupt the corruptor.

Consider bribery in relation to a tendering process. The bribe corrupts the tendering process; and it will probably have a corrupting effect on the moral character of the bribe *taker*. However, in addition, it might well have a corrupting effect on the moral character of the bribe *giver*.

Here we need to distinguish between a corrupt action that has no external effect on an institutional process or on another person, but which contributes to the corruption of the character of the would-be corruptor; and a *non-corrupt* action which is a mere *expression* of a corrupt moral character but which has no corrupting effect, either on an external institutional process or other person, or on the would-be corruptor himself. In this connection consider two sorts of would-be bribe givers whose bribes are rejected. Assume that in both cases their action has no external corrupting effect on an institutional process or other person. Now assume that in the first case the bribe giver's action of offering the bribe weakens his disposition not to offer bribes; so the offer has a corrupting effect on his character. However, assume that in the case of the second bribe giver, his failed attempt to bribe generates in him a feeling of shame and strengthens his disposition not to offer bribes. So his action has no corrupting effect, either on himself or externally on an institutional process or other person. In both cases, the action is the expression of a partially corrupt moral character. However, in the first but not the second case, the bribe giver's action is corrupt by virtue of having a corrupting effect on himself.

Notice further that the despoiling of moral character or the undermining of institutional processes, roles, or conditions would typically require a pattern of actions, not merely a single, one-off action. So although a single free hamburger provided to a police officer on one occasion does not corrupt and is not therefore an act of corruption, nevertheless, a series of such gifts to a number of police officers might corrupt, for example, if the hamburger joint in question in effect ended up with exclusive, round-the-clock, police protection and if this was the intention of the owner.

However, there are some cases in which a single, one-off action would be sufficient to corrupt an instance of an institutional process. Consider a specific tender. Suppose one bribe is offered and accepted and that the tendering process is thereby undermined. Suppose furthermore that this is the first and only time that the person offering the bribe and the person receiving it are involved in bribery. Is this one-off bribe an instance of corruption? Surely it is, since it corrupted that particular tendering process.

Naturally, a single action might be sufficient to corrupt an instance of an institutional process, for example, a specific tender, and might, in addition, be an element in a pattern of corrupt actions. Moreover, the pattern of actions in question might involve a number of individuals; there might be a network of bribe givers and bribe takers in relation to the tenders offered by a given organization over a period of time. If so, the tendering process in that organization might be said to have been corrupted by virtue of the tendency for the outcome of tenders offered by that organization to be influenced by bribes.[4]

Note also that in relation to institutional processes, roles, and conditions, we have insisted that, if they are to have the potential to be corrupted, then they must be *morally* legitimate, and not merely legitimate in some weaker sense, that is, lawful. No doubt there are nonmoral senses of the term "corruption." For example, it is sometimes said that some term in use in a linguistic community is a corrupted form of a given word or that some modern art is a corruption of traditional aesthetic forms. However, the central meaning of the term "corruption" has a strong moral connotation; to describe someone as a corrupt person or an action as corrupt is to ascribe a moral deficiency and to express moral disapproval. Accordingly, if an institutional process is to be corrupted, it must suffer some form of moral diminution, and therefore in its uncorrupted state, it must be at least morally legitimate. So although marriage across the color bar was unlawful in apartheid South Africa, a priest, Priest A, who married a black man and a white woman was not engaged in an act of corruption. On the other hand, if another priest, Priest B, married a white man and a white woman, knowing the man to be already married, the priest may well be engaged in an act of corruption. Priest B's act was corrupt because it served to undermine a lawful and morally legitimate institutional process, namely, marriage between two consenting adults who are not already married. But Priest A's act was not corrupt, because a legally required, but morally unacceptable, institutional practice—refraining from marrying a man and a woman merely because they belong to different race groups—cannot be corrupted. It cannot be corrupted because it was not morally legitimate to start with. Indeed, the legal prohibition on marriage across the color bar is in itself a corruption of the institution of marriage. And so Priest A's act of marrying the black man and the white woman not only was not corrupt but was also a refusal to engage in corruption.

In the light of the diverse range of corrupt actions and of the generic nature of the concept of corruption, it is unlikely that any precise definition is possible; nor is it likely that the field of corrupt actions can be neatly circumscribed by recourse to a set of self-evident criteria. This explains the futility, or at least limitations, of narrow definitions, such as that of corruption as the abuse of power by a public official for private gain, or of attempts to identify or contrast corruption with specific legal and/or moral offenses such as bribery or fraud.[5] No doubt the abuse of public offices for private gain or engaging in bribery are paradigms of corruption. But when police fabricate evidence out of a misplaced sense of justice, this act is corruption of a public office, but not for private gain. And when a punter bribes a boxer to "throw" a fight, this act is corruption for private gain, but it does not necessarily involve any public officeholder; the roles of boxer and punter are not necessarily public offices.

Indeed, there is a whole range of different forms of corruption outside the public sphere. Consider corruption in relation to the role of father within the social institution of the family. Suppose a father persuades his naive but nubile thirteen-year-old daughter to provide sexual favors to middle-aged businessmen in exchange for payments to him and gifts for her; this act is corruption, but it is not abuse of a public office. Or consider a gold digger who marries a lonely, wealthy man for his money and thereby deceives him and subverts the purposes of marriage as a social institution.

It seems that we should content ourselves with the somewhat vague and highly generic definition—in effect, a conceptual analysis—of corruption that we have just provided, and then proceed in a relatively informal and piecemeal manner to try to identify a range of moral and/or legal offenses that are known to contribute under certain conditions to the despoiling of the moral character of persons and/or to the undermining of morally legitimate institutions. Such offenses obviously include bribery, fraud, nepotism, and the like. But under certain circumstances they might also include breaches of confidentiality that compromise investigations and the making of false statements that undermines court proceedings or selection committee processes or the earned reputations of public figures, the selective enforcement of laws or rules by those in authority, and so on.

The wide diversity of corrupt actions has at least two further implications. First, it implies that acts of corruption have a correspondingly large set of moral deficiencies. Certainly, all corrupt actions will be morally wrong, and morally wrong at least in part because they despoil moral character or undermine morally legitimate institutions (or both). However, since there are many and diverse offenses at the core of corrupt actions—offenses such as bribery, fraud, nepotism, making false statements, and breaching confidentiality—there will also be many and diverse moral deficiencies associated with different forms of corruption. Some acts of corruption will have the moral deficiency of deception, others of theft, still others of not being impartial, and so on. Second, the wide diversity of corrupt actions implies that there may well need to be a correspondingly wide and diverse range of anticorruption measures to combat corruption in its different forms, and indeed in its possibly very different contexts.

Notwithstanding the diversity of corruption and the diversity of its moral deficiencies and possible remedies, there are various generalizations that can be made about corruption. In order to facilitate our discussion of such generalizations, let us return to the discussion of our examples of corruption.

It is sometimes suggested that corruption is essentially an economic phenomenon and that therefore the remedies for corruption need to be the sorts of economic solutions that economists propose for economic problems.[6] Certainly, many forms of corruption involve financial transactions and are motivated by a desire for financial gain. But many do not involve money and are not motivated by money; there are many forms of corruption that are not economic. Accordingly, it seems far-fetched to suppose that the remedies for such noneconomic forms of corruption would turn out to be economic remedies.

An academic who plagiarizes the work of others is not necessarily committing an economic crime or misdemeanour, and might be doing so simply to increase his or her academic status; there might not be any financial benefit sought or gained. Many academics are more strongly motivated by status than they are by wealth. A police officer who fabricates evidence against a person whom he or she believes to be guilty of pedophilia is not committing an economic crime, and the officer might do so because he or she believes the accused to be guilty and does not want the person to go unpunished; economics is not necessarily involved as an element of the officer's crime or as a motivation. When police do wrong, they are often motivated by a misplaced sense of justice, rather than by financial reward. Again, a political leader who abuses his or her power by meting out cruel and unjust treatment to those subject to his or her authority, and who does so out of sadistic pleasure, is not engaging in an economic crime and is not motivated by economic considerations. Many of those who occupy positions of political authority are motivated by a desire to exercise power rather than for financial reward.[7]

We conclude that although economic corruption is an important form of institutional corruption, it is not the only one. There are noneconomic forms of institutional corruption, including many types of political corruption, police corruption, judicial corruption, academic corruption, and so on. Indeed, there are as many forms of institutional corruption as there are types of social institution that might become corrupted. Furthermore, economic gain is not the only motivation for corruption. There are a variety of different kinds of attractions that motivate corruption. These include status, power, addiction to drugs or gambling, and sexual gratification, as well as economic gain. Contrary to what Gordon Gekko said in the film *Wall Street*, greed is not good; it is bad. But greed is not the only vice.

These distinctions between economic corruption, political corruption, and so on, draw our attention to the different kinds of basic activities and associated institutions in which human beings participate. Within a social group, we can distinguish between different, albeit connected and overlapping, kinds of activity, including communicative, economic, educative, sexual, and religious. Let us refer to these different basic kinds of activity taking place within a society as *spheres of activity*. Most societies at most periods of human history have engaged in most of these basic kinds of activity, and they have done so because these activities are grounded in basic human needs.

Spheres of activity are able, to some extent, to be marked off from one another by their characteristic features; an economic transaction involving the exchange of goods is not the same kind of thing as a religious experience.[8] Moreover, these spheres of activity are necessarily regulated by, at the least, conventions, and thereby take on different specific forms according to the specific conventions that structure them—for example, conventions of language. Often they are also regulated by explicit rules, including laws. And they are also regulated by social norms, a social norm being a regularity in action that has moral force among some social group, with members of the group believing that they ought to conform to it. The regulation of these spheres of activities by conventions, laws, and social norms gives rise to specific, and often contrasting, institutional forms, for example, the English versus the French language, the liberal-democratic versus the one-party state, the Catholic versus the Presbyterian Church, the adversarial versus the inquisitorial court system, and so on.

As we have just seen, there are different forms of corruption, and one way of distinguishing these is by reference to the sphere of activity in which they are principally located. Thus, in the economic sphere we typically see forms of corruption such as bribery and fraud, in the political sphere we see abuse of power and vote rigging, and in the communication sphere we see insincere pronouncements and the spreading of falsehoods in order to destroy reputations. It goes without saying that since these spheres of activity overlap, so do many of the associated forms of corruption, for example, bribes paid by a land developer to a local politician to ensure that a specific land re-zoning policy is implemented, exist at the interface of the economic and the political spheres.

CORRUPTION AND REASONING

In the previous discussion, we implicitly distinguished between the types of corrupt actions and the types of motivation for those actions. Thus, police fabricating evidence is a type of corrupt action, but a type of action that might have different sorts of motivation. For example, one police officer might fabricate evidence in order to secure large numbers of convictions so that he can get promoted; another officer might fabricate evidence only if she is guaranteed a financial reward; finally, still another might do so only in order to ensure that those he believes to be guilty are punished.

So there is a distinction between the action and the motivation for the action. However, the matter is even more complex than this, for there is a further distinction between the goal, end, or purpose of the action, on the one hand, and the ultimate motivation, on the other. Thus, in our police example, the action is fabrication of evidence, the end or goal is to secure a conviction, and the ultimate motivation is either financial gain, professional status (by virtue of promotion), or a sense of justice (ensuring that the guilty do not go unpunished). The distinction between the ends or goals of an action and the various ultimate motivations involved can be thought of as a distinction between different kinds of reasons for the performance of the action.

The reason for fabricating the evidence is to secure a conviction; securing a conviction is the end or goal. This is *means-end reasoning*, pure and simple; the reason is, so to speak, a mere goal or end that a person is aiming at or trying to achieve. On the other hand, the ultimate reason for trying to secure the conviction might be a desire for money—that is, the motivation might be greed. Greed, fear, desire for power or status, sexual gratification, lust, love, hate, and so on, are all reasons for actions. However, these emotions and other affective attitudes are not mere goals or ends; they are not merely states of affairs that we aim at. They are also *desired* states or conditions or activities. Desires, emotions, and so on provide a second kind of reason for action; let us dub the sort of reasoning involved here *desire-based reasoning*.

There is a third form of reasoning that we will dub *moral reasoning*. Moral reasoning is not the same kind of reasoning as means-end or desire-based reasoning. Moral reasoning is reasoning based on belief in moral principles. Thus, one might decide not to fabricate evidence because one believed in the principle of a fair trial based on objective evidence. Here one's belief in a moral principle functions as a reason for one's action (or, in this case, for one's omission).

Notice that desire-based reasoning and moral reasoning often involve *nested* means-end reasoning. Assume that agent A's ultimate motivation for fabricating evidence is greed. However, A proceeds via an elaborate chain of means-end reasoning before coming to the ultimate stopping point, namely, A's desire for money. A reasons as follows: fabricating the evidence is the means to securing the conviction, which is in turn the means to securing the payment, and A desires money; accordingly, A will fabricate the evidence.

Consider another one of our other examples, the contractor's bribing the public official awarding tenders. Let us assume that the ultimate motivation of both parties is financial gain. Thus, the ultimate reasons are desire-based reasons, rather than, say, moral reasons. However, the goal of the contractor is to fulfill this desire for money by means of securing the tender, and he aims to win the tender by means of bribing the official: so there is nested means-end reasoning. Similarly, the official aims to secure the bribe by means of awarding the tender to the contractor in question: so he engages in means-end reasoning in the service of an ultimate desire-based reason, namely, greed.

We now have a distinction between actions and reasons for actions, and we have three different kinds of reasons for action. This arrangement allows us to distinguish between corrupt actions and three sorts of reasons for performing corrupt actions. Somewhat paradoxically, one of the possible kinds of reasons for performing a corrupt action is moral reason. What we have in mind here is the notion of noble cause corruption that will be explained shortly.

Before doing so, we need to introduce a further distinction. This is the distinction between a one-off discrete action—an action considered on its own—and an habitual action. Today Agent A gets out of bed at 7 A.M.—this is a single action. However, assume that every day A gets out of bed at 7 A.M., so there is a regularity in A's action of getting out of bed at 7 A.M. Assume further that on each of these days, A gets out of bed without going through a full and an adequate reasoning process designed to justify A's getting out of bed at 7 A.M. on that day. Rather, A just gets out of bed at 7 A.M. because that is what A always does, because that is A's habit.

This is not to say that A might not have a reason for A's habit of getting out of bed at 7 A.M. Occasionally, A might actually sit down and rationally think through why A has this habit of getting up at 7 A.M., rather than earlier or later. Assume that the process yields a compelling set of reasons to do with the time that A is due at work and the time that it takes A to wash, dress, eat breakfast, and drive to work. Accordingly, A resumes A's habit. So A's getting up at 7 A.M. is habitual, but the habit is rational, or at least it is reason-based.

Now we suggest that corrupt actions are typically habitual; a corrupt action is not typically a one-off action, because often a one-off action will not succeed in corrupting a person or an institution (or subelement thereof). On the other hand, some one-off acts are corrupt, because they do corrupt a process. Many bribes are a case in point.

Some one-off actions are not acts of corruption, even though if they had been elements of a pattern of corrupt actions, they would have been acts of corruption. The reason for this outcome is that these one-off actions do not necessarily, and did not in fact, corrupt, although they would have done so, if they had been one of a whole set of actions performed out of habit.

Accordingly, we claim that a corrupt action is typically—though not necessarily or invariably—an element of a pattern of corrupt actions and is performed out of habit. Naturally, the existence of this habit is itself in need of explanation. What is the reason that A has this habit? As we have seen, the possible motivations are many. A common one is greed. The public official habitually takes bribes and is motivated by greed.

In this connection, note that a public official who accepts one bribe to, say, grant an unwarranted license, does so on one occasion only and then relents and refuses further bribes, is not corrupt, even though his or her act of accepting the bribe did corrupt that single institutional process of granting a license.

A further point about the habitual nature of corruption concerns free will and autonomy. From the fact that an action is habitual, it doesn't necessarily follow that it is unfree. Habits can be difficult to break, especially bad habits. Nevertheless, if we decide to do so, we can break many of our habits, including many of our bad habits. Assume that a habit cannot be broken; perhaps it is a physiological addiction, for example, some forms of heroin addiction, or perhaps it is genetically programmed. If so, then the actions that flow from that habit—the habitual actions—are not freely performed.

So corrupt actions are a species of morally wrong, (typically) habitual actions. What of the motive for corrupt actions? We have seen that there are many motives for these, including desires for wealth, status, power, and pleasure, including sexual pleasure and the pleasure of fine food and wine. For example, in China, gluttony is associated with corruption, so that providing people with large, expensive banquets is one way of currying favor or inducing them to do what is wrong or unlawful.

However, there is *apparently* at least one motive that ought not to be associated with corruption, namely, doing wrong for the sake of good. Here we need to be careful. Strange as it may seem, some actions that are done out of a desire to achieve good *are* in fact corrupt actions, for example, acts of so-called *noble cause corruption.*[9] However, even in these cases—contrary to what the person who performs the action thinks—the "corrupt" action morally ought not to be performed; or at least *typically,* the "corrupt" action morally ought not to be performed. Accordingly, the person who performs it is either deceiving himself or herself, or is simply mistaken when he or she judges that the action morally ought to be performed. So the motive—to act for the sake of what is right—is tainted. The person is acting only for the sake of what he or she *believes* is morally right, but in fact it is not morally right; the belief is a false belief. That is, it is not true that he or she is acting for the sake of what is *in fact* morally right. So we can conclude that corrupt actions are habitual actions that are morally wrong and therefore are not motivated by the *true* belief that they are morally right. We will discuss noble cause corruption in greater detail in Chapter 5.

There is a further point to be made here following on our claim that corrupt actions are not motivated by the true belief that they are morally right. It might be thought that a habitual action that in fact had the causal effect of undermining some institutional process was an act of corruption, even though this causal effect was unknown to the person(s) performing the action and could not reasonably have been known by that person(s). We are disinclined to define corruption so widely as to embrace such causal processes. By our lights, if an agent A performs a corrupt act, then the corruption produced must be such that A intends it or that A believes that it will occur as a consequence of his or her action, or—at the very least—the corruption produced must be such that A reasonably ought to believe that it will occur as a consequence of his or her action.

A final related point to the one just made concerns persons—in the sense of institutional role occupants—who are corrupted. The contrast here is with *institutional processes and purposes* that might be corrupted. Consider a bribe giver and a bribe taker. Assume that both are corrupted by their actions; although the bribe giver may well intend to corrupt the bribe taker, without the reverse being the case. If an action has a corrupting effect on a person then the person who is corrupted is to some extent, or in some sense, a *participant* in this process of corruption; persons who become corrupted have to some extent allowed themselves to be corrupted. So both the bribe giver and bribe taker have allowed themselves to be corrupted by their respective actions. Please note that our use of the term "participant" is not meant to imply that they *intended* to become corrupted. In our view, to allow oneself to be corrupted is not necessarily to aim at, or otherwise intend, that one become corrupted. Indeed, we do not think that in general the corrupt *aim* at corrupting *themselves,* although they can and often do aim at corrupting others. At any rate, by virtue of allowing themselves to be corrupted (in general), those who have been corrupted are at least to some degree blameworthy for not resisting the process of their corruption. Naturally there are exceptions to this rule such as, for example, young children who may not be morally responsible for the process of corruption that they undergo.

TYPES OF CORRUPTION

Actions that are believed to be morally wrong are typically both a violation of social norms and unlawful acts. For example, murder, theft, and assault are unlawful because they are a violation of basic moral principles adhered to in all or most societies; that is, they are a violation of the social norms of most societies.

As we saw before, corruption is a species of moral wrongdoing, but not all wrongdoing is corruption. Moreover, most serious kinds of corruption are unlawful, but not all corruption is unlawful. We also need to distinguish between conventions, laws, and social norms, and between social norms and *objective* moral norms.[10] Although there are infringements of conventions, and of laws, and of social norms (whether objective moral norms or not), these infringements have different moral implications.

Conventions are ubiquitous. We conform to conventions of language, of money, of dress, of eating, and of politeness. There are conventions in government, in business—in fact in all walks of life. There are conventions connecting sounds and marks to meanings, conventions linking coins and bits of paper to quantities of goods, conventions determining how we should approach possible sexual partners, and so on.

Conventions are different from laws, rules, and regulations in that the latter are explicitly laid down by some authority somewhere. The laws of the land are written down and exist because, for example, a parliament passed them. Regulations and rules exist in manuals and rulebooks. By contrast, conventions are typically not written down anywhere, nor have they been issued by some authority, such as the government or a judge.

Conventions are typically regularities in action to which all or most of us, most of the time, conform. A speaker produces the noise or mark "philosopher" when he or she wants to refer to a philosopher (in part) because the speaker knows that is what is regularly done in his or her linguistic community, so the regularity is a linguistic convention in that community. We don't change the word for referring to philosophers on a daily basis, or from one hearer to the next treatment. That would be very unhelpful, to say the least.

Conventions serve collective ends. For example, conventions of language enable the collective end of communication; conventions of politeness facilitate the collective end of interpersonal interaction; and driving on one side of the road helps to ensure the collective end of preserving one another's lives. Thus, conventions are regularities in action that achieve collective ends.

As we have just seen, conventions are necessary for cooperative activity. However, the crucial point for our purposes here is that conventions are necessary for cooperative activity, irrespective of what kind of cooperative activity it is. Establishing this connection between conventions and cooperative activity might make it seem that conventions are always and necessarily a benign phenomenon. This is not so. In the first place, cooperative activity is not always and necessarily morally good. The members of Chinese Triads, for example, cooperate with one another to extort money, traffic in drugs, and derive profits from prostitution.

Second, the activities of a given society, culture, or organization can be conventionalised beyond what is reasonable and desirable. The conventional practice of gift-giving in Japan is (arguably) problematic, in part because it provides a conducive environment for bribery.

Let us now consider social norms. The distinction between laws and social norms is obvious enough. Laws are explicitly formulated, they are enacted by a specific authority (e.g., a parliament), and they are backed by physical sanctions (e.g., imprisonment). A social norm, by contrast, is a type of action or inaction that members of a social group believe to be morally right or morally wrong. For example, individuals in a community might believe that it is wrong to kill. Refraining from murder is then a moral norm for each of those individuals. It is not simply that each individual does not commit murder; in addition, the individual believes that he or she ought to refrain from murder. So moral norms are regularities in behavior, and if those regularities are in part sustained by the moral attitudes of approval and disapproval in a community, then they are social norms. Social norms are often, but not necessarily, enshrined in the laws of the community.

Social norms are regularities in action. So they are like conventions. Indeed, the boundaries between conventions and social norms are extremely vague. However, there is an important in-principle difference between these social regularities, and our invocation of the terms "conventions" and "social norms" is intended to mark this difference. In the case of norms, but not necessarily conventions, agents hold moral beliefs in relation to the action or omission prescribed by the social norms, for example, the norm of not killing others, not telling lies, offering condolences to the bereaved, not informing on corrupt police colleagues, and so on.

As we have just seen, social norms are regularities in behavior that a community adheres to because it believes that conformity is morally required; social norms are intersubjectively accepted. However, it would not follow from this that a social norm was objectively valid. An objective moral norm is a type of action or inaction that is, as a matter of objective truth, morally right. Naturally, the set of objective moral norms may coincide, or at least substantially overlap, with the social norms of a given society. Indeed, in an ideal society, this would be the case. Refraining from murdering people is both a social norm and objectively morally right. The way to determine what is objectively morally required—as opposed to what is merely widely socially accepted—is to analyze the practice in question: the method of critical reasoning. In relation to the distinction between subjectively held and objectively valid social norms or practices, Siddhartha Gautama, the historic Buddha, had this to say:

> Believe nothing just because you have been told it, or it is commonly believed, or because it is traditional, or because you yourself have imagined it. Do not believe what your Teacher tells you merely out of respect for the Teacher. But whatsoever, after due examination and analysis, you find to be conducive to the good, the benefit, the welfare of all beings—that doctrine believe and cling to, and take as your guide.[11]

As noted before, corruption typically involves wrongdoing motivated by individual gain. The gain is typically some benefit, such as money, status, power, or influence. However, notice that the corrupt act is not necessarily done to benefit the individual who commits it. Sometimes an individual may engage in a corrupt act for the sake of his or her family or friend. Accepting a bribe for doing someone a political favor is a species of corruption; it is doing wrong to benefit oneself. On the other hand, nepotism in relation to a work position on the waterfront may not benefit oneself, but rather one's (possibly unknowing) son. It is, nevertheless, a species of corruption.

We can distinguish between a corrupt action and a corrupt person. Some persons may only occasionally engage in minor acts of corruption; their corrupt action may be habitual but opportunistic.[12] Others are involved in serious corruption as a way of life; corruption is a deeply ingrained habit and central feature of their makeup, such that they seek opportunities to engage in corrupt behavior. We might hesitate to call the former corrupt persons, whereas clearly the latter are corrupt.

We can distinguish two types of corrupt persons. The first type commits wrong actions out of self-interest but does so knowing these actions to be wrong. The characteristic moral attitude of this kind of corrupt persons to their corrupt activities is cynicism. However, typically these corrupt persons are capable of experiencing shame, since they do still recognize that the actions are morally wrong, even if at times they try to convince themselves and others that their actions are not morally wrong.

Note here the pivotal role of habits. We have seen that corrupt actions are typically habitual. Yet, as noted by Aristotle, one's habits are in large part constitutive of one's moral character; habits maketh the man (and the woman). The coward is someone who habitually takes flight in the face of danger; by contrast, the courageous person has a habit of standing his or her ground. Accordingly, morally bad *habits*—including corrupt actions—are extremely corrosive of moral character.

The second type of corrupt person has gone a step beyond the wrong-doers who know they are such. These persons have become fully corrupt in that they do not really see their actions as morally wrong or do so only fleetingly. For this reason, <u>fully corrupt persons</u> might not experience shame in relation to their wrongful and unlawful actions. For such persons, the performance of corrupt activities entails <u>no loss of self-esteem</u>, since they no longer identify with the social norms not to thieve, assault, and so on. Rather, they identify with the attractive features of the morally wrong actions they perform, including the excitement, the respect accorded to them because they are known to be able to intimidate others, the wealth and consequent status that they gain, and so on.

Shame is the social analogue to guilt. Guilt can be felt when one does wrong even when others are unaware of it. Shame is experienced when one's wrongdoing is made public. Shame is the feeling triggered in most people when they do wrong and are exposed. As such, it is a powerful vehicle for combating corruption. Fear of exposure and the resultant feelings of shame are powerful motivators against corruption. This is one reason why transparency is so important a factor in relation to corruption reduction; wrong-doers often fear the disapproving attitudes of others. However, in relation to our second type of corrupt person—such as the hardened professional fraudster—it may well be that shame in relation to their immoral and unlawful actions can get no purchase, since they do not see their actions as immoral. Notwithstanding the fact that such persons are immune to being shamed, transparency remains an important factor when it comes to combating their corrupt activities. For it will typically be necessary that their wrongdoing be detected by law enforcement officials and others if it is to be eliminated; and detection is also a necessary precursor to punishment. We will explore the issue of transparency in greater detail in Chapter 2.

Here we need to insist on distinguishing three sorts of motivation for compliance with moral principles, including those embodied in social norms. One reason for compliance is the fear of punishment, hence the use, or threatened use, of the so-called "big stick." Agent A does do not steal from Agent B because A will get caught and locked up. A second reason for compliance arises from the benefit to oneself, hence the possible utility of the so-called "carrot" approach. B pays B's workers reasonable wages because by doing so, the workers are healthy and work productively, and B makes good profits. These two reasons are essentially appeals to self-interest. Taken in combination they constitute the "stick-carrot" approach much loved by many contemporary economists. However, there is a third reason for compliance. This is moral belief or desire to do what is right. A refrains from stealing because A believes that it is morally wrong to steal; B pays B's workers reasonable wages because B desires to be fair.

Here we need to note that appeals to moral beliefs are not to be assimilated to appeals to self-interest. Moreover, the notion of persons acting out of moral rectitude is completely at odds with the essentially manipulative approach of those who advocate only sticks and carrots.

It is evident that widespread and ongoing compliance typically requires appeals to self-interest (sticks and carrots) but also appeals to moral beliefs. Ideally, legal and regulatory regimes should have penalties for those who do not comply, should enable benefits to flow to those who do comply, and should resonate with the moral beliefs of the people thus regulated, for example, the laws should be widely thought to be just. Institutional design that proceeds on the assumption that self-interest is the only human motivation worth considering fails. It fails because it overlooks the centrality of moral beliefs in human life and therefore does not mobilize moral sentiment. In our view, contrary to one strand of the Western philosophical tradition, ultimately the only thing that can be extracted from self-interest alone is more self-interest.[13] Invisible hand mechanisms have limited applicability, but even they presuppose a framework of rules regarded as preserving certain moral values, such as individual freedom of choice and fairness. On the other hand, institutional design that proceeds on the assumption that self-interest can be ignored, and that a sense of moral duty on its own will suffice, also fails; it fails because self-interest is an ineradicable and pervasive feature of all human societies.

We can offer a taxonomy of institutional—as opposed to personal— corruption by recourse to the criteria of seriousness, extent, and degree of collaboration involved.[14] Thus, at one end of this scale, we have a small number of individuals acting alone and engaged in minor forms of corruption in a single organizational setting; we have a few not-so-rotten apples. At the other end of the scale, we have large numbers of well-organized individuals engaged in serious forms of corruption across a range of fundamental social institutions—such as government, the judiciary, and industry—and doing so at the highest levels of those institutions; we have grand and systemic corruption.

Some forms of institutional corruption exist outside organizations but nevertheless take place in one or more of the spheres of activity that we described. Thus, we have individual corruption in the economic sphere when one person fraudulently acquires the estate of a deceased person and does so to the detriment of the deceased person's nearest of kin. Moreover, such nonorganizational corruption can be collaborative in nature. For example, assume that the fraudster is in cahoots with the deceased person's lawyer.

Aside from individual and collaborative corruption outside organizational settings, there is such corruption within and between organizations. Assume that a fraudulent scheme in which Fraudster A working for a company is undercharging a client organization. However, Fraudster A has an accomplice in the client organization, Fraudster B, who falsely records that the higher correct amounts have been paid and pockets the difference, which Fraudster B in turn splits with Fraudster A.

Let us call these various forms of corruption engaged in by individuals, or by ad hoc collaborative arrangements, *individual* corruption. Let us now turn to organized corruption.

In addition to (possibly partially corrupt) organizations existing to serve morally desirable ends, there are those such as the Mafia, the Yakuza, and the Chinese Triads, which exist to engage in corrupt and otherwise immoral activities. But such corrupt activity is, so to speak, a core activity of these organizations. Other organized corruption involves both legitimate and illegitimate enterprises. Consider, in this connection, the so-called "jao pho" in Thailand. These rich and influential members of the legitimate business community also use their wealth and informal power to engage in a variety of corrupt and unlawful practices.[15]

In some cases, these organizations, such as the now infamous 14 Association (14K) in Hong Kong, existed for political purposes—the 14K were formed as part of the Chinese Nationalist Kuomintang to assist in the war against the communists—but degenerated into out-and-out criminal organizations or, as we might say, underwent a process of corruption.

At any rate, let us use the term "organized corruption" to refer to corruption pursued by an organization that exists for that purpose. (So *organized corruption* is closely connected to organized crime.)

There is a third form of corruption that pertains to an organization or a set of organizations. This is pervasive and interdependent corruption within an organization. However, the organization does not exist for the purposes of engaging in corrupt activities. Rather, a large number of corrupt individuals within an otherwise morally legitimate organization engage in ongoing and interdependent corrupt activity. Although the individuals do not constitute a criminal organization as such, corruption has, nevertheless, become a cooperative enterprise. Consider in this connection the Liberal Democratic Party in Japan in the early 1970s, some of whose members, including senior people, engaged in so-called "money politics," whereby the public interest was secondary to individual self-advancement and wealth acquisition. Let us refer to this form of corruption—corruption of an organization—as *organizational corruption.*

Further, there is what we might term "systemic corruption," and there is also so-called "grand corruption." The use of the term "systemic" indicates that the corruption is pervasive and interconnected across many organizations and institutions. *Systemic corruption* consists of the erosion of social norms and as such is widely dispersed across organizations, institutions, social groups, and societies. Systemic corruption typically feeds on the moral vulnerability of some group or groups of people. It is no accident that systemic corruption has been associated historically, and in many otherwise diverse cultures, with addictive drugs, prostitution, and gambling.

 Grand corruption involves large-scale corruption of a very serious kind, and the corruption in question exists at the highest levels of one or more fundamental institutions.

 Corruption that is both systemic and grand is the most pernicious of all species of corruption, because the reach of systemic, grand corruption is both wide and high. Systemic, grand corruption infects senior members of the government, the legislature, the police, public administration, industry, and finance. It may involve the framing of policies and laws. The very structure of institutions may be the object of corrupt interventions.

Moreover, systemic, grand corruption not only presupposes organizational corruption, but also may well involve organized corruption. The cocaine cartels in Colombia (organized corruption) corrupted and dominated the government and other organizations within the nation-state (organizational corruption) to the point where they eroded the commitment to social norms embodied in the law on the part of members of the political and criminal justice system, and of large sections of the population (systemic corruption). Moreover, the corruption in question was of the most serious forms and existed at the highest levels of these institutions (grand corruption).[16] (See Chapter 2 for further discussion of the Colombian cocaine cartels.)

 Systemic, grand corruption undermines the wherewithal to oppose corruption itself. The detection and deterrence of corruption is achieved in large part by institutional mechanisms of accountability, and by policing techniques such as complaints investigation, use of informants, auditing, and surveillance. However, in the case of systemic, grand corruption, it is not enough to try to introduce an elaborate system of detection and deterrence. For one thing, those who operate the systems of detection and deterrence, namely the police, judges, and politicians, are often themselves corrupt. There is grand corruption. For another thing, the ordinary citizens who could be expected to reject and oppose these forms of corruption often participate in them or are tolerant of them. There is systemic corruption.

CONCLUSION

We have argued that the concept of corruption is a somewhat vague and highly generic one, and that therefore the types of corruption are quite diverse. Accordingly, the goal of finding a neat definition of corruption has proved to be an elusive one. Therefore, we have opted for a loose and generic definition, a conceptual analysis, if you like. This is not to say that more precise definitions might not be available for specific act types—such as bribery or fraud—that typically constitute acts of corruption. As is well known, John T. Noonan has offered an exhaustive account of bribery. He defines the core of the concept of a bribe as "an inducement improperly influencing the performance of a public function meant to be gratuitously exercised."[17] And there are widely accepted definitions of fraud. Typically, acts of fraud are said to possess the following defining features: first, fraud involves providing oneself with a financial benefit; second, the financial benefit in question is one that the fraudster is not entitled to; and third, the means by which the benefit is secured involves deception.

We have further suggested that the moral deficiencies associated with different forms of corruption will be various and that the remedies will correspondingly vary. Nevertheless, we have drawn attention to a number of taxonomies of corruption, specifically in terms of spheres of activity (economic, political, and so on) and in terms of the seriousness, extent, and degree of collaboration (systemic, grand, and so on). We now suggest that, notwithstanding the diversity of types of corruption, there are a number of general conditions that have been shown to facilitate the corruption of persons and of institutions. Thus, we are insisting on a distinction between the definition of corruption—what corruption consists of—on the one hand, and the causes of, or conditions that facilitate or tend to produce corruption, on the other hand. Some of these conditions, such as imbalances of power and lack of transparency, have already been identified. In the following chapter, we will present a more comprehensive set of these conditions and will provide analyses of them. We will argue that if organizations, governments, and communities are to successfully combat corruption, then they need to rectify these conditions.[18]

chapter two

Contexts and Causes of Corruption

In this chapter, we discuss

- Three general conditions that facilitate or are conducive to corruption: (1) the moral, or rather immoral, environment; (2) the absence of accountability mechanisms; and (3) the lack of transparency.
- A number of specific forms or elements that each of these general conditions might take or have. For example, the moral environment might be one in which there was an imbalance of power, or it might be one in which there were great inequalities of wealth.

In Chapter 1, we argued that corruption is fundamentally a species of immorality, rather than, say, a species of illegality or of bad economic practice, and we offered a general, theoretical characterization of corruption. We also introduced a number of sets of distinctions, including between spheres of basic activity and organizations, and between conventions, laws, and social norms. This discussion enabled us to offer a number of taxonomies of corruption, including one in terms of individual, organized, organizational, grand, and systemic corruption. In this chapter, we focus not on the nature or definition of corruption, nor on the types of corruption, but rather on the contexts in which corruption takes place and on the causes of corruption. Our concern is not with what corruption is per se, but with what causes it or tends to bring it into existence and/or maintain it.

Let us begin with the notion of a moral environment.

MORAL ENVIRONMENTS

The moral environment consists of the sociomoral context in which corrupt and/or criminal activities might take place. It consists in part of the framework of social norms that are adhered to, or at least, are paid lip service to. This framework is a more or less coherent structure of social norms.[19]

As we saw in the last chapter, social norms are regularities in action or omission sustained in part by the moral approval and disapproval of the participants in those social norms. So the members of a social group not only behave in accordance with a structured set of social norms, but also believe that they ought to comply with these norms. These beliefs constitute a structured system of moral beliefs—in short, a worldview about what constitutes morally acceptable and morally unacceptable behavior.[20]

Naturally, there will be differences between the moral beliefs of individuals who share such a common society-wide moral worldview. They might interpret some of the social norms differently, and this variation might lead to some differences in terms of compliance. For example, some might interpret very strictly the belief that lying is wrong, but others less strictly. Moreover, there might be differences in relation to their ordering of the beliefs that sustain given social norms. Thus, some might believe that keeping one's contractual obligations is more important than assisting needy others. These differences in moral outlook between individual members of the same social group might be substantial and systematic. If so, we might be inclined to regard them as differences in *personal* worldviews. This would especially be the case if these differences were the result of some sustained process of individual moral reflection.

Whatever the differences in moral outlook or personal worldviews of individual members of a social group, there will inevitably be a high degree of commonality in their moral beliefs and the regularities in action consequent upon those beliefs; in short, social groups require social norms. This is the case because social norms are necessary for social life beyond a very basic level. For example, social norms against random killing enable cooperative economic and family institutions. Again, social norms of truth-telling and of providing evidence for statements are necessary for institutions of learning. (Even the Ik tribe in Uganda, whose members were notorious for engaging in behavior that most societies hold to be immoral, had moral norms, for example, they believed that a person ought to repay a favor, and they acted in accordance with this belief.) Social norms of individual freedom put important constraints on the power that one institution or individual might have over another institution or individual.

From this it does not follow that *all* social norms are productive of cooperation, let alone *always* conducive to law and order. For example, in Sicily there used to be norms of revenge that undermined cooperation, as well as law and order. Nevertheless, a substantial fragment of the framework of social norms adhered to by a given social group needs to facilitate cooperation and good order, lest the social group disintegrate as a social group.

In contemporary societies, social norms are in large part enshrined in the criminal law. Theft, assault, murder, rape, kidnapping, child molestation, fraud, and so on, are actions which violate social norms in contemporary societies, and they are also criminal acts. Indeed, it is because these acts are held to be profoundly morally wrong that perpetrators are held criminally liable.

There is a tendency to confuse social norms with other sorts of closely related conformist behavior. In the last chapter, we have already distinguished social norms from conventions. But social norms need also to be distinguished from conformist behavior such as following fashions.

The difference is as follows. In the case of fashions, the individual conforms because he or she desires to do what others approve of. In the case of social norms, the individual conforms because the individual believes that he or she morally ought to do what everyone (or most people) including the agent himself or herself morally approves of. Hence, in the case of a social norm, but not a fashion, failure to conform produces shame. Consider the corrupt police officers who were brought before the Royal Commission into Corruption in the New South Wales Police Service in Australia in the mid-1990s. Some of these police officers violated social norms by taking bribes, dealing in drugs, and selling child pornography. It was obvious that when many of these men were brought before the commissioner and their corruption was exposed in video and tape recordings, they experienced deep shame. This outcome indicates that it is not merely a convention or a fashion that they have flouted. So social norms go hand in hand with the social moral emotion of shame. Failure to conform to social norms elicits feelings of shame; and shaming is a powerful form of social control.

As mentioned before, the set of social norms adhered to by members of a social group constitutes a more or less coherent structure and embodies a shared worldview of moral values. Such a set of social norms constitutes the basic framework within which individuals, groups, and organizations interact in the various spheres of activity and thereby lead their individual and collective lives. This framework provides, in effect, a *moral environment*. Without such a framework, including compliance with basic social prohibitions on murder, assault, restricting the freedom of others, theft, fraud, and so on, social life would soon disintegrate.

As mentioned in Chapter 1, compliance with social norms is not based simply on the rational self-interested calculations of individuals. Rational self-interest does not necessarily dictate that the moral rights of fellow citizens are protected. Nor does it necessarily dictate that the well-being of future generations, including one's own offspring, are catered for. Moreover, the rational self-interest of members of one economic or social class, culture, organization, or nation-state does not dictate that the moral rights or the moral well-being of members of another class, culture, organization, or nation-state be respected or taken into consideration. This is no doubt especially the case when one of the parties to the interaction has overwhelming power and is prepared to exercise it. In short, the pursuit of individual rational self-interest, especially in a context of unequal power, can have catastrophic effects, whether the "interaction" consists of intervention, ongoing interaction, or abandonment.

As we saw in Chapter 1, there is a distinction between subjectively held social norms and objectively valid moral norms. An objective moral norm is a type of action or inaction that is not just widely believed to be morally right; it is, in fact, as a matter of objective truth, morally right.

It needs to be noted that the concept of an objectively corrupt action is the concept of an action that is objectively corrupt relative to a person and also relative to a set of circumstances. Lying can be morally right or morally wrong, depending on the circumstances. Police working undercover to expose the activities of the Triads in Hong Kong necessarily deceive and tell lies. Nonetheless, they may be morally correct in doing so. However, the mere fact that one was a member of a society that had certain social norms, or that the actions of those in the moral environment in which one found oneself were governed by certain social norms, would not in itself make performing the action prescribed by those social norms objectively morally right. In the past, revenge killings were a social norm for members of the Sicilian Mafia—but it does not follow that they are, or were, objectively morally right. From the point of view of objective moral norms, the fact that one is a member of a particular society, or that one is interacting with, or in, that society, is no more than a consideration to be given some (or no) moral weight in determining what one ought to do.

Finally, it needs to be pointed out that social norms are by definition the moral norms that are adhered to by the members of a particular society and by the members of a particular social group. They do not necessarily transcend that group in the sense that they are adhered to by other groups. Not all social groups believe that the social norms that they adhere to are in fact universal moral principles and/or rights that must be respected in all interactions between all members of all social groups. As it happens, most of the major world religions, including Christianity, Hinduism, and Islam, accept the existence of universal moral principles.

The absence of universal moral principles is especially a feature of long-established criminal organizations centered on families and groups of families. Such organizations include the Mafia and some Chinese Triad groups. To an extent, these organizations are governed by social norms—as distinct from conventions and the rule of fear—but these social norms are, for the most part, constitutive of predatory or parasitic activity, and therefore they are defined in opposition to the group being preyed upon. So these norms are necessarily nonuniversal, and nonuniversalizable, in character. Such norms include norms of revenge, loyalty to the group and disloyalty to others, obedience to the superiors, and disobedience to the social norms and laws of the group being preyed upon, maintenance of secrecy, and so on.

Social norms on the one hand, and immorality, including corruption, on the other, are intimately, if antithetically, related. Robust social norms—at least in the sense of regularities in action that embody ethical or moral attitudes—provide a barrier to corruption; widespread corruption corrodes social norms. This barrier is by no means a sufficient condition for combating immorality, including corruption. But it is a necessary condition. If members of a community or organization do not think that there is anything morally wrong with murder, assault, theft, fraud, bribery, and so on, then there is no possibility of these practices being resisted, let alone eliminated; indeed, they will flourish.

So shared beliefs in the moral unacceptability of these practices is a necessary, but not a sufficient, condition for combating them. Other necessary conditions are what might be loosely referred to as "accountability systems." An accountability system, as we use the term, involves the requirement that people explain and justify their actions to some authority, that there be adjudication by the authority of their actions, and that the people be punished if they are found to be responsible for unacceptable actions. In contemporary societies, the most basic and pervasive accountability system is the criminal justice system. Those who are thought to have failed to comply with the criminal code are investigated, tried, and—if found to be guilty—punished. But there are numerous other accountability systems to which people are subject, for example, organizational and professional ones. Sometimes people think of the informal practice in which one or more persons express their disapproval of another's action as an accountability system. Given what was said before, we are not using the term "accountability" in this sense; rather, we are operating with the more restricted sense of accountability as necessarily involving a formal institutional system.

The nature of accountability systems and their appropriate relationship to social norms is something that we take up briefly later in this chapter and also in greater detail in Chapter 7. Here we simply note that a framework of social norms without an integrated accountability system lacks teeth, but that an accountability system without a framework of social norms to underpin it lacks life—like the dentures on a skeleton, it has nothing to animate it.

So much for the sociomoral context of corruption, the moral environment. Our next task is to explore more specific features of the moral environment that cause, or are conducive to, corruption. In order to facilitate this exploration, we first present a dramatic illustration of a moral environment extraordinarily conducive to corruption—one in which the framework of social norms has in large part broken down.

CASE STUDY 2.1   **Pablo Escobar**

After one of the biggest manhunts in recent history, Pablo Escobar, the notorious drug baron from Colombia, was finally cornered and shot dead on the roof of his hideout in his hometown, Medellín, on December 2, 1993. There is some evidence to suggest that the precision shot to the head that killed him was delivered from close range after Escobar's escape was thwarted by a debilitating initial shot to the leg.[21] Executed, or killed in the line of fire as he was making his escape, the man who from the time of his rise to power in the early 1980s had terrorized a whole nation now lay dead at the feet of his triumphant pursuers.

The hunt, which lasted over four years and cost the United States and Colombian governments hundreds of millions of dollars and several thousand lives, involved members of the Colombian Search Bloc, a special police unit set up to capture Pablo Escobar, and special intelligence and antiterrorist units from the United States, including elite units of the CIA, Centra Spike, Delta Force, as well as the DEA, the FBI, and the Bureau of Alcohol, Tobacco, and Firearms (ATF). This was not merely a hunt for the capture of a criminal—albeit an international criminal who headed the largest cocaine cartel in Colombia accounting for up to 80 percent of the multibillion-dollar export of Colombian cocaine to the United States—but all out war. Indeed, the Colombian state, with the technical, military, and intelligence support of the United States, was fighting this war for the sake of its very own survival.

Declared by the Colombian government to be "public enemy number one," Escobar proved a mighty challenge for both Colombia and the United States.[22] For Colombia it was a challenge by virtue of the threat that Escobar posed to the survival of its democratic institutions, including the government and the judiciary, and its economic infrastructure; for the United States it was a challenge by virtue of the threat to the U.S. "war on drugs" posed by Escobar's export to the United States of large quantities of cocaine and other drugs. For both countries it was a war that they could not afford to lose—a war that had to be won by any means possible.

Those means included the "dirty means" of an unofficial alliance of the Colombian special police unit, Search Bloc, with a vigilante group or "civilian militia," *Los Pepes* (People Persecuted by Pablo Escobar), which comprised known drug criminals from other drug cartels and some disaffected ex-associates of Escobar. In their willingness to use the same unlawful and violent means to destroy Escobar as those used by Escobar himself against his enemies, Los Pepes wreaked havoc against Escobar's operations, killing many of his associates and members of his family, and destroying many of his estates. Agent Joe Toft, who was head of the DEA operation in Colombia throughout the years of waging war against the Medellín cartel, was at the end troubled by the involvement of Los Pepes in the manhunt for Escobar. Soon after Escobar was killed, he retired from the DEA and leaked information that linked the newly elected Colombian president, Ernesto Samper, with the Cali drug cartel. Cali was suspected all along of being responsible for the formation and operation of Los Pepes. Asked what the lesson of the Escobar story was, Toft replied, "I don't know what the lesson of the story is, but I hope it's not that the end justifies the means."[23]

Arguably the richest (*Forbes* magazine in 1989 listed him as the seventh-richest man in the world) and most violent criminal of recent times, Pablo Escobar rose from humble beginnings (he was the son of a teacher and a peasant) as a small-time gangster and car thief in Medellín to become the most powerful and feared drug baron in Colombia, controlling a worldwide billion-dollar drug trade that gave him a lifestyle of unimaginable wealth and luxury comprising airplanes, helicopters, boats, vintage cars, vast estates and properties, banks, and luxury residences in Colombia and throughout the world. His seventy-four-hundred-acre ranch on the Magdalena River near Medellín, which he called "Hacienda Los Napoles," had its own airport, heliport, six different swimming pools, several lakes, and a zoo that housed elephants, buffalos, lions, rhinoceroses, gazelles, zebras, hippos, camels, and ostriches. He could sleep a hundred guests at a time, and entertain them lavishly with food, music, games, and extravagant parties.[24] When he voluntarily and temporarily gave himself up to the authorities in 1991, he and his associates ensconced themselves in "La Catedral," a luxury prison that Escobar had purposely built atop a mountain for that occasion. As it turned out, "La Catedral" was no prison, but was a state within a state from which Escobar continued to run his drug empire and criminal activities.

At the height of his career, he was smuggling to the United States as much as 10,000 kilos of cocaine per flight in specially converted Boeing 727s and up to 2,000 kilos in specially built remote-controlled minisubmarines. His ambition extended to politics, and in 1982 he was elected to Congress. His election to Congress in 1982 marked the apogee of his popularity and power, for popular he was. The increasingly admiring Colombian press knew him as the "paisa Robin Hood"—a man of the people who spent millions of his drug dollars to build sports facilities, roads, and housing developments to house the poor who lived in slums. Escobar did not see himself as a criminal but as an outlaw, a social benefactor who used the money he made by selling drugs to the Americans for the improvement of the people of Colombia. Some believed that the exchange of cocaine for American dollars led to the social and economic improvement of Colombia and that therefore Escobar's drug enterprise was the strategy of a revolutionary figure. Escobar saw himself as an outlaw, like Robin Hood, who took from the rich to give to the poor. Indeed, one of Escobar's heroes was the legendary Pancho Villa, the Mexican revolutionary who had challenged the United States in 1916 when he led raids into Texas and New Mexico. Moreover, the Escobar period was a time of intense Marxist revolutionary activity; groups like FARC, Fuerzas Armadas Revolucionarias de Colombia, or the Revolutionary Armed Forces of Colombia, were very active. There was peasant unrest caused by years of intimidation at the hands of the wealthy who used their private paramilitary armies, the feared *autodefensas*, to subdue the peasantry. More generally, there was resentment in Colombia of the rich elite of 3 percent of the population that controlled 97 percent of the land and wealth of Colombia. Accordingly, the image of Robin Hood was a powerful and popular one that Pablo Escobar—the consummate populist who understood the importance of publicity and public relations—cultivated to his maximum advantage.

However, that image became tainted as Escobar's violence escalated. During his criminal reign, Colombia became a war zone of daily kidnappings; car bombs that killed and maimed indiscriminately; murders often preceded by torture; and bribery of the police, politicians, and the judiciary. Though prevented by other politicians from taking up his office in Parliament as an elected member of Congress, he nevertheless had the Colombian government bribed and bombed into acceding to his demands of banning the extradition treaty with the United States that would have seen Escobar tried and imprisoned in America for drug trafficking. His method of dealing with the authorities, or anyone else who dared challenge him, came to be known as *plata o plomo* (silver or lead). If he couldn't bribe those who opposed him, he had them killed.

Two of the worst crimes that he was suspected of orchestrating and that marked the beginning of his fall were (1) the murder of the Liberal Party candidate for the presidency, Luis Galan, a charismatic popular politician who had vowed to rid Colombia of drug traffickers; and (2) on the false assumption that it was carrying Galan's successor, the downing of an Avianca airliner killing 110 people, including two U.S. citizens. These were fatal mistakes. Killing Galan made Escobar enemy number one in Colombia. Downing the Avianca airliner—including killing two U.S. citizens—turned him into an international terrorist and a legitimate terrorist target for the United States.

By the time of Escobar's death, hundreds of people had been killed, including many innocent civilians, foreign citizens, police officers, judges, lawyers, government ministers, presidential candidates, and newspaper editors. In the first two months of 1991, there was an average of twenty murders a day in Colombia.[25] Assassinations included those of Justice Minister Rodrigo Lara; more than thirty judges killed after Lara's assassination; the editor of *El Espectador*—for speaking out against Escobar and his drug trafficking operations; Luis Galan (the Liberal Party candidate for the presidency); and at least 457 police officers during the period of the manhunt for Escobar (1989–1993). During the latter period, Pablo was offering 5 million pesos to each young man in Medellín who killed a cop. When he could not stop the hunt against him—and in keeping with his modus operandi of *plata o polo*—Pablo offered $6 million to Colonel Hugo Martinez, the leader of Search Bloc, to stop the manhunt. Martinez flatly refused the bribe. As Mark Bowden pointedly remarked, "sometimes the fate of a nation can hinge on the integrity of one man."[26] Martinez's integrity, however, would later come under a cloud through the alleged association of his Search Bloc with the death squads of Los Pepes.[27]

Mark Bowden provides a poignant image of these times. It is that of an inconsolable pregnant woman with a small child who throws herself on a police officer's coffin and refuses to let go until she is pulled away. The officer was her husband and the child's father. According to Bowden, the normally stoical DEA chief, Toft—who felt it was his duty to attend the funerals of police officers killed in the struggle against Escobar—went back to his apartment after this particular funeral, and cried.[28]

What sets Pablo Escobar apart from most other criminals in history is that he waged war against the state, not as a revolutionary but as a criminal seeking to overpower the legitimate institutions of the state in the service of his self-regarding desire for power, status, and wealth. Accordingly, the Colombian and U.S. governments must have welcomed his death. Nevertheless, for many Colombians, Escobar's death was an occasion for grief. Thousands of ordinary people attended the funeral and accompanied the procession through the streets of Medellín. Many ordinary peasants refused to see him as a violent criminal who had terrorized a nation; they preferred to view him as a latter-day Robin Hood. That tells us something about Escobar's past power and influence; it also tells us something about the social and economic plight of large sections of the Colombian people.

MORAL ENVIRONMENTS: CONDITIONS CONDUCIVE TO CORRUPTION

Our case study is illustrative of a breakdown in the framework of social norms, and notably of a failure of compliance with, and enforcement of, the moral principles enshrined in the criminal law. Such moral principles include ones not to murder, assault, infringe the freedom of others, steal, defraud, or bribe. But the state of Colombian society and its central institutions reveals a number of specific sociomoral features or conditions that facilitate corruption. If organizations, governments, and communities are to successfully combat the sort of grand, systemic corruption that exists in Colombia and elsewhere, then we suggest they need rectify these conditions.[29]

First, Colombian society comprises a high level of *conflict and factionalism*. For example, there is evidently a high level of class conflict. There is good empirical evidence that conflict-ridden societies, such as apartheid South Africa and the former Soviet Union, provide fertile ground for corruption.

The reason for this likelihood is that conflict-ridden societies are ones in which there is not a robust system of social norms that are adhered to by all. Rather, at most, members of a particular social group or class comply with social norms in regard to one another but not with "outsiders." At best, individuals are prepared to restrain their self-seeking behavior only in their dealings with members of their narrow social group or faction. Consider, in this connection, the treatment of blacks by whites in apartheid South Africa or of the poor by the rich in Latin American countries such as Colombia. Quite clearly then, the issue of conflict and factionalism needs to be addressed as part of any wider strategy to combat entrenched systemic and grand corruption.

A second, and often related, sociomoral condition that is conducive to corruption is *unjust and unequal systems of wealth and status*. If there are great disparities of wealth and opportunity and if differences in wealth and status are not perceived as fair and as contributing to the common good, then commitment to institutional roles and conformity to the law and to social norms will weaken. For example, in many countries, the poor and powerless have turned for assistance to local crime bosses ("godfathers") who provide this assistance, but they do so in return for "loyalty," which might take the form of voting for certain candidates or turning a blind eye to corrupt and unlawful activities. In this connection, note the popular support that Escobar managed to draw, indeed manipulate, on the basis of his presentation of himself as a Robin Hood–like figure taking from the rich and giving to the poor. In reality, Escobar was nothing of the sort, notwithstanding his occasional and selective "charity" to the poor. However, it is understandable how poor and downtrodden members of the populace could come to see him as such. So reduction of inequalities and injustice in wealth and status is, we suggest, an important element in combating systemic, grand corruption.

A third sociomoral condition that facilitates corruption is *moral confusion*. Moral confusion has a number of sources but typically involves a combination of an unclarity in relation to moral beliefs about what is right and wrong, and a tempting opportunity to do wrong.

In times of rapid social and economic transition, stable moral practices are upset, and a degree of moral confusion can set in. For example, rapid economic growth and wealth acquisition can undermine traditional practices of self-restraint and financial prudence. During the 1980s in Australia, "corporate cowboys" such as Alan Bond and Christopher Skase came to possess enormous wealth by engaging in corrupt practices. Yet their activities were dependent on the gross negligence of bankers, lawyers, journalists, and others. According to Trevor Sykes, "Never before in Australian history had so much money been channelled to so many people incompetent to lend it into the hands of so many people incompetent to manage it."[30] The result was a wave of corporate and banking collapses, as well as the squandering of huge amounts of the savings of ordinary Australians. The recent Asian economic crisis, including in the banking sector in Thailand, involves similar stories, as does the recent spate of corporate collapses in the United States and Australia. (See later for an account of the Enron scandal.)

In relation to so-called "victimless crimes," there is often moral confusion. Are recreational drug use, occasional drinking bouts, intermittent gambling, casual sex, or paying for sex when outside a stable relationship morally wrong? If not, under what circumstances does drug-taking or gambling and so on become morally wrong, and under what circumstances should these activities be criminalized?

Societies seem to oscillate between a permissive approach and a highly restrictive approach to drugs, prostitution, and gambling; but neither seems to be desirable. On the one hand, an addiction to, say, heroin can be deeply corrosive of a person's autonomy and well-being, so that permissiveness in relation to drug addiction may well be morally pernicious. On the other hand, so-called "recreational" drug use might be completely harmless, and therefore criminalization morally unacceptable.

Perhaps the truth is that these kinds of activities are morally ambiguous; they are morally innocuous if indulged in on an occasional recreational basis, but morally problematic if they become an addiction or otherwise come to take center stage in a person's life. If so, then there is often an initial lack of moral discernment between, say, the horrors of addiction and the harmless pleasures of recreational use; this lack of discernment can be a source of moral confusion.

At any rate, the point we need to make here is that historically corruption has been fueled by the existence of moral confusion in relation to gambling, prostitution, drugs, and the like. The restrictive, criminalization approach not only has failed to work but also has driven these activities underground and thus enabled the criminal suppliers to make huge profits and to corrupt police and other officials involved in enforcement. This corruption of officials is able to be achieved in part because there is often an understandable feeling that gambling, prostitution, and much drug use is not all that morally reprehensible; accordingly, it is easy to compromise and thereby to set in train a process of compromise and corruption. The end result can be a set of "lose/lose" options; a given official might never have intended to be involved in serious corruption and might want to abandon the path he is going down; but he is already compromised, and if he tries to quit, his corrupters can bring him down. On the other hand, an entirely permissive approach evidently fails to appreciate the very real damage that can be done to people's lives when they become addicted to drugs, gambling, and so on. Indeed, in some instances, the damage includes moral incapacitation: the loss of the ability to make moral judgments and to act on them.

It is no accident, we suggest, that the huge profits, power, and capacity to corrupt that were possessed by Escobar ultimately derived from selling cocaine and that there is considerable moral confusion in relation to the use of cocaine. Accordingly, we conclude that the Escobar case study is illustrative of the importance of moral confusion as a condition conducive to corruption.

A fourth, and final, very important general sociomoral condition that is conducive to corruption is *imbalance of power*. What Lord Acton said is now a cliché, but no less true for that: "Power tends to corrupt, and absolute power corrupts absolutely."

The massive human rights abuses and corruption perpetrated by autocrats such as Hitler, Mussolini, Suharto, Marcos, Idi Amin, and Pinochet are testimony to the importance of limiting, constraining, diluting, and dividing power. But there are plenty of other cases that involve the liberal democracies. Consider in this connection the cynical arrangement between Australia and Indonesia to carve up the oil deposits in the Timor Sea "owned" by the East Timorese. Evidently its interest in these deposits influenced Australia's indifference to the plight of the East Timorese. Consider also world trade agreements that have, it is claimed, favored the powerful and rich nations, at the expense of the powerless and poor nations. Perhaps the much-vaunted "level playing field" is a self-serving myth fabricated by powerful multinational companies and the governments of rich Western nations. Or consider the Watergate scandal, in which an occupant of the most powerful political office in the world, U.S. President Richard Nixon, and some members of his political clique, engaged in unlawful and corrupt practices—including a cover-up—in the service of their own narrow political self-interest.

The Escobar case study graphically depicts the nexus between power and corruption. Escobar was a ruthless killer who possessed considerable coercive power by virtue of his capacity and willingness to torture and kill in the service of his ends. In addition, by virtue of the enormous drug profits he generated for himself, he possessed great economic power. But it was the combination of coercive and economic power that provided him with not simply local power but also national, and indeed international, power: so much so that the nation-state of Colombia was referred to not as a democracy, or even as an autocracy, but rather as a narcocracy. Escobar used his enormous power to corrupt individuals and institutions, and these corrupt individuals and institutions in turn maintained and strengthened his power. He corrupted politicians, judges, police, administrators, businesspeople, and ordinary citizens. They in turn—and motivated by fear, greed, ambition, and false hopes—gave him power by taking his money and doing him favors, by turning a blind eye to his criminality, by voting for him, and so on.

So much, then, for the importance of the sociomoral features of the moral environment—including conflict; moral confusion; injustice; and inequalities of wealth, status, and power—as a generic condition conducive to corruption. We need now to turn to a detailed consideration of institutional accountability systems, or the lack thereof, as a second generic condition that is conducive to corruption. Before doing so, we present another case study, the Enron scandal, that will illustrate and assist our discussion of this issue.

CASE STUDY 2.2   Enron

Enron begun its life in 1984 as a pipeline company called Houston Natural Gas with Ken Lay as its Chairman and CEO. Under Lay's direction, it merged first with two other gas companies, Florida Gas and Transwestern Pipeline, and then with InterNorth, a pipeline based in Omaha, Nebraska. In 1986, the company changed its name to Enron and moved its headquarters to Houston where Lay, the new Chairman and CEO of Enron, lived. Enron at that time was both a gas and an oil company, but under Lay's entrepreneurial and innovative style of management, it gradually ceased to be just a traditional gas and oil company. Helped by the increasing deregulation of the energy industry taking place under the Reagan administration, it was transformed into a cutting-edge trading company dealing in a diverse range of goods and services, including natural gas, electric power, pollution permits, telecommunications, water, and Internet broadband. In the political climate of deregulation, free markets became Enron's religion.[31] Its corporate culture was inspired by two things. The first thing was profits, and the second was how to generate even greater profits. New deals were struck in the pursuit of higher quarterly earnings and to thereby drive Enron's stock up to the highest possible price; this practice allowed Enron's in-house deal-makers to claim huge profits for the company and to justify large bonuses for themselves. It also enabled them to launch further new deals in order to secure even higher quarterly earnings, and so on and so forth. Moreover, in this environment, there was a powerful incentive to devise schemes designed to inflate profits and hide debt; this environment was conducive to institutional corruption.

In 1990, Lay hired Jeffrey Skilling, a brilliant Harvard MBA from McKinsey and Company, one of the top consulting firms at the time, to pioneer Enron's trading operations. Skilling in turn hired Andrew Fastow, a financial wizard and senior director from Continental Bank in Chicago. Fastow became Chief Financial Officer (CFO). He was also the architect of the Special Purpose Entities (SPEs) that primarily drove Enron to financial collapse. (SPEs were complex off-the-balance-sheet partnership arrangements that had the effect of hiding debt and inflating earnings. See Chapter 7 for more detail.) Skilling created the "gas bank," making Enron the first company to buy and sell large volumes of gas from producers and then to resell to industrial customers on long-term contracts. Coinciding with the deregulation of the energy business, and with the willingness of financial institutions to provide large pools of funds through an array of schemes to finance deals— including "structured finance," which was used to finance Enron's SPEs—Skilling's innovative work in energy and other forms of market trading pushed Enron to the forefront of corporate success. In a bold move, Enron moved its gas and electricity trading online. Expanding beyond energy, Skilling's team of young MBAs from some of the elite universities in the country created unheard-of commodity markets offering anything from energy to weather derivatives (contracts that offered companies financial protection against the costs of heat waves and blizzards).[32]

Enron became the darling of Wall Street and the business press, which were dazzled by Enron's meteoric success (a dazzle that would blind them to Enron's increasing financial problems, mismanagement, and corruption). For six years running, *Fortune* magazine ranked Enron as the most innovative company in the nation. From 1998 to 2000, Enron's stock tripled in value, hitting an all-time high of $90 a share in August 2000. These were Enron's halcyon days. Skilling is reported to have told the University of Virginia professors that Enron was "the world's coolest company." He joked that Lay had even considered the idea of draping a giant pair of sunglasses around Enron's headquarters tower in Houston.[33] Enron was heavily into image making; unfortunately, the image did not match the reality. Back in 1986 when it was still operating as Houston Natural Gas and InterNorth, the company hired the consultants Lippincott and Margulie to come up with a new name for the organization. The name suggested was "Enteron," a name that was initially embraced with enthusiasm. However, it was discovered that the name had an unfortunate medical meaning, that is, "alimentary canal, intestines, or guts." Less than a day before the name was to be unveiled, the board informed the consultancy firm that it had to come up with a new name. The "te" was simply dropped from "Enteron," and thus the company adopted Enron as its new name.[34] This little anecdote also illustrates the importance that the company placed on its image. Perhaps if Enron had not so ignominiously collapsed, it would have substantiated

Oscar Wilde's ironic quip that "in matters of great importance it is style, not substance, that matters." And Enron had style in abundance. It paid its employees $750 million in cash bonuses in 2000, an amount close to the company's reported profit for that year. As even secretaries became paper millionaires, Porsches replaced pickup trucks in the company parking lot, and the company executives built multimillion-dollar mansions in Houston's posh and exclusive River Oaks neighbourhood, as well as holiday homes in Aspen.[35] Between January and May 2000, the stock price of Enron rose by 80 percent. Enron insiders, Lay and Skilling among them, had cashed out over $475 million worth of stock. So these executives and management personnel of Enron got very rich. Unfortunately, it turned out to be at the expense of the employees, the banks, and the investors, who lost hundreds of millions of dollars when Enron collapsed, and before they, unlike the high flyers of Enron, had time to cash in their investments. Even as late as July 2001, just five months before Enron's collapse, Lay and Skilling, with the backing of analysts, were preaching the Enron gospel and encouraging investors to buy more shares in the company. If anyone within the company, including Lay and Skilling, knew of the impending implosion of Enron, they were keeping it to themselves and not telling the investors.

As the company entered new markets, it needed new injections of cash to finance its profligate and ever-expanding trading operations. From 2000, a SPE named LJM (after Fastow's wife Lea and his two daughters) provided most of Enron's profits, though because of their off-the-balance-sheet nature, they remained invisible to outside investors. Andrew Fastow's dual role as CFO of Enron and manager of the SPEs (including LJM) involved a serious conflict of interest, one that Fastow, as the company's financial watchdog in his role of CFO, should have avoided. When Jeffrey McMahon, the company's treasurer, complained to Skilling about the conflict of interest, he was first confronted by Fastow, who was told of the complaint by Skilling; and then, a week later, he (McMahon) was transferred to another part of the company and replaced by Ben F. Glisan, a close aid and associate of Fastow. Although Enron had publicly identified Fastow as LJM's general manager in its proxy statements in 2000 and 2001, it had not done so in its quarterly and annual financial statements filed with the Securities and Exchange Commission. This omission was a breach of corporate disclosure regulations.

Enron's final year of operations, 2001, began with Skilling's assuming the post of CEO in February and Lay's remaining the chairman of the company. In March, a major broadband deal between Enron and Blockbuster collapsed, but in keeping with Enron's magical accounting tricks, Enron used aggressive mark-to-market accounting practices, and Enron recorded a $111 million profit—notwithstanding the fact that the deal did not go through.[36] In the same month, *Fortune* magazine printed a major article about Enron with the provocative title "Is Enron Overpriced?" Enron's stock continued its downward slide. In August, Skilling, after six months as CEO, resigned for "personal reasons," sparking intense speculation and rumors about Enron's true financial position. Ken Lay assumed the CEO position again with stock trading at around $42 per share and going down amid growing concerns over the accuracy of Enron's reported earnings.

The emperor's fine clothes were looking increasingly threadbare. Shortly after Lay took over as CEO, Sherron Watkins, an accountant in Enron's finance division, sent a memo to Ken Lay sounding the warning of potential accounting scandals ready to blow up in Enron's face. On October 17, Enron changed its 401(k) pension plan administrator, a move that had the effect (by accident or by design) of locking in the stock holdings of employees for 30 days and preventing them from selling Enron stock. This step proved financially catastrophic for those employees whose pension funds comprised a large proportion of holdings in Enron shares. Fastow took "leave of absence" on October 24 in the wake of controversy over his role in Enron's SPEs. A week later, Enron's shares fell to $11 per share, its lowest point in nine years. Chewco and LJM came back to haunt Enron on November 8, forcing the company to write down its equity by $1.2 billion. Enron's attempt to bail out of trouble by merging with Dynergy, its largest energy-industry rival, fell through when Dynergy got cold feet about taking on Enron's debts. By November 28, Enron's stock was downgraded to junk-bond status and was now trading at less than $1 a share. Shortly afterwards, on December 2, 2001, Enron filed for bankrupcy. Ken Lay resigned from the company on January 23, 2002. In the early hours of January 25, 2002, Cliff Baxter, who was vice chairman of Enron when he resigned for personal reasons in May 2001 and who had complained bitterly to Jeffrey Skilling about Andrew Fastow's LJM transactions, was found dead from a gunshot wound in his car not far from his house. A note found in his car suggests that it was a suicide, but the block-lettered suicide note, which did not have a signature, has aroused suspicions surrounding the circumstances of his death. Along with the thousands of Enron employees who lost most of their pension savings when the company's shares became worthless, this was the human face of Enron's corporate collapse.

INSTITUTIONAL ACCOUNTABILITY SYSTEMS

We have described the nexus between the power of autocrats and criminals such as Pinochet, Suharto, Marcos, and indeed Escobar, on the one hand, and systemic and grand corruption on the other. Moreover, our case study on the collapse of Enron illustrates the nexus between power and corruption within a large corporation. The corrupt practices, including the creation of SPEs, were the creatures of the CEO, the CFO, and other members of the management team. It was their position of authority within the organization that enabled the existence of corruption on such a large scale and with such devastating consequences.

Naturally, not only is such corruption dependent on the power of the offenders, but it is also dependent on their immorality; the Enron CEO and CFO, for example, had few moral scruples and little concern for the welfare of Enron's shareholders and employees. So the existence of this power/corruption nexus points to the importance of robust social norms: commitment and compliance on the part of individuals to moral principles. However, social norms by themselves are not enough; they are necessary, but not sufficient. The additional necessary condition for combating corruption is adequate institutional accountability mechanisms. In the case of Enron, the accountability mechanisms, including auditing controls, were inadequate, but let us try briefly to describe the various kinds of institutional accountability mechanisms needed to control corruption. We offer greater detail on anti-corruption systems in Chapter 7.

In relation to the power/corruption nexus, one of the most important accountability mechanisms is *democracy*, because democracy limits, constrains, and dilutes power—at least potentially, and often in fact. The past and present existence of autocrats such as those named earlier underlines the importance of democratic accountability both in government and in public institutions more generally. Again, in the absence of accountability mechanisms in relation to the powerful, hierarchies that are based on patronage, rather than merit, tend to develop; and thus benefits, such as promotion, are distributed on the basis of "loyalty" to the powerful, including complicity in corrupt schemes, rather than on the basis of high-quality performance. Nor does this point pertain only to government. It holds equally for other organizational settings such as large corporations. Indeed, this claim has been argued persuasively by Robert Jackall[37] in relation to large U.S. corporations in particular. When the notion of democracy is discussed, it is normally done so in the context of government. However, the power/corruption nexus provides good reason for democratizing many other institutions, including corporations.

A second very important institutional accountability system is that of the *separation of powers*. Institutional separation and institutional independence are of paramount importance in limiting and dividing power, and therefore in controlling corruption. At the extreme end of the spectrum, one institution, such as the military, which was established to perform one kind of function, say defense, overpowers a second institution, say the legislature (parliament) and takes over its function. Military coups in Thailand are a case in point. But other examples are less extreme. Consider in this connection the claims made by Athol Moffitt, one of the three Royal Commissioners to consider organized crime in Australia:

> Thus organised crime and corruption have added a factor to the process of the breakdown of these [judicial] institutions due to the rise of party power. These things have other consequences. The political handling of organised crime and corruption in recent years when it has more and more intruded into the political arena, and the manipulation of the administration of justice, have pointed up the underlying vulnerability of the independence of the institutions of justice and the insecure basis on which the separation of powers rest, at least so far as judicial power is concerned.[38]

Consider also Kerry Packer's corporate empire in Australia. It consists of a large number of print and electronic media outlets. But it also consists of huge tracts of land susceptible to Native Title claims. Can his media be relied upon to communicate the truth, the whole truth, and nothing but the truth in relation to, for example, the Aboriginal land rights debate in Australia? This is doubtful. Again, consider the cosy relationship in Japan between politicians, bureaucrats, and business leaders. For example, on retirement, former bureaucrats are typically hired and paid large salaries by the very companies that competed for government contracts overseen by these bureaucrats.[39]

A third aspect of accountability systems pertains to their relationship with the framework of social norms. Corruption is facilitated when *laws, regulations, and institutional roles do not track ethical/moral principles and ends.* One kind of case involves the inappropriate criminalization of certain acts, such as the use of harmless drugs. We mentioned this kind of example in the context of our discussion of moral confusion. But there are other kinds of cases that do not necessarily involve moral confusion.

One such category involves conflicts of interest in relation to an institutional role; the role has not been sufficiently circumscribed so as to rule out certain kinds of conflict of interest. We examine conflicts of interest in considerable detail in Chapter 3, but a few remarks are in order here. Consider the tradition in Thailand whereby tax collectors and police were paid low salaries in the expectation that they would supplement their own salaries from taxes gathered or from fines received.[40] The possibility of justice and probity is greatly reduced by allowing such conflicts of interest in relation to institutional roles.

As noted before in the Enron case study, Andrew Fastow's dual role as CFO of Enron and manager of the SPEs involved a clear conflict of interest, and one that greatly facilitated the corruption process at Enron.

Inadequacies in the investigation of corruption are self-evidently deficiencies in relation to institutional accountability. For example, in relation to some categories of fraud in Australia, the United Kingdom, the United States, and some other countries, there are insufficient police resources to investigate the massive amount of fraudulent activity that is taking place. One element of this situation is a traditional police preoccupation with street crime and a tendency not to put resources into investigating white-collar crime. In Japan, the streets are very safe, but there is a history of corruption in relation to public works projects, elections, and so on. Another element is police corruption. Historically, police corruption has existed in relation to morally dubious activities that have been criminalized but that yet have a high demand, such as drugs, prostitution, and gambling.

Another set of deficiencies in institutional accountability are *inadequacies in the court system,* or in other systems of adjudication, such as the adjudication of professional negligence by professional bodies. We deal with some of these issues in greater detail in Chapters 7 and 9. Here we simply note that the law courts in most countries often find it difficult to successfully prosecute wealthy fraudsters and crime bosses who employ high-quality, well-paid lawyers. And in some countries, there is a history of bribing or intimidating the judiciary, thereby perverting the course of justice; consider the Mafia in Sicily.

Relatedly, there are sometimes *inadequacies in the correctional and prison system,* or more generally, in the systems of punishment within organizations: for example, demotion within a police service. We deal with this issue in detail in Chapter 10; here we simply note that imprisonment for nonviolent offenses, such as fraud, bribery, theft, and the like, may be counterproductive. Prisons may simply serve as expensive, crowded incubators of criminality. There may well need to be a greater emphasis on establishing institutions and practices, including restorative justice practices, with a focus on reintegration back into the moral community.

Different institutions and organizations require different accountability systems. A police organization requires an elaborate accountability system in relation to the detection and apprehension of criminal offenders—hardly a priority in, say, a university. On the other hand, universities need to have accountability systems in relation to examinations and the like. Most organizations require accountability systems in relation to financial transactions. In this connection, consider the absence of accountability mechanisms in relation to kickbacks to government ministers in return for the awarding of contracts for large infrastructure projects in Japan, or simply the ability of heads of governments such as Suharto to transfer money from public accounts into ones wholly controlled by themselves, or the inadequacy of auditing controls in the Enron and WorldCom corruption scandals.

Accountability and Technological Development

In effect, we have been arguing for the importance of the organizational, social, economic, and so on, *context* in the structuring of institutional accountability systems. In this connection, one of the most challenging aspects is dealing with opportunities for corruption arising from changes in technology.

Over the last three decades, there have been changes that revolutionized the way in which business is done. Paper-based financial systems have given way to key information being transmitted and stored electronically. Banks and other financial institutions, as well as most business and government enterprises, in developed countries undertake the majority of their business transactions electronically, with billions of dollars worth of funds transmitted, stored, and analyzed every day. Associated with this is the global communication system of the Internet, whereby governments, businesses, and individuals can communicate with each other not only internationally but also *instantaneously*. All of this fits within a much broader process of globalization. Nation-states no longer serve as the corner stone for business—transnational corporations straddle the global economy, and the rich and powerful nations of Europe, Japan, and the United States all work together to break down the barriers to business caused by laws and administrative procedures based upon the nation-state.

These changes have had the effect of creating a global marketplace that is dominated by the countries just mentioned. This marketplace has created enormous wealth for the players but has also brought considerable problems. Without attempting to be exhaustive, the following are examples of fraud and corruption that have been caused, or at the very least facilitated, by the advent of emerging technologies:

- Nigerian-based groups flood the Internet with electronic messages asking the recipients for details of their bank accounts so that these groups can shift funds. The claims are bogus, and those people foolish enough to respond find that their accounts are emptied of funds.

- Nick Leeson, a Singapore-based employee of the United Kingdom–based merchant bank Barings, virtually destroyed that enterprise by hiding details of unsuccessful deals in temporary internal accounts that he had the authority to operate. His purpose was to boost his standing within the bank by appearing to generate earnings that were not there. Leeson was convicted and served a jail sentence in Singapore.

- In Australia, David Muir, an employee of the Commonwealth Department of Finance, abused his rights to operate certain accounts electronically. He illegally transferred 8.25 million in Australian dollars to a complex network of companies. The funds were not recovered, and Muir was convicted and jailed for defrauding the Commonwealth of Australia.

- The U.S. General Accounting Office cited estimates that the number of identity fraud cases is between 250,000 and 750,000 per annum. The report cited that the Federal Trade Commission's Identity Fraud Clearinghouse was receiving 3,000 calls per week in December 2001. Although not all of these are related to electronic financial transactions, the majority involve theft of credit card details or abuse of Social Security numbers for fraudulent purposes.[41]

On page 6 of the GAO report just mentioned an FBI source outlines how emerging technology has contributed to the incidence of identity theft:

> The availability of information on the Internet, in combination with the advances in computer hardware and software, makes it easier for the criminal to assume the identity of another for the purposes of committing fraud. For example, there are web-sites that offer novelty identification cards (including the hologram). After downloading the format, fonts, art work, and hologram images, the information can be easily modified to resemble a state issued driver's license. In addition to drivers' licenses, there are web-sites that offer birth certificates, law enforcement credentials (including the FBI), and Internal Revenue Service forms.

At the broadest level, governments have a great deal of difficulty in controlling these changes. Grabosky, Smith, and Dempsey have noted the following:

> ... many governments lack the capacity to control behaviour in cyberspace, on the part of their own citizens or those of other countries. This is also reflected in the limited ability of governments alone to protect personal property in the digital environment. Law enforcement resources are constrained, and there are relatively few skilled computer crime investigators and forensic accountants.[42]

A research project[43] conducted by two of the authors of this book into electronic corruption in the New South Wales government enterprises in Australia showed a high awareness of some of the dimensions of the issue—in particular employees misusing Internet access to view pornography—but indicated serious shortcomings at an institutional level of systems for preventing corruption though the use of emerging technology.

Although much of the literature examining the cross-over between crime and technology implies that technology has created a new form of crime, it is more productive to see technology as yet another context in which corruption can occur. The characterizing features of that context are that the accountability mechanisms are trailing the developments in technology, so that the technologically aware have much more opportunity to commit acts of fraud and corruption. An associated issue is that business has rapidly changed from its social form of face-to-face contact to dealing with strangers over a computer network. Although that may give the wrongdoer a sense of anonymity (often exaggerated), the basic issues of moral responsibility are largely the same.

TRANSPARENCY

We have dealt with the moral environment and with accountability systems, and we have identified a variety of conditions that facilitate corruption. Some of these are elements of the moral environment, such as imbalances of power, and some consist of inadequacies in accountability systems, for example, auditing controls. However, there is a further condition that greatly facilitates corruption that we have not yet dealt with, namely, secrecy or lack of transparency. This condition is one that pertains both to moral environments and to accountability systems.

Widespread corruption can flourish in secretive social and institutional environments, such as those encouraged by the likes of Obote, Marcos, and Suharto. Transparency enables existing corruption to be brought to light and discourages incipient corruption. The role of a free and independent media is important in this regard. Transparency is a potent anti-corruption measure. The importance of the role of transparency is something that has been known since the birth of civilizations. Let us consider the ancient Greek story about the Gyges Ring. The following is a brief exposition of that myth as related by Glaucon to Socrates in Book 2 of Plato's (428–347 B.C.) *Republic*.

Once upon a time, a certain shepherd from Lydia named Gyges, while tending to his sheep, found a ring that he put on his finger. Gyges soon discovered that by turning the ring on his finger, he could make himself invisible. By making himself invisible, Gyges seduced the Queen, killed the King, and eventually became the new King. Glaucon continues the story by asking us to imagine an ordinary person who, like Gyges, has the ability through possession of a similar magical ring to render himself invisible, thus allowing himself the opportunity to act unethically at will and with impunity.

Invisibility is often present in instances of corrupt activity. Invisibility seems to be at least instrumentally desirable, for without invisibility, one might not be able to evade detection and thus to escape possible social disapproval and punishment from others, or the state.[44] Like Glaucon's perfectly unjust person, the perfectly corrupt person is one who maintains an outward appearance of justice and probity, while carrying out his or her corrupt deeds in secret. In this way, the person maximizes his or her self-regarding gain, or that of the group to which the person belongs, with little or no instrumental cost to the person or to his or her group.[45] Invisibility, therefore, seems to be a condition that is highly conducive to corruption, at least for instrumentally rational, self-regarding agents. In general, then, it would be self-defeating for those agents to engage in corrupt activities openly and transparently, since that method would minimize, not maximize, their chances of achieving their corrupt goals at little or no ethical or legal cost to themselves. Consider in this connection the CEO and CFO at Enron.

On occasion, agents act in a corrupt manner but do so openly. Consider, in this connection, some of the activities of Escobar. Many people knew who he was and what he was doing; but yet many supported him or failed to oppose him. How is this phenomenon to be explained?

One kind of explanation concerns social norms. Notice that transparency succeeds in combating corruption only if transparency exists against a background of widely accepted social norms. Only if members of the community find corruption morally unacceptable will its exposure to the harsh light of the public domain bring about the downfall of the corrupt. If the community has a high tolerance for corruption—or at least for specific forms of corruption, such as, say, bribery—then both transparency and the consequent exposure of the corrupt will not necessarily be a powerful anti-corruption measure.

Accordingly, in the so-called "state of nature," conceived of by contract theorists such as the English philosopher Thomas Hobbes (1588–1679), one can openly be corrupt with impunity because there are no legal or moral sanctions. In such a state of nature, there is, as Hobbes tells us in his seminal work *The Leviathan* (1651), "a war of everyone against everyone" that ultimately benefits no one, since no one can efficiently and effectively maximize his or her own self-interest under these conditions. In the state of nature, the condition of invisibility becomes redundant as far as social disapproval and legal sanction are concerned. In the state of nature, social-moral attitudes do not matter, and legal sanctions do not exist. So social attitudes and legal sanctions are not to be feared, and there is no need to hide one's transgressions on their account.[46]

We have been discussing lack of transparency as a condition conducive to corruption, and consequently transparency as an inhibitor of corruption. However, it is important to note that transparency in relation to matters that ought to be kept confidential or that fall within the sphere of an individual's right to privacy can function as an aid—rather than as an inhibitor of corruption. Consider a situation in which a police officer leaks the details of an undercover operation to a newspaper and they are published. The operation is compromised; a legitimate process of investigation has been corrupted. Or consider the publication by a magazine of explicit nude pictures and personal details concerning a person's private sex life without the person's consent. The magazine makes money by pandering to the prurience of a section of the community. However, this publication is a violation of the person's right to privacy and a misuse of the channels of public communication; the magazine story, an otherwise legitimate form of mass media communication, has been corrupted.

CONCLUSION

In this chapter, our concern has been with what causes or facilitates corruption, rather than with corruption per se. We have discussed three general conditions that are conducive to corruption, namely, an immoral environment, the absence of accountability mechanisms, and lack of transparency. We have illustrated these three general conditions and various aspects of them by recourse to two case studies, Pablo Escobar and Enron. Moreover, these case studies have also served to contextualize our discussion. We are of the view that the phenomenon of corruption and its causes cannot be assimilated to the sorts of causal relations that might obtain in the physical world. Although the causes of earthquakes might not deviate much from one location to another, the causes of corruption vary enormously from one social context to another. Accordingly, we have not sought to provide a detailed theory of corruption causation. Rather, we have contented ourselves with general descriptions and have only offered (partial) analyses of particular instances of corruption.

In order to understand the causes of corruption, it is extremely important to focus on each of the three general conditions discussed. But it is also important to understand the relationships between these three conditions and their various elements, in specific social and institutional contexts. A particular form of corruption in some social setting is likely to have a number of mutually reinforcing causal factors. It might, for example, involve a moral environment conducive to that kind of corruption and might also involve the absence of specific and relevant accountability mechanisms.

In the next chapter, we focus on a relatively specific feature of the moral environment that is conducive to corruption, namely, conflicts of interest.

chapter three

Conflicts of Interest

In this chapter, we focus attention on one particular type of condition that is conducive to institutional corruption, namely, conflicts of interest. More specifically, we

- Provide an analysis of the concept of a conflict of interest.
- Explore a variety of conflicts of interest, for example, the Keating Five and Enron, and conflicts of interest in clinical trials.
- Explain the relationship between conflicts of interest and corruption.
- Show how to satisfactorily resolve conflicts of interest, for example, by avoidance or disclosure.

One very important cause of corruption is the conflict of interest. A conflict of interest occurs when a person's or a group's self-regarding interest comes into conflict with its fiduciary duties, or when a person or a group has two fiduciary roles, and the duties of one compete with the duties of the other. For example, if a member of the tax office decided to adjudicate his own tax return, he would have a conflict between his personal self-interest and his fiduciary duty. Again, if an accountant happened also to be the manager of a football club and as an accountant she was asked to audit the club's financial statements, she would have a conflict of interest.

Conflicts of interest are conducive to institutional corruption in a variety of ways, depending on the nature of the role of the person or group that has the conflict of interest. For example, a magistrate or police officer with a conflict of interest may fail to apply the law impartially, or a businessman who is a member of a local government body might vote to award himself a contract.

Sometimes it is hard to determine whether an apparent conflict of interest is real or not. And theoretically, a conflict of interest that is only apparent might not be problematic. However, often even the *appearance* of impropriety can be harmful not only to the reputations of persons but also to the confidence that people need to have in the propriety of institutional processes.

Accordingly, it is often very important to clarify and resolve *apparent* conflicts of interest, as well as to avoid real ones. Indeed, it may well be important to avoid even the appearance of a conflict of interest.

Furthermore, the precise nature and boundaries of fiduciary and other roles should be clearly delineated and rendered perspicuous, for if this process is not done, then role confusion can arise, and with it the possibility of real or apparent conflicts of interest.

WHAT IS A CONFLICT OF INTEREST?

Before we proceed further, let us determine what a *conflict of interest* is. According to the "standard view,"[47]

> A conflict of interest is a situation in which some person P (whether an individual or corporate body) has a conflict of interest. P has a conflict of interest if and only if (1) P is in a relationship with another requiring P to exercise judgment on the other's behalf and (2) P has a (special) interest tending to interfere with the proper exercise of judgment in that relationship. The crucial terms in this definition are "relationship," "judgment," "interest," and "proper exercise."

The relationship required must be fiduciary—that is, it must involve one person's trusting (or at least being entitled to trust) another to exercise judgment on his or her behalf. Judgment is the ability to make certain kinds of correct and reliable decisions that require knowledge or skill. Interest is any influence, loyalty, concern, emotion, or other feature of a situation tending to make P's judgment (in that situation) less reliable than it ought to be. What constitutes a proper exercise of judgment is usually a matter of social fact; it includes what people ordinarily expect, what P or the group to which P belongs invites others to expect, and what relevant laws, professional codes, or other regulations require.[48]

What is generally wrong with a conflict of interest is that it renders one's judgment less reliable than it should be and results in a failure to properly discharge a fiduciary duty. Generally, a conflict of interest can arise in at least one of two ways:

1. Person A has a self-regarding interest that is in conflict, at least potentially, with his or her fiduciary duty and therefore has the tendency to interfere with the proper exercise of A's judgment with regard to that duty.
2. Person A has two potentially competing fiduciary duties or roles that are in conflict with each other, at least potentially, and therefore one duty or role has the tendency to interfere with the proper exercise of A's judgment with regard to the other duty or role.

For example, there is a clear conflict of interest in the case of an accountant, Joe, who audits the financial statements of a club and who is also the manager of that club. Consider the interest in the club that Joe has as the manager. Joe as manager has an interest in maintaining the image of the club as financially viable. Now consider Joe's interest as an auditor in providing a true and fair statement of the club's financial situation. Joe's interest as a manager in maintaining the image of the club might have a tendency to make his judgment as auditor less reliable than it should be. Clearly there is a potential conflict of interest here, and one that arises from these two conflicting roles.

Crucially for our purposes in this book, conflicts of interest are conducive to institutional corruption. For example, a police officer who also moonlights for a security firm faces a conflict of interest when called upon to investigate criminal allegations against the manager of that security firm. The police officer's personal interest in keeping his additional job conflicts with the requirements of his role as a police officer and thus may interfere with the proper exercise of his judgment in fulfilling his fiduciary duty, as police officer, of upholding the law. He might be less zealous than he ought to be in his investigation of the criminal allegations against his boss. Again, a judge who presides over a criminal trial that involves her daughter as defendant in a rape case has a conflict of interest. Notice that both the police officer in the first case and the judge in the second case may in fact not act corruptly; each may well intend to do his or her duty—by investigating the criminal allegation thoroughly (in the case of the police officer) or conducting the trial fairly (in the case of the judge). However, in both cases, the conflict of interest remains, and therefore there is at least an apparent inability to properly discharge their role requirements.

The preceding examples illustrate that although not every instance of a conflict of interest necessarily results in corruption, nevertheless, conflicts of interest are conducive to corruption. Thus, it is best to avoid conflicts of interest; it is best, for example, that a judge with no familial connections to the defendant is appointed to the trial. In cases in which the conflict of interest is a minor one and/or could be avoided only with great difficulty, it may be acceptable for the person with the conflict to disclose it without avoiding it. If so, disclosure might need to be backed up by some suitably rigorous process of accountability.

VARIETIES OF CONFLICTS OF INTEREST

As we have already seen, many conflicts of interest involve a conflict between one's self-interest and the requirements of the role that one occupies. Others involve a conflict between two different roles that one occupies. Still others involve a degree of role confusion that serves to mask a conflict of interest.

Conflicts of interest involving self-interest are reasonably obvious, but what of *role conflicts?* By way of illustration, consider the following restrictions imposed in some organizations or professions: one cannot be both judge and advocate, or both editor and manager of advertising revenue of a newspaper, or both cashier-banker and manager of accounts payable and receivable in a large corporation. Underlying this institutional division of potentially conflicting roles is the *principle of the division and separation of responsibilities.* This principle is adhered to so that the proper exercise of one's judgment cannot be adversely affected by allowing one to occupy two potentially conflicting roles or functions. The role conflicts involve primarily a conflict between two roles, offices, or institutions. Traditionally, a Western democratic state is divided into distinct institutional "estates," for example, the government and the judiciary, whose functions are by design supposed to remain separate and independent. The separateness and independence of these institutions from one another is designed to ensure a division of power and also to ensure that potentially harmful conflicts of interest are avoided. Without this "separation of powers," we would have the intolerable situation in which a senior politician is the judge in a case involving a political opponent or in a case involving an adjudication in relation to the legality of a proposed government policy.

Let us now examine a variety of conflict of interest cases. We begin with some of the conflicts of interest involved in the Enron corruption scandal.

Conflicts of Interest in Finance

The Chief Financial Officer (CFO)

Traditionally, the CFO is the executive officer within an organization who is entrusted with ensuring that it operates with financial discipline and propriety. However, in a business environment where investors expect, and managers require, increased earnings in every financial quarter, CFOs come under pressure to "cook the books" and make them look better than they are in reality.[49] CFOs can come to have two potentially conflicting roles: (1) the traditional role of policing the integrity and accuracy of the accounts and financial statements of a company, and (2) the contemporary "role" of making sure that the quarterly earnings of the company look the best that they can, and even at times assisting this outcome by recourse to some "creative" accounting. This conflict of roles creates, in turn, a conflict of interest that has the tendency, at least potentially, to interfere with the proper exercise of the CFO's fiduciary duty of ensuring the integrity and accuracy of the company's financial statements—a duty entrusted to the CFO by the board of directors and shareholders of the company.

Andrew Fastow's dual role as CFO of Enron and manager of the Special Purpose Entities (SPEs), such as LJM for example (see Chapter 2), involved a serious conflict of interest—one that Fastow, as the company's financial watchdog, should have avoided.

The Deal-Makers

As we saw in Chapter 2, Enron's in-house deal-makers launched new deals irrespective of the risks involved. They did so in order to boost quarterly earnings and the value of Enron stock, and thereby to enable themselves to claim huge profits for the company, and, as a consequence, to earn large bonuses for themselves. These deal-makers had an interest in earning immediate big bonuses for themselves through risky deals. This interest was in conflict, at least potentially, with their fiduciary duty to enhance the earnings of the company in real terms and over the long term, that is, not simply by means of short-term paper profits.

The Auditors

The role of an auditor is potentially in conflict with the role of a financial adviser, when one accountant performs both roles for the same client. Thus, we have potential conflicts of interest in accounting firms that perform audits for the companies for which they also provide lucrative consultancy and other financial management services. Here the latter role has a tendency to reduce the auditors' independence and thus potentially to interfere with the proper exercise of an auditor's fiduciary duty of ensuring that a company's financial accounts present a true and fair view of its operations. In short, there is potential for the auditing process to be corrupted. The role of Arthur Andersen in Enron's collapse is a case in point; that role serves to highlight the fact that such conflicts of interest are conducive to corporate corruption.

In 2000, General Electric paid KPMG $23.9 million for audit work and $79.7 million for consultancy work. Similarly, J. P. Morgan Chase paid Price Waterhouse Coopers $21.3 million in audit fees and $84.2 million for other management services, including consultancy work. These examples invite the question as to whether, in such circumstances, the auditing function has been carried out with sufficient independence; has the auditing process been corrupted?[50]

Conflicts of Interest in the Media—Advertorials

Advertorials exist to further the commercial self-interest that advertisers have in the promotion and sale of products. However, unlike ordinary advertisements, advertorials trade heavily on the credibility that attaches to public news and current affairs services; this credibility rests on the fact that such services are not engaged in advertising but rather in the provision of objective and impartial news and comment in the public interest. This blurring of the distinction between advertisement and objective news/comment effectively masks the conflict of interest that arises when advertisers also presents themselves, at least implicitly, as impartial reporters of factual information or as objective commentators acting in the public interest.

Consider the role of journalists as objective reporters. Journalists have a fiduciary duty to provide factual information, as well as balanced and objective comment, to the public on matters of public interest. By contrast, advertising practitioners do not have any such fiduciary duty; advertisers as advertisers do not have these professional obligations of impartiality and objectivity in the public interest. Rather, advertisers are recognized to be partisan promoters of particular products.

Now consider *advertorials*. Advertorials, as the name suggests, are paid-for advertisements posing as information and editorial-style comment. However, unlike ordinary advertisements, advertorials pretend to offer balanced and accurate information, and/or objective comment in the public interest. The audiences of advertorials are not necessarily fully aware of, and may well be somewhat confused about, the advertising intent and design of these advertisements. And since the producers of advertorials know that this is the case, there are often elements of deception and manipulation involved. Can they, however, amount to corruption? Advertorials can undermine— and therefore corrupt—the institution of objective, impartial, public communication in the public interest by tending to corrode the distinction between such communication in the public interest and advertising per se. This process of corrosion works at two levels. On the one hand, advertorials can *deceive* audiences into believing that what is in fact an advertisement is a form of impartial, objective communication, that is, advertisements 'become' news/objective comment. On the other hand, the existence of advertorials can contribute to the lowering of the community's expectations in relation to what is in fact bona fide impartial, objective public communication; and this tendency can lead producers of such public communication into diluting their offerings to make them more appealing, that is, objective news/comment "becomes" advertising. This two-sided pincer movement can have the effect over time of undermining the institution of impartial, objective public communication in the public interest. Consequently, it may constitute a form of institutional corruption.

Case Study 3.1   John Laws and the Cash for Comment Case

In what has come to be known in Australia as the "Cash for Comment" case, John Laws, a well-known Australian radio celebrity with an audience of two million listeners, made an agreement in 1999 with the banking industry lobby that he would provide favorable comment on the banking sector, if the banks paid him the sum of 1.2 million in Australian dollars. This financial transaction between Laws and the banks was carried out in secret; in particular, it was concealed from the public, including his audience. Just a few weeks prior to making this deal, Laws had used his airtime to repeatedly criticize the banks; he claimed that they were acting unethically by imposing unjustified fees on their customers and cutting back on vital services.

Given that Laws would have been providing favorable comment in return for a payment, his comments would have been (in effect) paid advertisements. However, in light of the fact that he presents himself as a bona fide commentator—and given that his audience would not have known about the payments—his comments would have constituted a particularly insidious form of advertorial. To that extent, impartial and objective public communication in the public interest would have been undermined—indeed, corrupted. In the U.S., the cash for editorial comment phenomenon is known as "payola."

Advertorials conveniently illustrate the important conceptual distinction between *external instrumentalism,* on the one hand, and *internal instrumentalism,* on the other. According to Alan Gewirth;

> In an external instrumentalism, the means or instrument is external to the end, in that it need not have any of the distinctive characteristics of the end. In internal instrumentalism, on the other hand, the means or instrument is internal to the end: it is instrumental to the end not only causally but also conceptually in that its features are also constitutive of the end. It serves as an instrument to the end by enforcing, reinstating, or in some other way bringing about a certain result, while at the same time it embodies distinctive characteristics of the result.[51]

As an example of the two types of instrumentalism, Gewirth refers to a university lecture. If the lecture is given only for the purpose of earning money, then the lecture as a means or instrument is *external* to its end; there is no conceptual connection between a lecture per se and the property of earning money. By contrast, in the case of a lecture given for the purpose of providing understanding on the lecture topic, the lecture, as means or instrument, is *internal* to the end; being a lecture and being a source of understanding are conceptually connected.

Journalism is, or ought to be, akin to a university lecture. A good news story is accurate and balanced, and as such it is a means or instrument that is internal to its end of informing the public. By contrast, the purpose of an advertisement is to persuade its audience to buy the product being advertised, and the advertisement can consist of any claims or images that might serve as a means to this end; thus, the means (claims and images) are external to the end (buying the product).

Advertorials are a form of advertisement, and as such they conform to the dictates of external instrumentalism. On the one hand, they *present themselves* as journalism, and therefore as conforming to a principle of internal instrumentalism. However, this is merely a ruse to distract and confuse the audience in relation to their real character as advertisements—communications governed by a principle of external instrumentalism.

Conflicts of Interest in Clinical Trials[52]

Another example of a conflict of interest arises in clinical trials.[53] The primary role of Institutional Ethics Committees (IECs) in Australia, the United States, and other Western nations is to approve and monitor medical research involving human experimentation. To this end, IECs must ascertain that research proposals submitted to them for approval conform to generally recognized and accepted scientific and moral principles. Scientific validity is normally the first aspect of any research proposal examined by an IEC. The concern regarding scientific validity is to ensure that (1) the research proposal as presented in the research protocol—a lengthy document full of statistical data and esoteric scientific writing—can achieve its stated objectives through the application of an adequate methodology, and (2) those objectives—usually the introduction of a new drug, a surgical or other procedure, or a therapeutic or diagnostic device—will improve medical theory and practice, as well as benefit the health of the community. Once a research proposal passes the test of scientific validity, an IEC will next consider its ethical validity. This process usually involves a concern about informed consent. Given that a research proposal is scientifically valid, an IEC must ensure that all the relevant information contained in the research protocol is provided to the potential participants in the research project by way of a consent form—relevant information being that which a potential participant would require in order to enable him or her to decide whether or not to participate in the trial. It is, in other words, the kind of information that a potential participant in a clinical trial would consider relevant from his or her own personal perspective—as opposed to the perspective of the researchers of the clinical trial in which the participant is being asked to participate. The distinction between the participants' and the researchers' perspectives is fundamental, since it is the former and not the latter perspective that is the basis for informed consent with regard to participation in clinical trials.

The primary difficulty that confronts IECs with regard to informed consent is that in the context of clinical trials, there can arise a conflict between the requirements of scientific validity on the one hand, and the legitimate requirements of the participants on the other. Consider the following typical case. During a clinical trial of a new drug, the researchers discover that the drug has certain additional adverse effects that had not been anticipated prior to the commencement of the trial; and as a result, information about those adverse effects had not been provided to the trial participants through the consent form. Since the trial participants' continuing consent for participation in the trial is conditional upon provision of all the relevant information regarding the trial, and since the new information regarding the additional adverse events of the drug is relevant information to the participants, the researchers are ethically bound to provide that information to the participants. However, if the researchers provide the additional information regarding the new adverse events to the participants in the trial, the researchers risk rendering the scientific results of the trial invalid. There are two reasons for this. First, the withdrawal of a sufficient number of participants from the trial, who decide to discontinue their participation after being informed of the additional adverse events, might render the statistical sample of the trial (the number of participants in the trial) inadequate, thus rendering the results of the trial scientifically invalid. Second, even if enough participants continue with the trial, so that the adequacy of the statistical sample required for scientific validity is not affected in any way, the participants' knowledge of the adverse events could introduce bias into the results of the trial, thus rendering the scientific validity of the trial doubtful and uncertain.

A similar but personal conflict of interest faces the individual doctor involved in clinical trials who is invested with the dual role of both physician and researcher. As a physician, the doctor's primary responsibility is to the welfare of her individual patients. As a research scientist, however, her primary responsibility is the successful completion of the clinical trial in order to enhance scientific knowledge, and, as a consequence, benefit society at large. The doctor has in her role as physician both a professional and an ethical responsibility to inform her patients in a clinical trial of her concerns regarding the safety of the drug or treatment being tested, the drug or treatment that is likely to have caused an unexpected and serious adverse event during the clinical trial.

However, in her role as a research scientist, the doctor has a responsibility to safeguard the scientific validity of the trial. Although the drug-related serious adverse event may have led to the death of one participant, for example, let us assume that the occurrence of the serious adverse event is, as a matter of fact, not statistically significant. Because it is not statistically significant, the occurrence of the serious adverse event is, for the time being, irrelevant to the scientific validity of the trial. If the doctor, in her role as physician, were to inform her patients of her concerns regarding the safety of the drug being tested, she would be acting ethically but would vitiate the experiment from a scientific viewpoint. And perhaps in her role as research scientist, her primary responsibility is the scientific validity of the trial and its contribution to scientific knowledge for the greater good of society at large. Thus, the doctor faces a choice between two bad options. The point is not that she faces an ethical dilemma; presumably her way forward is clear—she ought to inform her patients of the threats to their safety. Rather, the point is that in her role as researcher, she has an interest in ensuring the scientific validity of the tests, and this might be a source of unnecessary pressure on her to make the wrong decision; she might put scientific validity ahead of the rights of the participants in the trial. In short, scientists or doctors/ researchers might find themselves in a conflict of interest arising from their distinct roles, and this problem might be conducive to corruption in that it tends to interfere with the proper exercise of judgment as a doctor, and thereby undermine one's institutional role as doctor. It is interesting to note that if the doctor failed to comply with her fiduciary duty to ensure the safety of her patients, she would have engaged in a form of corruption (since such failures undermine the institutional role of doctor) and in a form of rights violation (the moral rights of her patients).

Moreover, the case illustrates how a conflict of interest can be systemic, and not simply a one-off individual conflict of interest. It is systemic because it arises by virtue of the methodological design of clinical trials. It arises, that is, as a result of the fact that one and the same person—the doctor/ researcher, say—is required to undertake two possibly conflicting roles, for example, to ensure that the participants have given informed consent and to ensure also that the trial has objective scientific validity.

The critical question, however, as in the case of the other types of conflicts of interest we have been examining, is whether a conflict of interest in clinical trials potentially, if not actually, might lead to corruption. Presumably the answer here is in the affirmative. This view is reinforced by the consideration that there are very large sums of money invested in clinical trials by pharmaceutical companies in developing new drugs, and that there are considerable financial and other professional inducements for medical researchers to successfully complete clinical trials without running the risk of having their trials discontinued or rendered scientifically invalid through the possible withdrawal of participants from trials if they are informed of serious adverse events. To alleviate and mitigate this potential risk, it is important that a number of stringent and independently monitored controls are put in place to ensure that the risk of potential corruption in clinical trials is minimized, if not entirely eliminated.

Conflicts of Interest in Government

Case Study 3.2   The Keating Five[54]

> "The appearance of it was wrong. It's a wrong appearance when a group of senators appear in a meeting with a group of regulators because it conveys the impression of undue and improper influence. And it was the wrong thing to do."
>
> —*John McCain*

Take five senators and a controversial property developer who bankrolled the senators' political careers, and who owe him a favor or two, and you have the makings of a potential conflict of interest. Add to this the fact that two of the senators are American heroes; John McCain spent five-and-a-half years in a Hanoi prison camp after he was shot down over North Vietnam, and John Glenn was the first American astronaut to orbit the earth. Now you have the makings of a serious scandal.

It all started in March 1987, when the US government was set to seize Lincoln Savings and Loan, a subsidiary of Charles Keating's American Continental Corp. Keating, who for years had been generously contributing to the election and reelection campaigns of various politicians on the rise, called on his indebted political friends to get the government investigators off Lincoln's back. To that end, he instigated two meetings between the regulators and five senators who had been recipients of his generosity. The five senators came to be known as the "Keating Five": Alan Cranston (Dem., CA), Dennis DeConcini (Dem., AZ), John Glenn (Dem., OH), John McCain (Rep., AZ), and Donald Riegle (Dem., MI).

Together the five senators had accepted more than $300,000 in contributions from Keating. By 1987, John McCain alone had received $112,000 in contributions from Keating and his associates. McCain's wife and his father-in-law had invested $359,100 in a Keating-owned shopping center in April 1988, a year before McCain and the other senators met with the regulators. DeConcini, who had arranged the meetings, had other close ties with Keating, including $50 million in loans from Keating for himself and his aides.

Although upon completion of their audit the San Francisco regulators, under the direction of Chair of the Federal Home Loan Bank Board Edwin J. Gray, had recommended that Lincoln be seized, Gray was replaced as chairman, and the investigation was transferred to Washington for a new audit—much to the delight of Keating.

However, Keating's delight was short-lived. In April 1989, two years after the Keating Five meetings, the government seized Lincoln, which declared bankruptcy. In September 1990, Keating was charged with 42 counts of fraud, and his bail bond was set at $5 million. During Keating's trial, the prosecution produced several elderly investors as witnesses who had lost their life savings by investing in American Continental junk bonds. Lincoln's losses amounted to $3.4 billion. Federal regulators filed a $1.1 million civil racketeering and fraud suit against Keating, accusing him of diverting Lincoln's deposits to his family and to political campaigns.

The Senate Ethics Committee found that Senators Cranston, DeConcini, and Riegle had substantially interfered with the federal regulators' enforcement processes at the request of Charles Keating.

Cranston's conduct in the Keating Five affair was noted by the committee as reprehensible, whereas the conduct of the other four senators was noted as questionable.

As Thompson[55] points out, the Keating Five case involved (1) the provision, or at least the appearance of the provision, of an improper service on the part of legislators (the senators) to a constituent (Keating), namely, interfering with the role of a regulator (Gray) on behalf of Keating; (2) political gain in the form of campaign contributions (from Keating to the senators); and (3) a link, or at least the appearance of a link, between (1) and (2), namely, the service being offered *because of* the political gain. Accordingly, the case study involves at least the appearance of corrupt activity on the part of the senators. Moreover, we agree with Thompson that such an appearance might be sufficient for institutional corruption, in that (1) damage has been done to a political institution by virtue of a diminution in public confidence in that institution, and (2) the senators ought to have known that their actions might have this effect, and therefore they ought not to have performed those actions.[56] Moreover, this institutional corruption resulted from the appearance of a conflict of interest, albeit in the context (as it turned out) of Keating's fraudulent activities, the collapse of a major financial institution and the subsequent damage done to elderly investors. As legislators, the senators have a duty to provide a service to their constituents. However, the appearance of a conflict of interest arises when legislators use their office to provide a questionable "service" to a person upon whom they are, or have been, heavily reliant for campaign contributions.

A related kind of conflict of interest—and attendant corruption—in government involves the improper extension of a political role. Consider, in this connection, a case of alleged corruption involving the Prime Minister of Italy, Silvio Berlusconi. It appears that his government used its political power to introduce a controversial new law that would allow defendants to seek the transfer of their trial from one court to another, if *they* felt that the first court was likely to be biased against them. Berlusconi's lawyers indicated that they would avail themselves of the "legitimate suspicion" law to have their client's trial on charges of bribing Roman judges to be moved from Milan (where it is felt that the court would be biased against Berlusconi) to Brescia (where Berlusconi enjoys widespread political support). There was a suspicion that the new law was deliberately introduced by Berlusconi's government in order to assist his defense against charges of corruption and thereby to enable him to escape prosecution. The attempt by the Italian government to introduce the legitimate suspicion law can be seen as a case in which the legislative role has been used to improperly interfere with the judicial function. If so, this practice amounts to political corruption of a judicial process, namely, the process of determining what matters should be heard in what courts.

How to Deal with Conflicts of Interest

Avoidance

The most obvious way to deal with conflicts of interest that might result in corruption is to avoid them. In cases in which there is a potential conflict between an institutional actor's self-interest and the duties of his or her institutional role, regulations requiring avoidance of these conflicts need to be introduced, and some form of accountability mechanism established.

Role conflicts can best be avoided through a strict division of duties and responsibilities that does not allow one person to occupy both roles. For example, there is a traditional division of accounting responsibilities between the cashiering and banking functions on the one hand, and the accounts payable and receivable functions on the other hand.

In the case of chief financial officers, one and the same person should not be permitted to occupy the role of auditor and that of financial adviser. In the case of accountancy firms, conflicts of interest might be avoided through the strict division and separation of the auditing and financial consultancy functions within the firm. However, this control may not be adequate to avoid conflicts of interest if fees from financial consultancy services far exceed auditing fees. One possible solution to this problem is to increase audit fees substantially so that they at least match those from financial consultancy services. If that solution is not possible, perhaps it should be impermissible for an accounting firm to provide auditing and consultancy services to the same client.

The potential conflict between the requirement for objectivity and impartiality in news reporting and editorial comment, on the one hand, and the commercial demands of advertising, on the other hand, can be avoided by having a strict division between those two functions in a media organization.

Disclosure

It is not always possible to avoid conflicts of interest. The next best solution is to disclose them. However, disclosure is acceptable only in the case of otherwise ethically acceptable practices. It would not be ethically acceptable for a politician to be a judge. Accordingly, disclosure would not be a solution to that conflict of interest.

On the other hand, the mandatory disclosure of advertorials as being in fact advertisements—and, therefore, in no sense to be regarded as sources of impartial and objective information—might be sufficient to eliminate the pretense that they are anything other than advertisements. In the aftermath of the Cash for Comment scandal, the Australian Broadcasting Authority (ABA) has introduced new binding regulations that require media organizations to make full disclosure about all relevant sponsorship arrangements to their audiences when comments made during normal programming refer to the sponsors of the presenters, or to the media organizations that employ them. In this particular type of conflict of interest, disclosure has almost the same effect as avoidance, because it eliminates the deceptive cloak and requires the advertorial to be seen for what it is—an advertisement.[57]

In the case of clinical trials, participants could be informed prior to their participation in any given trial that the disclosure of information concerning unexpected adverse events would be left to the discretion of the researchers in consultation with members of the relevant Institutional Ethics Committee. Although participants under this arrangement may still not be informed of adverse events occurring during a trial, especially if there is a risk that disclosure may render an otherwise ethically acceptable trial scientifically invalid, they would at least know, prior to making their decision to enter a trial, that such restricted conditions of disclosure apply.

As we have seen, some *apparent conflicts of interest* can be as ethically problematic as real ones because of their potential to generate either a loss of confidence in institutional processes or a loss of trust in institutional actors. One way of eliminating these untoward effects of apparent conflicts of interest is disclosure. Often full and frank disclosure reveals that the apparent conflict of interest is not a real conflict of interest, and this disclosure is sufficient to satisfy relevant parties that there are no grounds for loss of confidence or trust. Consider, in this connection, full disclosure of all donations to political parties.

CONCLUSION

This chapter has examined conflicts of interest, both in themselves and as a cause of corruption. We have outlined a number of different types of conflict of interest in a variety of settings. There are real and apparent conflicts of interest, conflicts of interest that arise from self-interest, and role-based conflicts of interest. Moreover, conflicts of interest arise in most, if not all, major social institutions, including government, the public sector, the criminal justice system, the media, industry, business and finance, and the medical sector. Conflicts of interest are sometimes best dealt with by avoidance and sometimes simply by disclosure. Whatever method, or combination of methods, is chosen, great care must be taken, because conflicts of interest are a perennial, as well as a pervasive, source of corruption.

chapter four

What Is Wrong with Corruption?

In this chapter, we address the question What is morally wrong with institutional corruption? In so doing, we

- Distinguish between what is morally wrong with corruption per se, for example, it undermines legitimate institutional processes, and what might be wrong with the action at the core of a corrupt action, for example, the action of breaching a confidence (that, say, undermines a criminal investigation).
- Discuss deontological, teleological, and consequentialist arguments against corruption.
- Consider various motivations for corruption, for example, self-regarding personal gain and amoral familism.
- Identify various harmful consequences of corruption, for example, the damage done to political institutions as a result of the Watergate scandal.

Institutional corruption is both morally wrong and (typically) unlawful. Moreover, it is unlawful because it is immoral (or unethical). As we saw in Chapter 1, what is illegal is not always unethical, and what is legal can sometimes be unethical. Moreover, what is ethical can sometimes be unlawful. For example, homosexuality between consenting adults was until recently unlawful in many jurisdictions in the Western world, yet it is now widely regarded as morally acceptable. So it is not the illegality of corruption per se that renders it morally wrong, at least in the first instance. Rather, it is the immorality of corruption that typically renders it unlawful. So the general reason why corruption is wrong is that it is immoral. That said, it may well be that an additional moral reason why corruption is wrong is that it is unlawful. At any rate, we need now consider in what specific ways corruption is morally unacceptable.

Here we need to note, as discussed in Chapter 1, that there are many different forms of corruption, ranging from types of economic corruption such as bribery and fraud, through types of political corruption such as the abuse of power, and on to types of communicative corruption such as plagiarism. Clearly, what is morally wrong with fraud is not necessarily the same thing as what is morally wrong with the abuse of power. Fraud involves deception and theft. By contrast, the abuse of power might involve openly perpetrating an injustice, such as blocking a subordinate's richly deserved promotion.

This large diversity of corruption types means that corruption has a correspondingly large set of moral deficiencies. Naturally, we can say that at the core of any act of corruption, there is an action that is morally wrong. And this is an important point to make; corrupt actions are morally wrong because the acts at their core are morally wrong. However, since there are many and diverse such acts at the core of corrupt activities, we will not be able to provide a fully adequate answer to the question, *What is wrong with corruption in general?*, if we were merely to focus our attention on these diverse acts. We will simply be left with the true, but limited, claim that what is morally wrong with corruption is whatever is morally wrong with the particular action that is at the core of any given act of corruption. That is, we are left with true, but limited, claims such as the following ones: an act of corruption that is also an act of bribery is morally wrong in large part because acts of bribery are morally wrong. Again, an act of corruption that is also an abuse of power is morally wrong in large part because abuses of power are morally wrong.

Notwithstanding the lack of specificity in relation to the moral wrongness of actions at the core of different acts of corruption, corrupt actions have something in common, namely, that they consist of the performance of a (typically) habitual act that is a despoiling of moral character or undermining of an otherwise morally legitimate institutional process, role, or purpose. Moreover, in Chapters 2 and 3, we identified a number of conditions that facilitate corruption. These included imbalances of power, inequalities of wealth, unwarranted secrecy, conflicts of interest, and so on. The definition of corruption and these facilitating conditions provide important additional guides for us in our endeavour to answer the question, What is wrong with corruption?

This task is further assisted by a consideration of the nature of the relationship between an action and the corruption it causes. Some actions might be only loosely, and contingently, connected to the corruption that they cause. As such, they might be acts of corruption in certain specific contexts, but not typically. A manager's decision in a low-risk organizational setting not immediately to implement an expensive policy of password protection might be a reasonable, or at least an excusable, one. However, the same decision in a high-risk financial environment might constitute willful negligence that is tantamount to corruption. The general point is that failure to ensure, say, password protection, is not corrupt per se; whether it is corrupt is almost wholly context dependent. On the other hand, bribery is nearly always corrupt; the connection between an act of bribery and the property of being corrupt is very close and, in part, conceptual, because part of the *point* of bribery is to obtain a benefit by means of undermining some otherwise legitimate institutional process. Accordingly, bribery almost always has a corrupting effect.

Deontological, Teleological, and Consequentialist Moral Considerations

As with immorality in general, corruption can be shown to be wrong on the basis either that it is inherently wrong or that it has bad consequences (or both of the preceding). If the former, then corruption is wrong because of some inherent wrongness in corrupt practices themselves, and irrespective of their consequences. If the latter, corruption is wrong if it has consequences for oneself and for others, and irrespective of whether it is inherently wrong. The reasons for claiming that corruption is inherently wrong are various. They might be *deontological* reasons, or they might be *teleological* reasons.

Roughly speaking, deontological reasons are ones that pertain to the action considered in itself and are independent of the purpose, goal, or end that it was performed in the service of. So physically harming someone by punching the person would normally be considered morally wrong by virtue of a deontological principle to the effect that physically harming people is wrong.

By contrast, teleological reasons pertain to the purpose, goal, or end of an action. So if one punched someone solely for the purpose of defending oneself against an unprovoked assault, then the action might be morally justified by virtue of a teleological principle to the effect that injuring an attacker for the purpose of self-defense is morally permissible. If, on the other hand, it is stated that corruption is wrong *only* because of its bad consequences—and therefore, irrespective of whether those consequences were intended or not—the reason adduced in support of that statement is a *consequentialist* one.

"Deontological," "teleological," and "consequentialist" are three terms used by philosophers to refer to three different sets of reasons offered in support of the moral evaluation of actions. The following deontological, teleological, and consequentialist arguments can be adduced to show why specific forms of corruption might be morally wrong.

Deontological Arguments

Moral Principles

Human societies have always recognized and been guided by moral principles. There has been some divergence in relation to the set of such principles, especially when it comes to adhering to them in relation to social groups other than the group to which one belongs. But the list of such moral principles is relatively familiar and includes prohibitions on killing, raping, enslavement, theft, deception, and the breaking of promises. It also includes moral requirements to assist the needy and to do one's duty as a parent, doctor, businessperson, soldier, leader, and so on. Some of these moral principles embody moral rights, but some do not, for moral rights generate especially strong moral obligations. To say that one has a right is to make a moral claim that overrides most other moral claims. For example, persons have a right to life, and this right overrides moral reasons to help out at the local soup kitchen. Accordingly, forced to choose between going to work tonight at the soup kitchen and taking a person to the hospital to save the person's life, a person must choose the latter. As Ronald Dworkin says, "Rights are trumps."

The infringement of some, perhaps all, of these moral principles can in certain circumstances constitute corruption. This is perhaps most obviously the case in relation to duties that attach to institutional roles to which special powers are also attached. Many such duties are fiduciary duties—duties that one is *entrusted* to perform for the benefit of others. For example, members of the professions, such as lawyers and accountants, have fiduciary duties to their clients, and directors of companies have fiduciary duties to their shareholders. Furthermore, politicians, police, and other public officials are said to hold positions of public trust and to have special duties to the citizenry at large—duties that others not so entrusted do not have. Such duties arise in institutional settings and typically depend on implicit or explicit acceptance; the person who has the duty has freely accepted it, either by explicit consent, for example, swearing an oath of office, or at least by virtue of freely taking up the institutional position to which the duty attaches. The acceptance of special duties goes hand in hand with the conferring of special powers. Lawyers have powers that others do not have to act on behalf of their clients; politicians, but not others, have powers to enact laws; police have powers of seizure and arrest not granted to others; and so on. Naturally, the possession of special powers affords opportunities for abuse, exploitation, and personal gain—opportunities that are not available to those without these powers. So institutional positions of trust are susceptible to corruption.

Moral Rights

Human beings have various moral rights, including the right to life, the right to freedom, and the right to property. The violation of these rights by others is a moral wrong. As we saw before, moral rights are "trumps," and therefore the violation of rights is an especially egregious form of moral wrongdoing.

So in general, an action that is a violation of a person's rights is morally wrong. Nevertheless, it is still only a prima facie wrong, not an absolute wrong; that is, it is not wrong under all circumstances. Consider killing.

Killing is morally wrong; it is a violation of a person's right to life. On the other hand, killing someone in self-defense might be justified in a situation in which there was no other recourse to save one's own life. Where the "violation" of someone's rights is, under specific circumstances, justified, as for example, when the state imprisons a criminal for the protection of society at large, then it might be said to be an *infringement* rather than a violation of rights. Generally speaking, we will assume that if an action is a *violation* of someone's rights, then it is morally unjustified; but if it is merely an *infringement* of someone's rights, then it may well be morally justified, or at least morally excused. Here an excuse provides a mitigating reason for an otherwise morally unacceptable action; but the reason does not fully justify the action. The burglary of one's house by a thief is a *violation* of one's right to property. By contrast, the confiscation of one's assets under a court order for the payment of an outstanding loan that one (unreasonably) refuses to pay is a fully justified *infringement*, and therefore not a violation, of one's right to property. Unintentional killing of an intruder might be an excusable, but not a fully justified, infringement of the killer's right to life. Other forms of corruption, such as the abuse of power, might involve the violation of certain rights to freedom, as in the case of harassment of a subordinate. Still others might involve a violation of the right to privacy or confidentiality, as in the case of compromising a criminal investigation by a breach of confidentiality, for example, by prematurely making known the identity of a witness to an offender.

If it can be shown that specific forms of corruption involve the violation of rights, such as the right to property, then that will be a morally significant feature of corruption. Moreover, if specific forms of corruption involve the violation of fundamental universal rights, such as the rights to life and freedom, then that will demonstrate that at least these forms of corruption ought to be regarded as basic moral wrongs by all people and at all times.

The Categorical Imperative (CI)

There are a number of important substantive moral principles that acts of corruption typically violate. These include moral rules against deceit, theft, breaking promises (including explicit legal contracts), and the infringement of various individual freedoms. Bribery and fraud, for example, typically involve deception, and fraud by itself typically involves theft. The abuse of power often involves the infringement of a subordinate's right to autonomy. So these different types of action—deceit, theft, infringement of autonomy, and so on—break different moral rules. However, they arguably have something in common; they all violate the so-called "Categorical Imperative."

According to the German philosopher Immanuel Kant (1724–1804), a moral rule must be one that is capable of being a universal law—a law that applies to everybody in all places and at all times without exception. Kant referred to this *formal* moral principle as the *Categorical Imperative.* According to Kant's principle, we must act only according to rules that we can at the same time will or comply with as universal laws. Kant thought that an essential feature of *moral* rules or principles is their *universalizability*—their capability of being applied universally under relevantly similar conditions. Two formulations of the Categorical Imperative (CI) are worth noting:

1. Always act in such a way that you can also will that the rule or maxim of your action should become a universal law;
2. Act so that you treat humanity, both in your own person and in that of another, always as an end and never merely as a means.

Although the preceding formulations are supposedly formally equivalent, the first illustrates the need for moral principles to be universalizable, that is, to be capable of being applicable to everyone at all places and times under relevantly similar conditions. The second draws a sharp distinction between *things* and *persons,* and it emphasizes the necessity to respect persons for themselves and not simply for what they can do for us. Under this formulation, the Categorical Imperative is designed to show that treating other people purely as a means for the advancement of our own self-interested ends is morally wrong.

Applying the first formulation of the Categorical Imperative, can we consistently will that, say, committing theft, breaking promises, telling lies, or infringing the autonomy of others become universal laws? It seems not, for any such laws would be detrimental and impractical, both for oneself and for others. If everyone engaged in theft, then the right to property would be undermined; if everyone broke promises, then the institution of promise-keeping would collapse, since no one would trust anyone else to keep the promises that had been made; if everyone lied, then the possibility of communication would cease to exist, since no one would believe what anyone else said; and, if everyone violated everyone else's autonomy, then no one would have autonomy.

In sum, Kant's CI principle is designed to show that telling lies, breaking promises, committing theft, violating the autonomy of others, and the like, are inherently unethical because they are inherently irrational. And they are inherently irrational because they are self-defeating, and therefore it is not possible for all of us to consistently comply with them. In short, according to Kant, only universalizable laws can form the basis of moral conduct.

Teleological Arguments

Teleological arguments focus on the ethical or moral goal or end or purpose of a process, occupation, or institution. By ends, goals, or purposes, it is here meant states that are intended, or otherwise *aimed at,* by a person or persons. Accordingly, when an end or goal or purpose is realized, it is not the mere unintended consequence of a person's or persons' action or actions; rather, it is a consequence that was intended, or was otherwise aimed at.

Thus the purpose or end of the criminal justice system is to deliver justice, that of journalists to unearth and communicate the truth, and so on. Moreover, these ends, goals or *teli* are held to be in part definitive of the processes, occupations, or institutions in question.[58] Accordingly, to undermine or obstruct the realization of these goals or ends is to strike at the heart of the process, occupation, or institution. Thus, a teleological argument can demonstrate what is wrong with corruption, if it can demonstrate that bribery, fraud, breaches of confidentiality, the abuse of office, and so on, undermine the acknowledged *purposes* of particular processes, occupations, or institutions.

Or at least such a teleological argument is available in cases in which the end or goal of the role, process, or institution was a morally desirable goal or end. Clearly, the Mafia as an organization has morally unacceptable goals, and therefore the alleged "duties" of the occupants of Mafia roles, for example, the role of "soldier" (enforcer), are not moral duties. Moreover, because the duties that attach to such roles are not moral duties, but rather immoral ones, they cannot be corrupted. As we saw in Chapter 1, corruption presupposes a *morally legitimate* institutional role, purpose, or process, and a *morally legitimate* institution.

Specifically, this teleological argument against corruption posits a connection between the various fiduciary duties attached to institutional roles, on the one hand, and the moral purposes of institutions, on the other. Both the roles and their attendant duties exist to facilitate institutional purposes or ends.[59] Accordingly, culpable failures on the part of role occupants to discharge their fiduciary duties subvert, indeed corrupt, institutions.

Thus, the role of a police officer is to uphold law and order and to provide assistance in the criminal and judicial process; the role of a journalist is to inform the public truthfully and fairly on matters of public interest; the role of a doctor or a nurse is to provide medical care to her patients for the benefit of their health; the role of a priest or a minister is to provide pastoral care to members of his congregation; the role of a politician is to provide good and just government to her electorate; and the role of the director of a public company is to safeguard the assets and profitability of the company for the collective benefit of its shareholders.

Accordingly, to the extent that bribery, the abuse of power, fabrication of evidence, fraud, nepotism, conflicts of interest, and so on, defeat the purposes or ends of legitimate occupational roles and institutional processes, then they corrupt these roles and processes, and they corrupt, therefore, the larger institutions of which these roles and processes are constitutive elements.

Consequentialist Arguments

According to the ethical theory of consequentialism—utilitarianism being the predominant species—the morality of an action depends exclusively on its consequences, irrespective of whether those consequences were intended or otherwise aimed at. Thus, according to utilitarianism, an action is morally good if it results, overall, in good consequences for the greatest number of people affected by that action. To put it another way, an action is morally good if it results in a maximization of utility (utility is typically understood as preference satisfaction or happiness or pleasure) for the greatest number of people. Similarly, an action is morally bad if it results, overall, in bad consequences—especially harm or reduction of utility—for the greatest number of people. Therefore, according to the consequentialist argument, corruption, such as bribery, fraud, or abuse of power, is morally wrong only to the extent that it results, overall, in bad consequences for the greatest number. In contrast to the deontological arguments, the consequentialist argument does not focus on the inherent moral wrongness of any particular form of corruption, nor does it focus on the intention or goal behind an action. Rather, according to the consequentialist argument, corruption would be counted as unethical only if, overall, it resulted in bad consequences or a reduction in overall utility for the greatest number of people. In fact, under consequentialism, corruption that resulted overall in good consequences would count as morally right and therefore desirable. Theoretically then, a consequentialist could be in favor of some corrupt practices, namely, ones that overall had good consequences. This kind of consequentialist argument has been advanced in relation to corruption. For example, it is sometimes claimed that bribing public officials "greases the bureaucratic wheels" and leads to greater efficiency than otherwise would be the case; so bribery, it is argued, is actually a good thing, at least in certain contexts. In point of fact, the evidence is overwhelmingly against the proposition that corrupt practices result overall in good consequences. Widespread corruption, especially systemic, grand corruption, is extraordinarily harmful in its effects. We deal with this issue in the final section of this chapter.

Armed with the knowledge of the various kinds of ethical argument, namely, deontological, teleological, and consequentialist arguments, as well as with knowledge of the various defining features and causes of corruption, we can now address more directly the question as to what is wrong with corruption. We do so by examining corruption in relation to its three main elements, namely, the *motivation* for corruption, the *act* of corruption per se, and the *consequences* of corruption. We begin with the motivation for corruption.

MOTIVATION FOR CORRUPTION: SELF-REGARDING GAIN

We have already noted the existence of so-called "noble cause" corruption, that is, corruption motivated by a desire to do good. In Chapter 5, we examine the notion of noble cause corruption in detail. The existence of noble cause corruption is sufficient to demonstrate that corruption cannot be *defined* in terms of the motivation of self-regarding gain. Nevertheless, self-regarding gain is a pervasive motivating feature of corruption. Indeed, we suggest that not only frequently, but indeed typically, individuals, groups, and organizations act corruptly for their self-regarding gain; self-regarding gain is evidently one of the most important, perhaps the most important, general motivation for engaging in corrupt activity. Let us consider some case studies that are illustrative of some of the motivations for corruption.

CASE STUDY 4.1   Motivation for Corruption

Surely, Lord, your law punishes theft, as does that law written on the hearts of men, which not even iniquity itself blots out. What thief puts up with another thief with a calm mind? Not even a rich thief will pardon one who steals from him because of want. But I willed to commit theft, and I did so, not because I was driven to it by any need, unless it were by poverty of justice, and dislike of it, and by a glut of evildoing. For I stole a thing of which I had plenty of my own and of much better quality. Nor did I wish to enjoy that thing which I desired to gain by theft, but rather to enjoy the actual theft and the sin of theft.

In a garden nearby to our vineyard there was a pear tree, loaded with fruit that was desirable neither in appearance nor in taste. Late one night—to which hour, according to our pestilential custom, we had kept our street games—a group of very bad youngsters set out to shake down and rob this tree. We took great loads of fruit from it, not for our own eating, but rather to throw it to the pigs; even if we did eat a little of it, we did this to do what pleased us for the reason that it was forbidden . . .

When there is discussion concerning a crime and why it was committed, it is usually held that there appeared a possibility that the appetites would obtain some of these goods, which we have termed lower, or there was fear of losing them. These things are beautiful and fitting, but in comparison with the higher goods, which bring happiness, they are mean and base. A man commits murder: why did he do so? He coveted his victim's wife or his property; or he wanted to rob him to get money to live on; or he feared to be deprived of some such thing by the other; or he had been injured, and burned for revenge. Would anyone commit murder without reason and out of delight in murder itself? Who can believe such a thing? Of a certain senseless and utterly cruel man it was said that he was evil and cruel without reason. Nevertheless, a reason has been given, for he himself said, "I don't want to let my hand or will get out of practice through disuse." Why did he want that? Why so? It was to the end that after he had seized the city by the practice of crime, he would attain to honours, power, and wealth, and be free from fear of the law and from trouble due to lack of wealth or from a guilty conscience. Therefore, not even Catiline himself loved his crimes, but something else, for sake of which he committed them.

(Augustine, *Confessions,* Book II, Section 9 [any edition])

CASE STUDY 4.2   Watergate[60]

"I had no prior knowledge of the Watergate break-in. I neither took part in nor knew about any of the subsequent cover-up activities; I neither authorized nor encouraged subordinates to engage in illegal or improper campaign tactics. That was and is the simple truth."

Nixon (in a speech to the American people), August 15, 1973

Dear Mr. Secretary,
I hereby resign the Office of President of the United States.

Sincerely
Richard Nixon

With these words, Richard Nixon, the thirty-seventh President of the United States, resigned on August 9, 1974, so as to avoid impeachment proceedings against him, after the House Judiciary Committee recommended Articles of Impeachment to the full House of Representatives.

Nixon's path to resignation began in the early morning of June 17, 1972, when Frank Wills, a security guard at the plush Watergate Hotel in Washington, D.C., alerted police, who discovered five intruders inside the headquarters of the Democratic National Committee. It was later revealed that they were there to adjust bugging equipment that they had installed during an earlier break-in for the purpose of photographing the Democrats' documents. The burglars worked under the direction of G. Gordon Liddy, a former FBI agent and finance counsel at Nixon's Committee for the Reelection of the President, known as CREEP. The burglars were E. Howard Hunt, a former CIA spy who had participated in the Bay of Pigs invasion, and members of Miami's Cuban exile community who had also participated in that invasion.

By October 1972, FBI agents had established that the Watergate break-in involved a widespread campaign of political intrigue and sabotage conducted on behalf of the Nixon reelection effort. Ironically, while the investigation into the burglary was gathering momentum, Nixon won the next presidential election on November 7, 1972, with one of the biggest recorded landslides.

The investigation that followed owed much of its initial rigor and momentum to the media, and in particular to two *Washington Post* journalists, Bob Woodward and Carl Bernstein. They went on to win the Pulitzer Prize for their reporting of Watergate. In February 1973, the Senate established a committee to investigate Watergate. The committee uncovered the existence of the secret White House tape recordings that provided the smoking gun that eventually led to the House of Representatives' passing a resolution on February 6, 1974, authorizing the Judiciary Committee to initiate impeachment proceedings.

The coup de grâce came in July to early August 1974 with the decision by the Supreme Court to order Nixon to release tapes that he had initially refused to release. The tapes revealed that he had participated in the Watergate cover-up as far back as June 1972. Nixon was now checkmated. He had no other choice but to resign or face impeachment. He chose to resign on August 9, 1974. He died in 1994.

As we pointed out earlier, self-regarding gain need not necessarily involve the pursuit of financial rewards or gains. Rather, the motives are multiple. It can be motivated by political gain, as in the case of Nixon in our Watergate case study. Or it can, as in the case of the sexual abuse of children by priests or ministers, be motivated by the desire for sexual gratification. And it can be motivated by a desire for professional success and status as when, for example, an academic plagiarizes someone else's work, or when a scientist fabricates his or her research results so as to appear more successful and therefore worthy of more peer recognition and professional status than he or she truly deserves.

Naturally, self-regarding gain is not in itself necessarily morally unacceptable. It becomes morally problematic only when it involves breaking moral principles; violating the rights of others, having as a consequence loss or harm to others; and—given the concerns of this book—corrupting institutional processes, roles, purposes, and—ultimately—institutions themselves.

Needless to say, there are many examples, such as that of Watergate and Enron, of self-interest being pursued at the expense of the public interest and to the detriment of social institutions. The Watergate break-in and subsequent attempts at cover-up were clearly at variance with the public interest in open and fair political processes in which rights to confidentiality, property, and so on are respected. Indeed, Watergate was a clear threat to the integrity of U.S. political institutions.

The key players responsible for Enron's collapse had—in their respective roles as auditors, accountants, directors, and executives of Enron, as well as financial advisers and investment bankers to Enron—a responsibility to investors and shareholders to protect Enron from corporate malfeasance and not to contribute to it, either through professional negligence or by venal design. Enron and similar corporate collapses are a clear threat to the integrity of U.S. economic institutions.

Susan Rose-Ackerman says that

> ". . . there is one human motivator that is both universal and central to explaining the divergent experiences of different countries. That motivator is self-interest, including an interest in the well-being of one's family and peer group. Critics call it greed. Economists call it utility maximization. Whatever the label, societies differ in the ways they channel self-interest."[61]

This might overstate the case somewhat in relation to self-interest. Moreover, it conflates individual and collective self-interest, and it runs together a myriad of self-regarding motives, including desire for wealth, status, power, and well-being. However, there is no doubt that self-interest, broadly understood, is a powerful and pervasive human motivator, and one that needs to be taken into account in understanding and combating institutional corruption.

As we saw in Chapter 3, when the pursuit of one's own private gain comes into conflict with one's moral responsibilities, including those constitutive of one's institutional role, there is the *potential* for corruption. But when the *policies* adopted in an organization such as Enron reward self-interest at the expense of discharging legal, institutional, and moral responsibilities, then organizational corruption is almost *certain* to follow.

As has been mentioned before and as is evident from many of our case studies, self-regarding gain has a number of different forms, including the desire for excessive power, wealth, and status. The desire for power, wealth, and status is often the driving force in corporate corruption. This was plainly so in the case of Enron. Enron's directors, board members, and senior managers adopted an aggressive push in the pursuit of corporate power, wealth, and status, which in turn led to the adoption of corrupt means to achieve those ends. The ultimate consequences of all this was financial disaster for shareholders, creditors, and Enron employees.

When excessive, the desire for political power can lead people to engage in unlawful and immoral activities. Consider the Watergate scandal described earlier. The desire to hold onto power led President Nixon et al. to engage in unlawful and immoral activities of a kind that justified impeachment.

An instrumentally rational agent whose primary objective or goal is to maximize his power, wealth, and status might be tempted to use unlawful and/or immoral means to achieve his desired goals, if the agent thinks that the cost of being caught is far exceeded by the benefits consequent upon the achievement of the ends and/or if he thinks that he can act with impunity. Moreover, if this inclination leads a person to act and to do so habitually, then we have a pattern of immoral behavior properly describable as corruption. It is easy to see the importance of external accountability mechanisms in this situation; such external controls prevent agents from acting with impunity. What is less obvious but no less important is the existence of "internal" attitudinal controls. If the external environment is conducive to corruption, then it is almost inevitable that one will engage in corrupt behavior, unless one is possessed of a strong internalized moral code: hence the importance of moral character and the inculcation of the moral and civic virtues—preferably at an early age.

In Chapter 2, we introduced you to the myth of Gyges. Even though under Gygean conditions of perfect injustice, one could in theory avoid detection and thus act corruptly with impunity, it would not follow that one would necessarily avoid moral sanctions, because the moral cost to a Gyges-like character operating corruptly under conditions of perfect injustice might well be one of emotional and cognitive dissonance. This is likely to be the case if we assume that the Gyges-like character in question is at least moderately rational and is possessed of the beliefs and emotions of a normal, socialized person. Such a person is likely to suffer distress by virtue of the dissonance between their real corrupt motives and actions on the one hand, and their false and merely apparent moral reputation on the other. Like Macbeth, the person would be liable to inner conflict and the loss of inner peace. Perhaps the capacity for self-deception can defeat the onset of inner conflict; one convinces oneself that one's corrupt actions are not really corrupt. However, many agents lack the capacity for such self-deception, especially when others force them to confront the corrupt nature of their actions.

So engaging in corruption with *impunity* does not guarantee *immunity* from moral sanctions in the form of inner conflict and the consequent loss of inner peace. Perhaps integrity of character provides indemnity against the moral sanction of inner conflict and is thus a force that resists corruption, even under Gygean conditions of perfect injustice. Certainly, integrity of character is an important factor that needs to be mobilized in the devising of anti-corruption measures. A fundamental failure of the stick-carrot approach to combating corruption—an approach based purely on appeals to self-interest in the form of incentives (benefits) and disincentives (punishment and other burdens)—is that it ignores the importance of moral integrity as a basic human motivational force.

CORRUPT ACTIONS: ABROGATION OF DUTIES AND CORRUPT CULTURES

Many forms of corruption are breaches of fiduciary and related duties, and therefore they corrupt institutional processes, purposes, and roles and—ultimately—undermine institutions. For example, the due process of law in a criminal investigation is perverted when a police officer fabricates evidence or plants false evidence on a suspect, in order to obtain a conviction that the officer would otherwise not be able to secure because of the lack of sufficient evidence. In so doing, the police officer has not only failed to discharge his or her duty but also has abused his or her position as a police officer and has contributed to the undermining of an important institutional process. Such behavior is paradigmatic of corruption.

As noted before, fiduciary and related duties attach to institutional roles, and those roles exist to serve various purposes, notably the provision of various human goods. Thus, the role of a police officer is to serve the purpose of, say, law and order, that of a doctor the goal of physical well-being, and so on. So fiduciary and related duties are teleologically grounded; they derive from the moral purposes served by the roles to which they attach. Moreover, the occupants of such roles engage in corruption when they fail to fulfill these duties and use the powers attached to these roles for illegitimate purposes. Thus, the institutional role of a welfare officer might be to care for the elderly. The welfare officer acts corruptly if he or she exploits the vulnerability of an infirm, elderly person in the officer's care by, say, fraudulently diverting funds from the person's bank account into his or her own account. This is an act of fraud and an abrogation of the duty of care. But it is also an act of corruption, for by defrauding the client, the welfare officer has subverted the purposes of his or her institutional role and has thereby culpably undermined that role.

One important aspect of corruption is its relation to institutional culture. This trait is obvious in the case of a company like Enron. Enron's cutthroat corporate culture was inimical to ethical values and the pursuance of the public good. The cultural ethos at Enron evidently involved an overriding commitment to profit maximization and increasing the share value of Enron stock. Profit incentives and generous bonuses ruled supreme—moral principles and ethical values ran a poor second. However, at the end of the day, Enron's ethical breaches precipitated its financial collapse. To this extent, the Enron story vindicated the maxim that ethics is good for business and corruption is bad for business. We do not endorse this maxim as a *universal* statement true for all time in all places and in all business situations. Nevertheless, the maxim clearly has a reasonably *wide* application.

Although the importance of the relation between culture and corruption is often noted, the relationship is often not well understood. However, there is a growing literature on this relationship. One such exposition is contained in Francis Fukuyama's book *Trust*,[62] and another is to be found in Lipset and Lenz's "Corruption, Culture, and Markets."[63] These authors attempt to shed light on the relationship between culture and corruption by means of Edward Banfield's notion of amoral familism.

According to Banfield, corruption is to a large measure an expression of particularism—the felt obligation to help and give resources to members of one's family above all, but also to friends and members of the social group to which one belongs. This solidarity with members of one's family and social group can produce a self-interested culture that is hostile to the interests of outsiders. To this extent, it is analogous to individual self-interest; it is collective self-interest. Nepotism is one of the clearest examples of such collective self-interest.

Banfield argues that in a society of amoral families, there is little or no loyalty to the larger community, and there is only weak acceptance of social norms of behavior. Accordingly, amoral familism tends to facilitate corruption. An extreme form of amoral familism is the Mafia.[64] Although Banfield's research concerns specifically the people of Southern Italy, Fukuyama in his book makes similar observations about various other cultures and subcultures outside Europe, including Asia. The concept of amoral familism can be extended to some close-knit professional groups such as the police, where references to police corruption have often been related to perceptions of police solidarity and a police culture.

So a culture of amoral familism is conducive to corruption. Moreover, the *invisibility* of forms of corrupt practices within closely knit families creates problems for the detection and deterrence of such corruption. The problem is exacerbated by weak criminal justice institutions.

It is interesting that in these familial-based forms of corruption, a morally misguided understanding of the fiduciary relationship between members of a family can motivate corrupt practices. In many forms of corruption, the violation of a well-understood fiduciary relationship is driven by individual self-interest, for example, financial gain. However, in the case of corruption arising from amoral familism, a morally misguided understanding of one's fiduciary duty to other members of the family drives the corruption.

The explanation for such morally misguided understanding of fiduciary duties to members of one's family (or professional group) lies in the strength of group loyalty in solidaristic groups with a deeply felt collective self-interest. Misplaced, particularist fiduciary "duties" to family, friends, or professional colleagues override any commitment to universal moral principles or to actual fiduciary duties. The Watergate scandal is a clear illustration of one kind of amoral familism, namely, the political clique prepared to go to extreme lengths, including immoral and unlawful actions, to achieve its collective political ambitions. Members of such a clique act in part out of a misplaced loyalty and sense of obligation, both to their professional colleagues in the clique and to the leader of the clique. Consequently, their actual fiduciary duties to, say, the American people are downplayed or ignored, sometimes with the assistance of rationalizations, for example, that the end (a Nixon-led U.S. government—since this is allegedly in the public interest) justifies the means (unlawful break-ins and a cover-up). (See Chapter 5 on corruption and rationalizations.)

Fiduciary and related institutional duties presuppose relations of trust between those empowered to undertake these duties and those who entrust them with these powers. Accordingly, trust is fundamental to the survival of basic institutions such as government, the criminal justice system, and the economic system.

Corruption is typically parasitic on trust. It is only because a police officer, company director, or politician has been entrusted with particular powers that the officer can engage in corruption. On the other hand, corruption undermines trust. If directors, auditors, judges, politicians, journalists, and so on are not trusted, then there will be a reluctance to provide them with the requisite powers to enable them to perform their institutional roles, and even if powers are reluctantly agreed to, there will be a strong desire to unduly hamstring them with excessive regulatory and accountability mechanisms. Alternatively, citizens may simply "opt out" of public institutions, for example, give up on political participation as a lost cause, abandon the buying of shares, turn away from the communications of journalists, settle their disputes privately, and so on. Such retreat into the private sphere and its accompanying cynicism can only serve to further undermine public institutions.

Watergate and the resignation of President Nixon in the face of probable impeachment was a blow for the office of the American presidency, although it would have been a far worse blow had he continued in office. The collapse of Enron, WorldCom, and Arthur Andersen has seriously undermined public trust in the corporate sector. Widespread sexual abuse of children by ministers and priests undermines trust in the church; police corruption undermines trust in the criminal and judicial process; and the likes of the Jon-Benet Ramsey case in the United States and of the Lindy Chamberlain case in Australia undermine trust in the media.

The relationship between trust and political corruption is of particular importance, since the undermining of political institutions impacts powerfully on all or most of the other social institutions, and therefore on the framework of social norms that holds a society together. This is the case because government has a leadership and governance role in relation to other institutions and in relation to the citizenry at large.

In this connection let us consider a teleological argument that has traditionally been used in political philosophy to justify political authority. Although the earliest version of the argument first appears in Book 2 of Plato's *Republic,* its modern version comes down to us from Thomas Hobbes. An outline of the argument, which appears in Hobbes's *Leviathan,* is as follows.

As mentioned in Chapter 2, Hobbes conceived of a precivilized *state of nature* in which there are no rules to govern human behavior and individuals are free to act as they please. In such a state of nature, *each individual is at war with every other individual.* Under such circumstances no one can get on with one's own business, because everyone is always subjected to interference from others. In this state of *the war of all against all,* there is no law to protect anyone's life or property. In such a lawless state, each person is a law unto themselves.

However, people in the state of nature can come to realize that it would be in everyone's interest if they had some common moral rules to guide individual conduct. Such commonly recognized rules would allow people to get on better with each other, and in consequence, each person would be able to pursue his or her business without fear of interference from others. Thus, they come together and agree to a set of common rules of social conduct in order to achieve the *telos,* "commodious living." To ensure *compliance* with those rules, they endow someone among them with political authority and with sufficient power to ensure that this authority is exercised for that purpose. In Hobbes's time, the authority and power to ensure compliance were invested in the king or queen. In our times, that authority and power is invested in a democratically elected government. In summation, according to Hobbes, it is this social contract among individuals within a society that establishes rules of moral conduct and justifies the authority of political power as a means of ensuring compliance with these rules.

Now we have deep reservations about the adequacy of any attempt—including that of Hobbes—to arrive at fundamental moral principles by way of the deliberations of rational self-interested contractors. Nevertheless, Hobbes has undoubtedly provided important insights into *political* institutions. In the light of this Hobbesian contractarian conception, we can see one of the main reasons why political corruption, in particular, is morally unacceptable. If those entrusted with the authority and power to frame and to ensure compliance with morally legitimate laws in fact fail to legislate such laws into existence, or violate those laws, then a loss of trust will inevitably follow. Such a loss of trust in political institutions can have profound consequences. It has the potential to undermine the authority of political institutions and therefore of the capacity of governments to provide leadership and governance in relation both to other institutions, and to the citizenry at large. In such circumstances, Hobbes's state of nature beckons. On the contractarian model, serious and widespread political corruption tends to undermine the very foundations of the state. In extreme examples, this condition may lead to anarchy or the kind of political, institutional, and moral chaos that existed in Colombia during Pablo Escobar's time. (See Case Study 2.2.)

THE HARM CONSEQUENT UPON CORRUPTION

The following are, in summary, some of the types of harm associated with corruption:

1. Harm to self (personal)
2. Harm to family (familial)
3. Harm to profession (professional)
4. Harm to organizations (organizational)
5. Harm to society (social)

The harm involved in corruption will typically involve a combination of a number of these types of harm.

Personal harm may take the form of loss of reputation, financial loss through fines, loss of freedom through imprisonment, or, in some extreme cases, for example, that of Pablo Escobar, loss of life. Moreover, one may suffer harm through the corruption of one's character.

Familial harm, as in the case of personal harm, may take the form of loss of reputation, shame through being publicly disgraced, financial loss to one-self and one's family, as well as general hardship to one's family.

Professional and organizational harm may take the form of loss of public trust and confidence in the corrupt professional person and/or his or her organization, and/or his or her profession as a whole. In the case of Enron, for example, Enron's auditors, the giant international firm Arthur Andersen, suffered a significant loss of professional reputation, a loss of many of their established clients, and a consequent financial collapse. Indeed, ultimately Arthur Andersen went out of existence.

Social harm may take the form of financial loss, as in the case of the Enron investors, creditors, and employees, as well as loss of trust in the social, professional, or other institutions in which the corruption takes place. For example, widespread police corruption undermines trust in the criminal justice system. As we argued in the last section, political corruption may have especially profound consequences, including the destabilization of the state.

The preceding types of harms associated with corruption are clearly illustrated in the Enron, Watergate, and Pablo Escobar case studies. In each of these case studies, there is personal, family, professional, organizational, and social harm consequent upon corrupt activity.

Personal harm resulted with regard to both the perpetrators, or at least alleged perpetrators, and the victims of corruption in both the Enron and Escobar cases. In the case of Enron, the most tragic loss was the death of Cliff Baxter, vice chairman of Enron, who was found dead from a gunshot wound. (See Case Study 2.2.) We can also note the scene in the Escobar case study (Case Study 2.1) involving the inconsolable pregnant woman with a small child who throws herself on her husband's casket and refuses to let go until she is pulled away.[65] Tragic loss of life goes well beyond any financial loss or gain that may accrue to victims or corrupt actors. Corruption is not, as is sometimes thought, merely a financial or an economic problem. Corruption has implications for human rights, including the right to life.

With regard to personal financial loss, tens of thousands of Enron employees and retirees lost a staggering $1.3 billion. For example, former Enron employees and retirees Janice Farmer and Charles Prestwood lost $700,000 and $1.3 million (respectively) of their pension savings; the money had been invested in Enron stock.[66] Another less well-known corporate collapse is that of the Baptist Foundation of Arizona (BFA). BFA filed for bankruptcy in 1999, after mismanagement and corruption resulted in 13,000 of its mostly elderly investors collectively losing in excess of $590 million—a heavy blow for elderly pensioners that put their trust in the integrity of that organization. As in the case of Enron, the auditor of BFA was Arthur Andersen.[67]

Familial harm that results from corruption is in most cases an extension of personal harm. Consider the emotional and psychological, let alone financial, harm that Cliff Baxter's death (allegedly) through suicide must have brought to his family. And presumably the picture of Andrew Fastow in newspapers in October 2002, which showed him being led handcuffed by FBI agents into court to face charges of fraud, money laundering, and conspiracy, must have caused his family significant emotional and psychological harm; this is in addition to the personal harm that he himself must have suffered. Like the thousands of Enron employees and investors who were harmed by Enron's collapse, the families of the corrupt actors themselves are also usually among the victims.

The family of Pablo Escobar, and specifically his wife and two children, suffered emotional and psychological harm as a result of Pablo's crime and corruption. Even if his family were aware of Escobar's corrupt activities, we can still feel some degree of pity for their plight after Pablo's killing. Interviewed by a Bogota TV crew in their suite at the Hotel Tequendama where they had been isolated for weeks after Escobar's death, his wife, Maria Victoria, looking haggard but composed, portrayed herself and her children as just more victims of the country's violence. "There's no positive response to any of this," she said. "I don't know if you notice, but we are also a family who feel we've gone through the same despair the country has. And psychologically, I'm very concerned whether my children will be able to survive this complex situation."[68]

It is obvious that *professional and organizational harm* can ultimately result in *social harm*. On the one hand, there is the loss in terms of public trust in those professions and organizations; on the other hand, there is the direct loss in terms of the undermining of the actual institutional processes and roles themselves.

In the case of Escobar, there was widespread bribing of police officers, politicians (including mayors, councillors, and congresspersons), judges, and army officers that undermined the proper and efficient functioning of those institutions to the overall detriment of government and those governed. Escobar's modus operandi, *plata o plomo* (silver or lead), was an effective method of getting what he wanted, either through generous bribes or murder. Most, like a judge who arranged for the charges against Escobar and his associates to be dropped, took the bribes. Others, like the newspaper editor of *El Espectador* and Lara, the justice minister, who denounced Escobar's criminal operations, were murdered. Escobar's power was such that no social or political institution in Colombia remained untainted by corruption.

As has often been observed, corruption undermines the legitimacy of government. This was certainly the case in Colombia during Escobar's time, a time when Escobar's power to corrupt was enhanced by a population that had little trust or respect for the preexisting political and economic institutions. Indeed, Escobar saw himself as a Colombian Robin Hood or a new Pancho Villa.[69] This view was shared by some poor and oppressed Colombians who benefited from Escobar's largesse in the form of handouts and social works programs. Unfortunately, his "generosity" had very little positive effect on social and economic deprivation in Colombia, although its negative effects were significant.

Here, as elsewhere, the benefits of corruption need to be factored into the equation, alongside the harms. Unfortunately, the benefits of corruption are typically far outweighed by the harms. In relation to the purely economic ledger of benefits and burdens, there is increasing empirical evidence that the costs far outweigh any benefits. As Bukovansky notes,

> The dominant rationale for the emerging international anti-corruption regime has been economic and institutional rather than normative: the argument is that corruption hurts economic development either by siphoning off resources and discouraging foreign investment, or because corrupt elites select public financing projects in order to maximise their opportunities for monopoly rents rather than encourage sustainable growth.[70]

We concur, but note that economic well-being and institutional functionality are human *goods*; Bukovansky is (albeit unknowingly) offering a (partial) *normative* argument.

In the case of the Enron collapse, the professional and institutional harm is manifest. It included harm to the professions of auditor, accountant, director, corporate manager, and so on. It also involved harm to organizations, notably to Enron itself and to Arthur Andersen.

Susan Rose-Ackerman correctly claims that "corruption that involves top-level officials can produce serious distortions in the way government and society operate."[71] In the case of Escobar, this is obvious enough. But what of the type of corporate corruption that we encounter in Enron and similar cases? Though the U.S. institutions are robust and are relatively resistant to the type and level of systematic and pervasive corruption encountered in Colombia under Escobar's reign of terror, their perceived probity and relative invulnerability is questioned by the public when companies like Enron and WorldCom collapse in a quagmire of corruption and mismanagement, and in so doing profoundly harm ordinary citizens. Indeed, these collapses might engender considerable public mistrust in key elements of the market economy, the financial pillar of contemporary Western democracies. As more and more people invest their life savings in pension funds in public companies—amounting now to billions of dollars—the potential for harm not only increases but also rightly becomes a matter of public concern.

As Rose-Ackerman points out, it is true that "credible reform must start at the top" and "a crackdown should reach the rich and powerful."[72] This of course is happening with regard to Enron; the top officers of that company are now under investigation for corruption and face litigation from aggrieved shareholders and ex-employees. But in the process of setting an example by going after the people at the top, the possibly systemic nature of the problem should not be ignored. The problem may be wider and deeper than the existence of a corrupt management; it may extend to the lower echelons and to external agencies, including regulators and auditors.

Accountability is necessary for the control of corruption, and accountability with regard to corporate corruption needs to exist at a number of levels. It requires not only proper and effective internal controls and an independent and a credible auditing process at the micro level, but also an array of institutional mechanisms at the macro level. These include effective regulators, a robust and independent judiciary, and a vigilant and free press that is not averse to exposing the corrupt, no matter how rich or powerful they are. Most of all, it requires a government with the will to ensure that appropriate accountability mechanisms at these various levels are established and maintained. These important issues of responsibility and accountability will be taken up in detail in Chapters 6 and 7.

CONCLUSION

In this chapter, we have argued that the moral problems with corruption are multiple and contextual. They are multiple in that they pertain to the inherent nature of corruption, to the intentions and motivations that lie behind corruption, and to the harms consequent upon corruption. Moreover, they are multiple in respect to the varieties of motivation and to the variety of harms consequent upon corruption, for example, harms to self, family, profession, and organization.

The moral problems with corruption are contextual in that whether or not a specific act is corrupt depends on its causal contribution to the undermining of a specific, socially and historically located, institution. The same act might corrupt in one institutional or social setting but not in another. That said, there are some actions, such as bribery, fraud, and the abuse of power, that will invariably result in the undermining of institutions. Such actions are more or less inherently corrupt.

chapter five

Rationalizing Corruption

In this chapter we

- Identify a number of different rationalizations used to justify corrupt actions.
- Introduce a number of case studies of corruption involving such rationalizations, including the "Dirty Harry" scenario, and the Bhopal and Lockheed scandals.
- Provide a detailed analysis of noble cause corruption and of transcultural corruption.

Corrupt practices are often rationalized by those who engage in them. For example, Person A might argue that if he, A, does not accept the bribe, someone else will. So the world will not be a better place if A refuses the bribe, and A will lose out if A refuses it. So A should accept the bribe. Such rationalizations can make corrupt practices seem reasonable and thus tend to reinforce rather than undermine them. Rationalizations are particularly potent if they cohere with a personal, community, or occupational worldview, albeit one that is not objectively sustainable. Accordingly, one important source of rationalizations is an alleged role responsibility. In these sorts of cases, people convince themselves, or are convinced by colleagues, that a manifestly wrongful act is justified in terms of their professional duty—it is somehow justified by virtue of some larger moral purpose of their institutional office.

CASE STUDY 5.1   Corruption of Institutional Role

For years a bitter dispute raged between the two men who both claimed to have been the discoverer of the virus that causes AIDS, the American Robert Gallo, head of the National Institute of Health's Laboratory of Tumor Cell Biology, and the Frenchman Luc Montagnier of the Pasteur Institute. More than personal pride was involved: the dispute became a matter of institutional and even national prestige. In the late 1980s, Gallo finally conceded that the virus he identified (in work done in 1983 and 1984) was from a sample contaminated by a sample sent to him by Montagnier. A National Institutes of Health Investigation found Gallo's report of the work full of falsifications of date and misrepresentations of method.

It is in this context that we should examine the actions of Dr. Michael Garretta, former Head of the National Blood Transfusion Centre in France. In the spring of 1985, it was clear that the French supplies of a blood-clotting substance needed by hemophiliacs were contaminated by the AIDS virus. French hemophiliacs could have been protected if then-available techniques for decontaminating blood tainted with HIV had been used or if the tainted supplies had been replaced. The technology was developed in the United States. So, either way, the French would have been relying on American science—something that the French government was loath to do, especially given the dispute between the two countries over the discovery of the AIDS virus—and the cost would have been substantial (one estimate put it at $40 million).

Although Garetta was aware of these possibilities, he ordered that the supplies be used until they were exhausted. (They were withdrawn in October 1985, after the French decontamination process was available.) As a result, some 1,500 hemophiliacs were infected; at least 300 have since died. In October 1992, Dr. Garetta was convicted of "fraudulent description of goods" in the distribution of tainted blood and was sentenced to four years in prison (the maximum allowed). In Garetta's defense, it was argued that his superiors were aware of the dangers and that he acted as an agent within a bureaucracy committed to safeguarding the prestige of French science. In short, he was fulfilling his role responsibilities.

(Adapted from Daniel E. Wueste (Ed.), *Ethics and Social Responsibility,* Lanham, Maryland: Rowman and Littlefield, 1994, pp. 15 and 24.)

Unlike the one manifest in this case study, some rationalizations have a basis in reality; they are not mere rationalizations, but rather plausible justifications, or at least excuses. As such, they are not violations, but only infringements, of moral principles or moral rights. Perhaps A is extremely poorly paid and the main breadwinner for a large extended family; therefore, A needs to engage in minor forms of corruption (bribery) to avert a morally unacceptable outcome.

And there are other rationalizations that are neither plausible justifications nor mere rationalizations. These include ones that arise when a person is put in a very difficult situation that calls for moral courage or even heroism. Suppose Person B is working in a corrupt environment and is offered a bribe. B does not want to accept, but if B does not, then B will be ostracized by B's colleagues and subjected to harassment.

At any rate, the widespread existence and influence of rationalizations for corrupt practices, as well as the confusion that they create, make it important to subject them to philosophical scrutiny.

In this chapter, we consider in detail two prevalent forms of rationalization. The first arises in relation to so-called "noble cause" corruption. Noble cause corruption is corruption in the service of a good end. Consider a police officer seeking to put away a known serial pedophile. Perhaps the evidence is not quite as strong as it could be, so the pedophile might escape conviction. Accordingly, the police officer "enhances" or "loads up" the evidence. In so doing, the officer rationalizes his course of action by recourse to the good end that he believes it will realize.

The second kind of rationalization that we consider occurs when an individual is placed in an environment in which the practices are "different" from those that she is used to—indeed, the practices are ones that the person would normally regard as corrupt. However, the person reasons that "This is the way things are done in this cultural context" and that therefore the appropriate principle to follow is "When in Rome do as the Romans do." This is an especially seductive rationalization when it is in one's personal interest or the interest of the organization for whom one is working (or both) and when engaging in these corrupt practices apparently has few, if any, untoward consequences. Indeed, it might seem that failure to engage in the corrupt practices will have untoward consequences. We will refer to this form of corruption as transcultural corruption.

NOBLE CAUSE CORRUPTION

CASE STUDY 5.2   Dirty Harry

The "Dirty Harry" problem draws its name from the 1971 Warner Brothers film *Dirty Harry* and its chief protagonist, antihero Inspector Harry Callahan.

A 14-year-old girl has been kidnapped and is being held captive by a psychotic killer. The killer, "Scorpio," who has already struck twice, demands $200,000 ransom to release the girl, who is buried with just enough oxygen to keep her alive for a few hours. Harry gets the job of delivering the ransom. At the meeting, Scorpio decides to renege on his bargain, let the girl die, and kill Harry. Scorpio escapes, but Harry manages to track him down and finally confronts Scorpio. Harry shoots him in the leg as he is trying to escape. Standing over Scorpio, Harry demands to know where the girl is buried. Scorpio refuses to disclose her location; demanding his rights to a lawyer. As the camera draws back from the scene, Harry stands on Scorpio's bullet-mangled leg to torture a confession of the girl's location from him.

(Carl B. Klockars, "The Dirty Harry Problem" in *The Annals*, No. 452, November 1983, pp. 33–47.)

Many forms of moral wrongdoing involve harming people in various ways, for example, killing, assaulting, lying, taking property, invading privacy, and so on. But sometimes harming people is morally justified by the good end that is achieved, for example, a surgeon's cutting you up to save your life, police surveilling a pedophile, a person's killing an attacker in self-defense, and a German citizen's lying to the Nazis to save the lives of Jewish people. The preceding Dirty Harry scenario outlines what to many is a perfectly justified course of action. In fact, Harry's action is difficult to justify, notwithstanding the emotional appeal of such rough justice to audiences weaned on unrealistic cop shows. For one thing, the girl was already dead, and so Harry's action did not achieve its end; for another thing, torture as a routine practice in policing is demonstrably inconsistent with upholding law and order.

Sometimes harming people has a good end, but the harm caused is still not, or not obviously, morally justified, for example, dropping an atomic bomb on Hiroshima to end World War Two, napalming a Vietnamese village to end the Vietnam war, fabricating evidence against a known pedophile to secure a conviction, establishing vigilante death squads to murder known drug dealers, torturing a spy to save the lives of one's own people, and so forth. Noble cause corruption involves performing corrupt actions—and thereby typically harming someone or other—but doing so for good ends. So noble cause corruption is a species of doing evil to achieve good.

Some occupations seem especially vulnerable to noble cause corruption, for example, those of politicians, the military, and police officers. This tendency is in part because these occupations at times necessarily use methods or means that are harmful and that would under normal circumstances be immoral, for example, killing people or intrusively surveilling them.

Noble cause corruption often involves not only doing evil to achieve good but also breaking the criminal law to achieve good. Here it is important to remind ourselves that the criminal law and morality are not necessarily the same thing. Sometimes there are morally repugnant laws, for example, the South African apartheid laws. Nevertheless, the criminal law typically "tracks" morality. There are laws against murder, rape, assault, and theft precisely because these practices are regarded as morally wrong.

What is the difference between the *morally justified* harming of people for a good end by, say, the police, and noble cause corruption/wrongdoing? Morally justified harming typically meets the following three conditions:

1. The action is harmful but is morally justified by virtue of complying with some objective moral principle(s), for example, killing someone who will kill you unless you kill that person and who is not justified in trying to kill you.

2. The action is lawful.
3. The action is of a kind consented to by the community.

Here we need to note that laws enacted in democratic communities are typically viewed as having been consented to by the community, because the community elected the legislature—the law-making body—and the community is in a position to reject the legislature if the laws that it enacts are felt to be immoral or unreasonable.

Acts of noble cause corruption do not comply with all three conditions. The act of noble cause corruption is performed in order to realize some morally worthy end, and the action is therefore believed to be morally justified. However, the action fails to comply with one or more of the three conditions just listed. That is, the action is not objectively morally justified, and/or it is unlawful, and/or it is not in accordance with the community's will. Thus, fabricating evidence against a suspect infringes the suspect's moral rights and is unlawful. Moreover, although it may be in accordance with the private judgment of a police officer, it does not reflect the will of the community.

Moral dangers arise when (1), (2), and (3) come apart. For example, moral dangers arise when the law does not track objective ethical principles or when such principles are inconsistent with the community's attitudes. Perhaps mandatory sentencing is objectively morally wrong, but the community wants it, and politicians enact laws requiring it. Again, the legal rights of suspects might exist at the expense of the moral rights of victims, for example, the legal right of war criminals such as Milosevic or of fraudsters such as the Australian Christopher Skase, not to be extradited.

In order to enable us to explore further the philosophical issues associated with noble cause corruption and to focus our discussion, let us consider the following case study.[73]

CASE STUDY 5.3   Noble Cause Corruption

A young officer, Joe, seeks advice from the police chaplain. Joe is working with an experienced detective, Mick, who is also Joe's brother-in-law, and who is looked up to by Joe as a good detective who gets results. Joe and Mick are working on a case involving a known drug dealer and pedophile. Joe describes his problem as follows:

> Father—he has got a mile of form, including getting kids hooked on drugs, physical and sexual assault on minors, and more. Anyway, surveillance informed Mick that the drug dealer had just made a buy. As me and Mick approached the drug dealer's penthouse flat we noticed a parcel come flying out the window of the flat onto the street. It was full of heroin. The drug dealer was in the house, but we found no drugs inside. Mick thought it would be more of a sure thing if we found the evidence in the flat rather than on the street—especially given the number of windows in

the building. The defense would find it more difficult to deny possession. Last night Mick tells me that he was interviewed and signed a statement that we both found the parcel of heroin under the sink in the flat. He said all I had to do was to go along with the story in court and everything will be sweet, no worries. What should I do Father—perjury is a serious criminal offense.

> (This case study was provided in a suitably disguised form by Father Jim Boland, Chaplain to the New South Wales Police.)

In this scenario, there are two putative instances of noble cause corruption. The first one is Mick's intentionally unlawfully loading up the evidence and committing perjury in order to secure a conviction. As it is described here, this instance of noble cause corruption is not morally sustainable, because there is a presumption against breaking communally sanctioned ethical principles enshrined in the law, and this presumption has not been offset by the moral considerations in play here. Indeed, it is by no means clear that in this situation Mick's unlawful acts are even necessary in order for the drug dealer to be convicted. Moreover, achieving the good end of securing the conviction of the drug dealer is outweighed by the damage being done by undermining other important moral ends, namely, due process of law and respect for a suspect's moral rights.[74] (For a detailed account of a suspect's rights, see Chapter 9.)

Nor is there anything to suggest that this is a one-off unlawful act by Mick, and that he had provided himself with what he took to be a specific and overriding moral justification for committing it on this particular occasion. Indeed, the impression is that Mick loads up suspects and commits perjury as a matter of routine practice. Furthermore, there is nothing to suggest that police powers in this area—at least in Australia—are hopelessly inadequate; that police and others have failed in their endeavors to reform the law; and that therefore police officers have no option but to violate due process law, if they are to uphold (so-called) substantive law. Of course, it is a different matter whether or not current Australian antidrug policies are adequate to the task. Evidently they are not. But this situation in itself does not justify an increase in police powers in particular, for if anything is clear, it is that a policy of criminalization is by itself inadequate. Accordingly, Mick and likeminded detectives do not have available to them the argument that noble cause corruption is justifiable, because there is a discrepancy between what police powers ought to be, by the lights of objective ethical principles, and what they in fact are. In the first place, there is no such discrepancy, although arguably current antidrug policies are failing. In the second place, loading up suspects, perjury, and the like could never be lawful procedures grounded in objective ethical principles. Last, if in fact an increase in police powers were morally justified, then the appropriate response of the police ought to be to argue and lobby for this increase, not to engage in unlawful conduct. It might be the case that an irredeemably obstructionist political system that consistently failed to provide police with adequate powers in spite of sustained and well-put arguments and lobbying by police and others, might justify police exercise of unlawful powers of a kind that ought to be lawful, for example, detaining a suspect for a period longer than was lawful.

There is a second possible example of noble cause corruption in our scenario that is more morally troublesome. This is Joe's committing perjury in order to prevent a host of harmful consequences to Mick, Joe, and their families. If Joe does not commit perjury, Mick will be convicted of a criminal act, and their careers will be ruined. Moreover, the friendship of Mick and Joe will be at an end, and their respective families will suffer great unhappiness. The second example is a candidate for justified, or at least excusable, unlawful behavior on the grounds of extenuating circumstances. Let us assume that were Joe to commit perjury, his action would be morally justified, or at least morally excusable. The question to be asked now is whether it is an act of noble cause corruption.

Certainly, such an act of perjury is unlawful. But here we need to distinguish a number of different categories. Some acts are unlawful, but their commission does not harm any innocent person. Arguably, such unlawful acts are not necessarily immoral. The drug dealer will be harmed in that he will go to prison, but he is not innocent; he is a known drug dealer and pedophile who deserves to go to prison.

But the fact that the drug dealer is guilty of serious crimes does not settle the issue. Consider Joe's actions. Some acts are unlawful, but their commission does not infringe anyone's moral rights. Joe's act will certainly infringe the drug dealer's moral rights, including the right to a fair trial based on admissible evidence. Moreover, perjury undermines a central plank of due process law; without truthful testimony, the whole system of criminal justice would founder; perjury is a species of institutional corruption. Considered in itself, the act of perjury is both a serious moral wrong and an act of corruption. Unfortunately, as we have already seen, the moral costs of Joe's not committing perjury are also very high—perhaps higher than those involved in perjury.

We can conclude that Joe faces a genuine moral dilemma; he will do moral harm whatever he does. Does it follow that we have found an instance in which noble cause corruption is justified? Here there are really two questions. First, is Joe's action an instance of noble cause corruption? Second, is his action morally justified? The distinction between corruption—including noble cause corruption—on the one hand, and immorality, on the other hand, is a fine distinction in this context; but it is no less real for that. As we have seen in earlier chapters, corruption is a species of immorality, and corrupt actions are a species of immoral actions; nevertheless, not all immorality is corruption, and not all immoral actions are corrupt ones.

Most corrupt actions have a number of properties that other immoral actions do not necessarily possess. First, corrupt actions are typically not one-off actions. For an action to be properly labeled as corrupt, it has to in fact be corrupt and therefore is typically a manifestation of a disposition or habit on the part of the agent to commit that kind of action. Indeed, one of the reasons most acts of noble cause corruption are so problematic in policing is that they typically involve a disposition to commit a certain kind of action. Acts of noble cause corruption are typically not simply one-off actions; they are habitual.

Now Joe's action is not habitual. However, as we saw in Chapter 1, some acts of corruption are one-off. So the fact that Joe's action is a one-off, nonhabitual action does not settle the question as to whether it is corrupt or not.

Second, most corrupt actions—involving as they do a habit to act in a certain way—are not performed because of a specific nonrecurring eventuality. Rather, they are performed because of an ongoing condition or recurring situation. In the case of noble cause corruption in policing, the ostensible ongoing condition is the belief that the law is hopelessly and irredeemably inadequate, not only because it fails to provide police with sufficient powers to enable offenders to be apprehended and convicted but also because it fails to provide sufficiently harsh punishments for offenders. Accordingly, so the argument runs, police need to engage in noble cause corruption; that is, they need to develop a habit of bending and breaking the law in the service of the greater moral good of justice, given the irremediable features of the criminal justice system.

Now although Joe is motivated to do wrong to achieve good, or at least to avoid evil, he is responding to a highly specific—indeed extraordinary—circumstance that he finds himself in, and one that is highly unlikely to recur.[75] He has not developed a disposition or habit in response to a felt ongoing condition or recurring situation. However, again the point has to be made that some corrupt actions are one-off, nonhabitual actions that are responses to a highly specific, nonrecurring circumstance. Accordingly, we cannot conclude from the nonrecurring nature of these circumstances that Joe's action is not a corrupt act.

Third, corrupt actions are typically motivated, at least in part, by individual or narrow collective self-interest. In the case of policing, the interest can be individual self-interest, such as personal financial gain or career advancement; or it can be the narrow collective self-interest of the group, such as in the case of a clique of corrupt detectives.

Certainly, Joe's action is not motivated by self-interest. However, it is a defining feature of acts of noble cause corruption that they are not motivated by self-interest (or narrow collective self-interest), and so this feature of Joe's action does not prevent its being an act of corruption—and specifically, an act of noble cause corruption.

Given that Joe's act of perjury undermines a legitimate institutional process and given the possibility of one-off acts of noble cause corruption, it might seem that Joe's act is corrupt. But this move is a little too quick. Certainly, Joe's action undermines a legitimate institutional process. However, as noted in Chapter 1, for his act to be corrupt, Joe has to be morally culpable in some degree. Now Joe is aware that his act of perjury will undermine a legitimate institutional process; it is not as if he is ignorant of the institutional damage that he is doing. On the other hand, he is well-motivated; he is aiming at the good, albeit by doing what is prima facie morally wrong.

This action is an instance of noble cause corruption. In order for his action to be an act of noble cause corruption, it has to be corrupt, and in order for it to be corrupt, it must fulfill the following two conditions. First, it must have a corrupting effect. Second, the agent must have intentionally performed an act that corrupts, or one that the agent knew would corrupt or ought to have known would corrupt. Joe's act meets these two conditions. By virtue of being an act of perjury it will corrupt the criminal justice process, and Joe intends that this be so.

However, it seems to us that Joe faces a genuine moral dilemma. Perhaps it would be morally wrong for him to commit perjury. However, even if this is so, we do not believe that he would be culpable in the required sense, if he committed perjury in these circumstances, because the dilemma is such that we cannot confidently claim that Joe ought to have known that committing perjury *in these circumstances* would be morally wrong. We conclude that Joe's act of perjury is corrupt and might be morally wrong, but that Joe is not morally culpable.

We have seen that corrupt actions, including acts of noble cause corruption, are typically—but not necessarily or invariably—habitual actions; typically, they are not one-off actions performed in accordance with moral principles that have been applied to a particular nonrecurring situation. So in most cases of noble cause corruption, the motivating force is in part that of habit, and there is no attempt to perform a rational calculation of the morality of means and ends on a case-by-case basis. Accordingly, there is an inherent possibility, and perhaps tendency, for such acts of noble cause corruption not to be morally justified when individually considered. After all, the police officer who has performed such an individual act of noble cause corruption has simply acted from habit and has not taken the time to consider whether or not the means really do justify the ends in the particular case. Moreover, given a presumption against infringing communally sanctioned and legally enshrined ethical principles, this failure to engage in moral decision-making on a case-by-case basis is surely morally culpable by virtue of being—at the very least—morally negligent.

What we have said thus far points to the morally problematic nature of doing wrong to achieve good as a matter of unthinking routine. This discussion does not show that noble cause corruption is motivated by individual (or narrow collective) self-interest—noble cause corruption remains noble (in some sense). However, there is a weaker claim to be made here, namely, that most acts of noble cause corruption are motivated, or at least in part sustained, by a degree of moral negligence.

The officer who habitually performs acts of noble cause corruption does not feel the need to examine the rights and wrongs of his or her (allegedly) ends-justified immoral actions on a case-by-case basis. Yet given the presumption against infringing communally sanctioned ethical principles enshrined in the law, surely decision-making on a case-by-case basis is typically morally required. Moreover—as we saw before—acts of noble cause corruption have not been communally sanctioned; they are actions justified—if they are justified at all—only by some set of moral principles held to by the individual police officer or group of officers. Furthermore, this set of alleged ethical principles is typically not objectively valid; it is not a set that ought to be enshrined in the law. Rather, these allegedly ethical principles are in fact typically spurious; they are the kind of principle used to justify actions of the sort that Mick commits, namely, loading up suspects and perjury.

Accordingly, there is a strong possibility of, and perhaps tendency to, moral arrogance, moral insularity, and the application of unethical principles being inherent in noble cause corruption. Accordingly, noble cause corruption is both dangerous in its own right and likely to be, at least in part, self-serving.

In short, although acts of noble cause corruption are by definition not motivated by individual (or narrow collective) self-interest, insofar as they are habitual actions, they are likely to be indirectly linked to, and in part sustained by, self-interest. Indeed, this conceptual claim of an indirect connection between noble cause corruption and self-interest seems to be supported by empirical studies. It appears to be an empirical fact that police who start off engaging in noble cause corruption often end up engaging in common or garden-variety out-and-out corruption.[76]

TRANSCULTURAL CORRUPTION

A social group consists of a set of individual persons who are (at least) the current participants in some common structure(s) of conventions (including at least a structure of linguistic conventions).[77] We noted in Chapter 1 that conventions are essentially facilitative and instrumental social forms, whereas social norms embody the moral principles and values of a social group. For that reason, social groups by definition also involve a common structure of *social norms.*

Such a structure of social norms is necessarily embedded in the fundamental institutions of the social group in question.[78] Hence, there is a further condition for being a social group, namely, a common structure of fundamental institutions, including at least linguistic, kinship, legal (or quasi-legal), and economic ones.

Most English and German people speak English and therefore share a structure of conventions, namely, the conventions of the English language. They also share a common structure of social norms, including those embodied in the criminal laws of both countries. Furthermore, they share a similar set of structures of fundamental institutions, including those of the modern nuclear family, capitalism, and the liberal democratic state. But the Germans and the English do not constitute a single social group. One reason for this difference is the lack of a common intergenerational history. The history of the English certainly intersects with that of the Germans, but they are nevertheless relatively distinct. Let us then add the following condition for being a social group: a common stretch of intergenerational history.

The resulting definition remains inadequate. Many minorities with strong claims to being distinct social groups have shared a common stretch of intergenerational history with the larger community of which they are a minority, and they have participated in common structures of conventions (including linguistic conventions), social norms, and at least some fundamental institutions. However, their point is that they have done so under duress and that there are important "cultural" differences that have been suppressed. Consider the Kurds in Turkey or Iraq.

Here we need to distinguish two conditions. The first condition is that (1) the membership of the social group in question is able to be differentiated from the membership of other social groups in virtue of (a) their common ancestry and (b) their participation over generations in some common set(s) of joint actions, activities, and/or projects, including joint (so to speak) epistemological and narrative projects (roughly, joint, intergenerational attempts to understand "the world," that is, their worldview). In short, condition (1) expresses the proposition that a set of individual persons have shared a common life over generations. The second condition is that (2) their moral rights have been violated, and violated because they are members of a specific social group. Roughly speaking, social groups that meet condition (2) are oppressed peoples.

Clearly (1), but not (2), is a condition for being a social group. Condition (2) presupposes the existence of a social group. So condition (2) cannot be a necessary condition for being a social group. On the other hand, condition (1) ought to be sufficient to mark off minority social groups from the members of an oppressive "host" social group. Typically, the former will not participate with the latter in the same joint activities and projects—and especially not the same narrative projects. Moreover, even where they participate in the same joint activities and projects, "fault lines" of social tension and dissent will indicate that joint "participation" is coercive in character.

Transcultural interaction is, and always has been, a pervasive feature of social groups.[79] Most societies at most periods of human history have engaged in most of the various kinds of generic joint activity that comprise spheres of activity and underpin social institutions, and they have done so because these activities are grounded in basic human needs. Moreover, throughout the course of history, many, if not most, social groups have interacted with some other social groups communicatively, economically, sexually, and so on. So a sphere of activity is not by any means necessarily an intrasocietal or intracultural phenomenon.

Since communicative, economic, and so on, interactions—at least to the extent that they are voluntary—are to some extent structured by conventions, so transsocietal and transcultural communicative, economic, and so on, interactions will be structured by conventions, conventions to which the members of both interacting social groups will be party. Dialogue between members of different social groups, societies, and cultures presupposes a common language. This requirement remains true notwithstanding problems of differences in interpretation. For example, French used to be the international language, and now English is. Trade between societies presupposes a commonly adhered to system of exchange, whether it be a barter, monetary, or some other type of system. Let us call mere *convention-governed interaction* between distinct social groups, *transsocietal* interaction.

The existence of transsocietal interaction displays the distinction between social groups and mere participants in a sphere of activity. A social group consists of a set of particular individuals who participate in a number of the same spheres of activity and who therefore are party to a number of the same networks of conventions (each network regulating the interactions in a given sphere of activity). In addition, however, members of a social group (by our preceding stipulative definition) share a common intergenerational history and have been inducted into a common structure of social norms and institutions.

What of the interaction between organizations belonging to different social groups? Historically, there has been a great deal of political and economic (cooperative) interaction between economic or business organizations, and between political organizations, such as governments. However, a good deal of it has been coercive in character. Consider nineteenth-century British gun-boat diplomacy pursued for the purpose of ensuring that opium traders had access to China. On the other hand, much of the interaction has been broadly cooperative in character. And the current predilection for regional trading blocs, economic communities, and the like indicates a belief that cooperation can be mutually beneficial. But as with individual persons, including individual members of the same organization, cooperative interaction between different organizations, and between organizations belonging to different societies, presupposes a common set of conventions, such as ones governing the exchange of goods. Accordingly, one species of transsocietal interaction is *transsocietal organizational* interaction.

However, there is a different kind of transsocietal interaction involving organizations. Historically, as well as in the contemporary world, there have been many different kinds of *transsocietal organizations,* including empires, military and religious organizations, and multinational corporations. Such transsocietal organizations presuppose not only that the two or more social groups have an overlapping sphere, or spheres of activity, and an adherence to a common set of conventions, but also that they belong to at least one of the same organizations. Insofar as such organizations have a minimal impact or are unwanted impositions on a preexisting social group, they do not necessarily destroy the identities of the different social groups that belong to the transsocietal organizations in question. Accordingly, the notion of transsocietal interaction within a given organization is quite coherent. What about transsocietal institutions?

There are transsocietal institutions. The English language is a case in point. However, the notion of a transsocietal institution contains an inherent tension because a social group is in part defined in terms of a particular set of social institutions. So two different social groups could not have all, or even most, of their institutions in common; if they did, it would cease to make sense to claim that they were in fact different social groups.

Armed with this characterization of social groups and of transcultural interaction, let us now turn to transcultural corruption. As we have seen, corruption is a species of immorality. Not all wrongdoing is corrupt activity, but much is. An action could be morally wrong but not corrupt. However, like immorality more generally, corrupt acts are corrupt relative only to certain moral principles.

Here we need to invoke a distinction that we made in Chapter 2. The distinction in question is that between subjectively valid social norms and objectively valid moral norms. A social norm is a type of action or inaction that members of some social group *believe* to be morally right. However, they are not necessarily objectively valid. An objective moral norm is a type of action or inaction that is, as a matter of objective truth, morally right. It needs to be noted that the concept of an objectively corrupt action is the concept of an action that is objectively corrupt relative to a person and relative to a set of circumstances. Lying can be morally right or morally wrong, depending on the circumstances.

In Chapter 1, we distinguished various species of corrupt actions and activities. First, there is *individual* corruption, which essentially involves individuals working on their own. For example, a motorist might pass money to a traffic police officer to avoid a fine for speeding.

Second, there is *organized* corruption in the sense of corrupt activities carried out by an organization that exists for the purpose of undertaking that corrupt activity. For example, a criminal organization such as the Mafia, the Chinese Triads, or the Yakuza might have a concerted and ongoing practice of bribing politicians to ensure that their drug-trafficking activities were not unduly interfered with.

Third, there is *organizational* corruption. This is pervasive and interdependent corruption within an organization. However, the organization does not exist for the purposes of engaging in corrupt activities.

Furthermore, there is *systemic* corruption, and there is also *grand* corruption. The use of the term "systemic" indicates that the corruption is pervasive and interconnected across many organizations and institutions. Systemic corruption consists of the erosion of social norms, and as such it is widely dispersed across organizations, institutions, social groups, and societies. Grand corruption involves large-scale corruption of a very serious kind, and it exists at the highest levels of one or more fundamental institutions.

Transcultural institutional corruption can take any of the preceding forms. It can be individual, organized, organizational, systemic, and/or grand in character. Moreover, by virtue of the nature of the relationship between cultures—and especially the nature of social norms—transcultural corruption is especially problematic. It is so because it offers a number of attractive rationalizations not necessarily available to those engaging in other forms of corruption.

Commitment to social norms—as well as the feelings of shame generated by nonconformity—often weakens when dealing with members of another society. "What do I care what they think?" ("I only care what *we* think.") Correspondingly, members of the other society are going to be less concerned to express disapproval of one's actions. "What do they care what I do?" In short, there is more likely to be an "us-them" mentality, a lack of trust, and a willingness to bend or break moral norms in the service of self-interest.

Furthermore, social norms are often norms for a *given* social group. Many social norms are near enough to being universal moral norms. But some are not. For example, social norms of honor can differ greatly from one society or culture to another. Again, a level of deception is typically involved in business dealings—a seller tries to make out that the goods are superior than they might in fact be, the buyer that he or she is less interested than is actually the case, and so on. But now an issue can arise concerning the nature and degree of deception that is acceptable in given cultural contexts. Not being bound by one's initial word might be morally acceptable to a Japanese businessperson but might be morally unacceptable to an Australian counterpart. What is an Australian businessperson to do when dealing with the Japanese in Japan? For the businessperson to "do as the Romans do when in Rome" might well be against his or her conscience, against his or her social norms. It can be viewed as corrupt, and thus as corrupting. On the other hand, to refuse to accept the social norms may be to court disaster—one may as well have stayed home. Again, individual property rights in relation to intellectual goods—including copyright—might be a social norm in the Anglo-Saxon world, but in China intellectual property might be regarded as essentially a socially owned good. This view might partly explain the recent dispute between the Chinese and U.S. governments. But in that case, is a Chinese person's copying material "owned" by a U.S. company really doing something morally wrong? Issues like this one indicate the importance of agreements in relation to moral disputes. Where social norms clash, it might be necessary to delineate new transnational and transcultural laws, which then might give rise to new social norms. At any rate, the general point is that the real or apparent differences in conventions and social norms can give rise to a greater or lesser degree of moral confusion in transcultural interaction. And as we saw in Chapter 2, moral confusion is a condition that is conducive to corruption.

There are typically, or at least often, jurisdictional problems in transcultural interaction, including in relation to legal accountability. Transcultural interactions of the corrupt kind are often transnational and therefore—in the absence of special agreements—transjurisdictional. (Extradition agreements are one attempt to deal with this kind of problem.) Pornography that is placed on the World Wide Web or is beamed by satellite emanating from the United States but that is accessible by someone in Malaysia creates jurisdictional problems. Pornography is legal in the United States but illegal in Muslim Malaysia. And law enforcement may be effective only if it is the senders who are subject to sanctions. But in that case, should the United States legislate against international communication of pornography when it does not legislate against domestically distributed pornography? And if it should, who should be the one to make that decision? The United States? Why not an international body? Such jurisdictional problems provide loopholes for corruption—at least from the point of view of the Malaysians.

Laws differ from one society to another. Health and safety regulations in industry might be stricter in an affluent society. This might be the case because health and safety equipment, pollution control, and/or the training of personnel are expensive. Again, minimum wages are higher in affluent societies than in poorer ones. Should multinationals pay the same wages from one country to the next? Should they insist on the highest health and safety standards, including in relation to personnel, from one country to the next? Surely one is under an obligation to obey the reasonable laws of one's own society. But to what extent is one under an obligation to obey the laws of another country? As a visitor, one is present in that country. However, these are not the grounds on which one has an obligation to obey the laws of one's own country. And in any case, why does merely being in a place obligate one to fall in line with the laws that it happens to have? But the point is, in the absence of a moral justification for obeying the laws of a foreign country, is there not increased scope for corruption? And even if there is some adequate moral justification for obeying the laws of another society, it might not feel as though there is; there might not be adequate psychological compulsion. Once again, we have a species of moral confusion, a condition that we identified in Chapter 2 as being conducive to corruption.

The relationship between macroentities such as nation-states or societies is not the same as that between individuals in a society. Individuals in a society participate in a moral order embodied in a structure of institutions, and they do so, at least potentially, as equals. Moreover, individuals within macroentities such as societies, nations, or organizations are driven along to some extent by the momentum—including the structure and goals—of that macroentity. However, in these macroentities, there may be no moral order embodied in an institutional structure, or such institutions as exist may be too weak to be effective. In particular, the institution of international law may be too weak to function as an institution for enforcing morality in relation to the "actions" of macroorganizations (such as nation-states and multinationals) in the international arena.

The relationships between individual human beings, especially ones who are part of the same macroentity, only faintly resembles the relationship between macroentities—between a huge and an authoritarian entity such as China and, say, a small fledgling democracy such as Taiwan, or between Indonesia and East Timor, or between the United States and Grenada. Morality does not disappear in such lopsided power relationships. If anything, moral questions become more pressing because of the likelihood that overwhelming power will be abused. But there is, nevertheless, a real issue as to what to do when one finds oneself in such a lopsided power relationship. It is not as if the power relationship can be overcome or even significantly reduced. But the point is that the potential for corruption is extraordinarily high. Perhaps the United Kingdom's handing over of Hong Kong to China was nothing other than an instance of corruption, given that a majority of the people living in Hong Kong did not wish to return to Chinese rule, and given the triadic power relationship that existed between China, the United Kingdom, and Hong Kong.

In order to enable us to further explore the philosophical issues associated with transcultural corruption and to focus our discussion, let us consider the following case study.

Case Study 5.4   Lockheed Corporation

In 1972, Prime Minister Kekuei Tanaka of Japan was bribed with $7 million by the Lockheed Corporation to secure a lucrative Tri-Star Jet contract for planes for Japan's domestic carrier, All Nippon Airways. Other Japanese officials, politicians, and businesspersons were also bribed. Lockheed's Swiss subsidiary funneled money through its Swiss bank account and then onto an international foreign currency firm, Deak and Co., which had an office in Hong Kong from which its courier service transferred millions of dollars worth of yen in air travel bags to Japan. In 1983, Tanaka received a four-year prison sentence and a fine of $3.1 million. The chairman of All Nippon Airways got three years.

Lockheed was charged with failing to disclose payments to foreign officials and agreed, without admitting any wrong, to an injunction forbidding it to engage in any further activities of this type. After a three-year investigation by a U.S. Senate committee, Lockheed pleaded guilty to concealing payments to Tanaka and other officials and was fined $647,000. The Department of Justice then dropped further prosecution of Lockheed for misconduct. The investigation did lead to the Foreign Corrupt Practices Act of 1977 outlawing bribery of foreign officials. Lockheed subsequently reported $30 million in improper payments in various other countries.

Let us now analyze the Lockheed case study. The commitment to social norms is weaker than it otherwise would be, because agents do not strongly identify with the persons with whom they are interacting. This tendency looks to be the case with the Lockheed scandal. Evidently, Lockheed was unconcerned with the negative impact that its activities around the globe might be having. Unfortunately, although this weaker commitment might be a sociopsychological fact, it in no way justifies the actions of the Lockheed Corporation. In particular, Lockheed ought to have been concerned about the negative impact that bribing the prime minister of Japan would have on Japanese institutions. After all, Lockheed must have been aware that bribery—especially bribery of the prime minister—serves to undermine a democratic system in which publicly elected officials have positions not only of power but also of public trust.

In the Lockheed corruption scandal, there may well have been a certain amount of moral confusion. Transcultural interactions typically involve decision-making that, from the agent's perspective, is morally problematic partly in virtue of differences in the social norms adhered to by the interacting agents. Bribery and gift-giving were a widespread fact of life in Japanese politics and business at that time. This fact presumably muddied Lockheed's decision-making in relation to whether or not to bribe. However, bribery, as opposed to the convention of giving small gifts, is corrosive of public institutions. A competitive market system is undermined if there is a widespread practice of preventing fair competition by engaging in bribery. And if governments are complicit in such activity, then the problem is simply compounded. The fact that bribery might have been a widespread practice and that therefore it might have been in Lockheed's interest to bribe the Japanese prime minister, in no way morally justifies it, because compliance with immoral practices was not the only possible course of action for Lockheed. There are other alternatives open to powerful corporations such as Lockheed in these circumstances, including putting pressure on governments to enact anti-bribery legislation, and establishing accountability systems and other anti-corruption measures to combat the practice of bribery.

Transcultural interactions often take place in a context of unequal power, or at least contexts of insufficient power, that is, contexts in which one of the interacting agents is either not able to resist the morally excessive exercises of power on the part of the other one or is not able to ensure compliance with minimal moral standards. In the Lockheed scandal, the U.S. Senate and Department of Justice displayed extraordinary lenience of an order of magnitude consistent with yielding to external pressure. For example, the fines handed out to Lockheed for serious criminal offenses were quite trivial. Moreover, the scandal illustrated the power of those in the upper echelons of macroentities, such as Lockheed and the Japanese government, and their lack of accountability in relation to serious criminality to any community, be it the American or the Japanese community.[80]

But the existence of such lopsided power relationships conducive to corruption is hardly an argument justifying participation in corrupt actions on the part of the powerful. Rather, the powerful need to learn to curb the excesses that they are capable of, and the community, or at least the relevant communities, needs to establish institutional structures whereby the capacity of the powerful to engage in corrupt activities is minimized. Such institutional redesign is hardly a novel idea. Consider the notion of the separation of powers in the development of the modern nation-state. It may well be that the dangers of corruption on the part of large multinational corporations engaged in transcultural interaction call for various institutional changes. Perhaps the activities of such multinationals need to be made more transparent and their governance structures democratized to a greater extent. And perhaps governments need to combine to institute compliance regimes with more teeth.

Transcultural interactions typically give rise to jurisdictional problems. Jurisdictional problems were evident not only in relation to the absence of laws against transnational bribery but also in relation to the will to enforce transnational laws by handing out severe penalties, as opposed to the trivial fines imposed on Lockheed. And transcultural interaction gives rise to a host of other hard questions, such as whether the criminal act of bribery ought to be tried in the courts of the country to which the briber belongs or that to which the bribed person belongs. Can U.S. courts adequately take into consideration the attitudes and harm done to the Japanese community? On the other hand, should a U.S. citizen who never leaves the United States be tried in a Japanese court? These jurisdictional problems are far from insoluble. Governments can enter into agreements to resolve them. Indeed, this outcome is ultimately what happened as a result of the Lockheed scandal.

It might be thought that the Lockheed scandal was something of a one-off, at least in terms of our explanatory theory of conditions conducive to transcultural corruption. But there have been a significant number of large-scale transcultural corruption scandals, and we would argue that many are susceptible to our analysis. At any rate, let us consider one more of these, though one of a somewhat different kind than the Lockheed debacle. Let us consider the Bhopal disaster, in which the conditions conducive to institutional corruption in transcultural interaction (previously described) do seem to have obtained. But let us first describe the disaster.

CASE STUDY 5.5 Bhopal Disaster

In 1984 in Bhopal, India, 3,400 died (a conservative estimate—another estimate was 8,000), and more than 200,000 were injured when toxic gas escaped from Union Carbide's insecticide plant. Those who suffered most were slum dwellers living in the vicinity of the plant. Bhopal was the world's worst industrial accident—worse than Chernobyl in terms of death and injuries. Responsibility for the disaster was collective in the sense that it was negligence on the part of Indian managers and employees at Bhopal—safety procedures specified in the handbook were routinely ignored, albeit by undertrained staff—and Bhopal's management in the United States had not put in place an adequate accountability scheme. After the disaster, Union Carbide tried strenuously to pay out in compensation as little as possible. It blamed employee sabotage—a somewhat far-fetched claim—and wanted the matter to be tried in India, where leniency and lesser payouts would be forthcoming. In the end, a U.S. judge determined that the matter be tried in India but under U.S. legal principles. Union Carbide paid out $470 million, and the Indian government agreed to drop criminal charges against the company.

Let us now look at the Bhopal disaster in the light of our account of conditions that are conducive to corruption.

First, the commitment to social norms was apparently weak, partly by virtue of a lack of identification with Indian slum dwellers on the part of U.S. managers. It seems that Union Carbide managers in the United States did not identify with the plight of the slum dwellers in Bhopal to the same extent as they would have to, say, the plight of U.S. citizens similarly afflicted.

Second, there may well have been a degree of moral confusion. Transcultural interactions typically involve decision-making, which from the agent's perspective is morally problematic partly by virtue of differences in the social norms adhered to by the interacting agents and partly because of the unfamiliar situations in which they have to apply the moral principles to which they ordinarily adhere. The Union Carbide managers were confronted by different social norms in India, including in relation to levels of training and safety measures. For example, it was apparently "normal" in India to allow people to live in close proximity to a plant such as the plant in Bhopal. Accordingly, Union Carbide may not have felt that there was any obligation to ensure that these people were removed before operating the plant. Moreover, the view taken by Union Carbide managers was evidently that a higher level of risk is acceptable in a poorer country, economic benefits to all parties being forthcoming only when a local undertrained workforce is used.

Transsocietal and transcultural interactions often take place in a context of unequal power or of insufficient power. This tendency was evidently so in the case of the Bhopal disaster. Union Carbide, and to a lesser extent the U.S. and Indian governments, failed to exercise due care and/or a commitment to principles of justice in relation to the victims of the disaster. Surely this failure was in part because the victims were relatively powerless both in relation to Union Carbide and in terms of their capacity to influence the Indian government in its dealings with the U.S. government and Union Carbide. Indeed, the Indian government itself was relatively powerless in relation to the Americans, both company and government.

Finally, transcultural interactions often take place in a jurisdiction the authority of which at least one of the agents does not accept. The Union Carbide matter was decided in Indian courts on the basis of U.S. principles. This outcome was an attempt to overcome the jurisdictional problems, but arguably it served mainly to highlight them.

CONCLUSION

Corrupt actions are often rationalized by those who perform them. Two forms of corruption that are partly susceptible to such rationalization are noble cause corruption and corruption in transcultural settings. Noble cause corruption involves performing a corrupt action for a good end. Given the good motive, this form of corruption is highly susceptible to rationalization. Unfortunately, such actions—notwithstanding the good motive—are tainted. In particular, although the person who performs such an action might *believe* that he or she is doing what is morally right, this belief is a mistaken one; the action is morally wrong.

Persons operating in transcultural settings often find it easy to rationalize away their engagement in corruption by invoking arguments, such as "When in Rome, do as the Romans do." When one is operating in an environment in which one has, so to speak, no moral stake, such arguments can be tempting. This is especially the case if other conditions conducive to corruption, for example, power imbalances, are in play. Unfortunately, these rationalizations for corruption that arise in transcultural settings do not in fact justify it. Transcultural corruption is, needless to say, a form of corruption.

chapter six

Corporate Corruption and Collective Moral Responsibility

In this chapter, we

- Describe some of the more notable corporate collapses and corruption scandals, and periods of corporate corruption in the United States and Australia, in particular.
- Provide an analysis of the concept of collective moral responsibility.
- Apply the notion of collective moral responsibility to the special case of the modern business corporation.

INTRODUCTION

In the first part of this book, we examined the nature and causes of institutional corruption. We also addressed the question of what is wrong with corruption, and we looked at some of the rationalizations offered to justify corrupt behavior. In the second part, we turn to a consideration of some of the central problems that arise in combating corruption.

The first of these concerns the ascription of responsibility for corruption. The second concerns accountability and, specifically, anti-corruption systems. As law-enforcement personnel know only too well, it is one thing to have willingly performed an act of wrongdoing without excuse or justification, and therefore to be morally responsible for that wrongdoing; it is another to be called to account for those wrongful acts that one has in fact performed. The notion of accountability brings with it notions of investigation, interrogation, adjudication, and so on. In many contexts, it also brings with it the notion of a hierarchical system, in which each level is accountable to the level above it, for example, public-sector agencies that are ultimately answerable to a parliament.

In short, accountability in relation to corruption implies anti-corruption systems. We deal with anti-corruption systems per se in Chapter 7. In Chapter 8, we consider an important element of any adequate anti-corruption system, namely its complaints-handling process, and specifically the issue of whistleblowing. In Chapter 9, our focus is the moral rights of those who might be, rightly or wrongly, suspected of corruption, and therefore under investigation. In the second part, we also consider the endpoint of accountability—namely, punishment and rehabilitation; this is the subject of Chapter 10.

Our concern in this chapter is with the question of moral responsibility in relation to corruption, and specifically to corporate corruption. If corruption is to be successfully combated, we must first understand the concept, or rather concepts, of moral responsibility as these pertain to corruption in various contexts, including the context of the modern corporation. This task is more difficult than it might first appear to be, particularly when we are speaking of forms of corruption other than one-off cases of individual corruption.

Sometimes the people responsible for a spate of corrupt activity are a number of individuals functioning as individuals; this is the phenomenon of a "few bad apples." Individuals acting alone are individually morally responsible; individuals acting alone are individually to blame. However, individual corruption is increasingly being seen as relatively unimportant: unimportant, that is, by comparison with large-scale collective corruption—organized, organizational, grand, and systemic corruption. Moreover, as we ought to expect, given our analysis in Chapter 2 of the conditions conducive to corruption, the extraordinary power and wealth of large corporations—taken in conjunction with the inadequacy of accountability mechanisms in terms of resources, degree of independence, and so on—have brought with them unprecedented opportunities for collective corruption and criminality. The modern corporation has become a key site of collective corruption. Accordingly, we shall argue, there is a need for a concomitant shift from notions of individual moral responsibility—and correspondingly, individual accountability—to notions of collective responsibility (and collective accountability).

CORPORATE COLLAPSES

In Chapter 2, we outlined the collapse of the U.S. corporation Enron. The collapse had a devastating effect on shareholders and employees. It revealed a corporate culture characterized by greed and contempt for regulations and

moral standards; and it highlighted the inadequacy of institutional accountability bodies, including auditors and regulators. Moreover, the Enron collapse was only one among a number of recent corporate corruption scandals,
including WorldCom and the giant accounting firm Arthur Andersen.

Now consider a significant corporate collapse in Australia.

CASE STUDY 6.1   HIH Collapse

HIH was the second largest insurance company in Australia, and it collapsed in March 2001 with debts of 5.3 billion in Australian dollars. At
the time of its collapse, HIH had some two million policyholders who
were adversely affected. Up until the mid-1990s, HIH had focused
upon liability insurance, at one stage holding 50 percent of major
insurance risks in Australia. As a result of a number of business factors
(the advent of class actions, lawyers' contingency fees, and a 25 percent
increase per annum growth in claims), HIH sought to broaden its insurance base by a series of purchases of other insurance enterprises. As
a result of a disastrous buying spree, HIH's equity holdings fell from a
healthy 17 percent in 1993 to 6 percent in 1998. Long before HIH went
into liquidation, its losses were widely known.

Prior to HIH's collapse, the Australian government, conscious of the
impact upon the economy of the failure of the company, agreed to what
turned out to be a futile rescue package of 640 million in Australian
dollars. The collapse of HIH has had such an adverse impact upon the
Australian insurance industry that the government has undertaken a
Royal Commission into the reasons for the collapse, including why the
regime of corporate and insurance regulation failed so spectacularly.

The Australian corporate regulators have laid charges against the
CEO, Ray Williams; a former non-executive director, Rodney Adler;
and the chief finance officer, Dominic Fodera. Although the root causes
of HIH's collapse were bad business decisions, a number of parties are
alleged to have been involved in corrupt practices. The CEO is charged
with having recklessly and dishonestly borrowed large amounts of
money in the knowledge that the company was insolvent. He is also
charged with neglecting his director's duties by making business decisions that failed the test of good faith and proper use of company
resources. In one particular deal, HIH purchased Pacific Eagle Equities
for 10 million Australian dollars. That entity was a family-owned company of Rodney Adler, who then allegedly committed an offense under
the Corporations Act by manipulating the stock market in buying 4 million Australian dollars of HIH shares in Pacific Eagle Equities' name.

The complex dealing between Ray Williams and Rodney Adler
included the purchase of FAI Insurance, a company in which Adler had

significant interests. FAI held interests in a company called Home Security International. Adler allegedly arranged to have a U.S. investor buy 48,000 shares in Home Security International, which caused a 30 percent spike in the value of the stock. As a result of this deal, 12 million Australian dollars were added to FAI's value, and soon after, the company posted a yearly profit of 8.6 million dollars. As a result of this profit, the price paid by HIH for FAI when it purchased the company was far in excess of its true value.

The Royal Commission into HIH has found that, as the company lurched toward collapse, it engaged in corporate excesses involving travel, entertainment, charitable donations, and executive gifts. These excesses stripped over 32 million Australian dollars out of its assets. Staff were given gold watches, and a tip of 700 dollars was paid at a dinner attended by the CEO and HIH executives at Port Douglas (Port Douglas is an expensive tropical resort some 1,500 miles away from Sydney, where HIH was based). Just weeks before the collapse, 180,000 dollars was paid to a Melbourne football club that was in some financial difficulty.

The HIH collapse has sparked a lively debate into the ethical responsibility of company directors and the role of corporate regulators. The laying of charges against the principal parties has been widely applauded by the media. The corporate regulators, particularly the Australian Prudential Regulation Authority, claims that it was profoundly misled by HIH, and thus it, in turn, had inadvertently misled the government about the seriousness of the crisis facing the company. The Federal Opposition has questioned how the collapse was not anticipated by the regulatory authorities, given the amount of material showing that HIH was in trouble up to two years before the collapse.[81]

The corporate collapses and corruption scandals of the late 1990s and early 2000s in the United States, Australia, and elsewhere appear to be part of a recurring cycle. Recall the corporate scandals of the 1980s in the United States and elsewhere. That period was notable for a stock-market crash, a junk-bond collapse, the bankruptcy of numerous highly leveraged clients, the prevalence of the unlawful practice of insider trading, and the fining and imprisonment of the likes of Michael Milken and Ivan Boesky. Milken paid fines in excess of $600 million, Boesky over $100 million.[82]

Nor was the U.S. economy the only one to suffer from the so-called "Decade of Greed." According to Trevor Sykes, financial journalist and historian, the corporate collapses of the 1980s were the most devastating in Australian history. It's worth quoting Sykes at length on this:

> The collapses included Australia's largest industrial group (Adelaide Steamship); the ninth largest enterprise in the nation measured by revenue

(Bond Corporation); nearly half the brewing industry (Bond Brewing); all three major commercial television networks (Bond Media, Qintex, Channel Ten); Australia's largest car renter (Budget); the second largest newspaper group (Fairfax); Victoria's largest building society (Pyramid); and Australia's largest textile group (Linter) . . . Total write-offs and provisions by banks and financiers amounted to $28 billion. Australia's three largest merchant banks (Tricontinental, Partnership Pacific and Elders Finance) had to be rescued by their parents. Two of Australia's four state banks (State Bank of Victoria and State Bank of South Australia) suffered devastating losses and had to be investigated by Royal Commissions . . . The four major trading banks (Westpac, National, Commonwealth and ANZ) had to write billions of dollars off their loan books.[83]

During the 1980s "corporate cowboys"—or "bold riders," as Sykes calls them—such as Boesky and Milken in the United States, and Bond, Skase, and Elliott in Australia, enjoyed enormous wealth, power, and indeed prestige, though of course since then their images have been somewhat tarnished by the corporate collapses and by the extensive ongoing media coverage of alleged corruption.[84] At any rate, self-evidently, the corporate collapses and excesses of the 1980s were extraordinarily damaging economically. Moreover, as Tomasic and Bottomley point out, they may well be symptomatic of underlying systemic deficiencies in corporate law and regulation, and indeed of structural deficiencies in the corporate sector itself, including the mechanisms of corporate governance.[85]

In this connection, we should be suspicious of sharp dichotomies between corrupt cowboys, on the one hand, and inefficient work practices on the other, and also between the collapses on the one hand, and the general health of the corporate sector on the other. In the first place, we should not confuse rhetoric and reality. It needs to be remembered that throughout this period, the rhetoric included a great deal about the importance of competitiveness and best practice. Of more importance, it is evident that the corporate collapses were not simply aberrations wholly attributable to the corrupt actions of a few bold riders. Rather, corruption worked hand in hand with incompetence and poor business judgment.

The responsibility for the corporate disasters extends far beyond the corrupt practices of the corporate cowboys. For one thing, the cowboys relied on loans from incompetent bankers. Nor were the bankers the only ones to blame. Accountants and auditors failed to detect and expose unlawful and dubious practices; and lawyers, brokers, and so on were also implicated in what amounted to theft.

Moreover, some measure of responsibility lay with the regulatory/legal system and therefore government, though perhaps the regulators might be excused on the grounds that they were underresourced. But in relation to an ongoing series of corporate collapses and corruption scandals, it is difficult to find excuses for those in government. Ultimately, in a nation-state such as the United States or Australia, the government of the day must shoulder responsibility for an inadequate regulatory system, and for failing to intervene speedily and effectively to prevent its economic system from becoming infected with the level of corruption and incompetence that evidently characterized the corporate sector in the 1980s, and indeed in the late 1990s and the first few years of the twenty-first century as well.

According to many commentators, a very important feature of such periods is the shift in what might be referred to as "ethos."[86] Roughly speaking, the ethos of an institution, company, group of companies, or indeed entire institutional systems, is the spirit that pervades the institution and informs the decisions and activities of its members. So the ethos of some rather puritanical business community might consist of hard work, frugality, and strict adherence to procedures and codes of conduct. Apparently, the ethos of the 1980s in the corporate sector was one of greed, recklessness, and abandonment of procedures and codes of conduct. Part of the explanation for the collapses of the 1980s was a change in the ethos of the corporate sector. Many of these collapses became probable, or at least more probable, given that directors, bankers, auditors, and so on engaged in corrupt practices or were negligent and reckless on an unprecedented scale; which is to say, these collapses became likely, given this shift in ethos.

Ethos must be sharply distinguished from the framework of ethical virtues, principles, and ends that ought to determine the character and activities of any given institution and its members. The ethos of an institution needs to be adjusted to the appropriate ethical framework, rather than the reverse. If the ethos is so adjusted, it will contribute to the strengthening and reproduction, rather than the undermining, of that ethical framework. One of the features of the 1980s is that ethos came apart from ethics; the driving spirit was not grounded in the ethical virtues, principles, and ends definitive of a healthy corporate sector. As a consequence, many corporate actors lowered their ethical standards and lost sight of ethical ends. While others continued to pursue ethical ends and to maintain ethical standards, they often had to do so in spite of, rather than in keeping with, the prevailing ethos.

No doubt a large *part* of the explanation for the excesses of the 1980s and the more recent corporate collapses is simply that many people either did things that they knew were wrong or, through moral weakness, failed to draw attention to the wrongdoing of others. Perhaps deregulation and a business boom simply provided many people with the opportunity to do wrong. However, if we grant, as we must, that the average corporate manager, financier, banker, lawyer, auditor, and so on is not wholly bereft of a commitment to professional obligations, then greed, corruption, and incompetence triggered by deregulation and a business boom may not constitute the whole of the explanation for the emergence of the gap between ethos and ethics.

Another *part* of the explanation may lie in the inadequate ethical understanding on the part of corporate actors of their institutional roles, especially in a context of changes to corporate institutions, and to the business environment more generally, as a result of a variety of processes, including globalization. Perhaps it was not simply a case of forgetting old-style ethics, nor simply a matter of becoming more competitive by freeing up the marketplace—as the ideology of hardline economic rationalism would have us believe—but rather a matter of <u>simultaneously rethinking</u>, on the one hand, corporate institutional mechanisms, practices, and regulations, and on the other, ethical virtues, obligations, and ends. Such rethinking—and a subsequent process of internalization—is at times necessary in order to put in place that mix of regulation and deregulation, of competition and cooperation, and of incentive-driven self-interest and ethical commitment to professional obligations, which would enable the corporate sector to secure its ethical ends, such as the generating of long-term, equitably distributed wealth and job creation.

Here it is important to stress that the ethical dimension of the corporate sector, or any other human institution for that matter, does not simply consist of a timeless set of principles and virtues that people from time to time forget and need to be reminded of—would that it were that simple. Nor does the ethical dimension simply consist of rules that either constrain economic activity or provide the minimal standards for it to be undertaken. Of course, there *are* relatively timeless ethical virtues and rules, such as not engaging in fraud, or not stealing from the till, or not pushing your competitor off a high building. Many of these rules have been enshrined in the law for centuries, and others are expressed in nonjudiciable ethical codes. Indeed, there is evidently a set of very general ethical values, such as freedom, justice, truth, compassion, and so on, which are timeless, and which ought always to inform both individual and institutional life. Naturally, some of these values have a more central place in a given institution than others. For example, justice is more central to the institutions of the law than, say, material well-being, and perhaps the reverse is so for corporations. However, no institution can afford to ignore these timeless ethical values in the design of its structure or in the pursuit of its day-to-day constitutive activities.

The ethical dimension of business activity does not consist simply of constraining rules and minimal standards, and certainly not simply of legally enforceable rules and standards. In the first place, many principles and standards are not legally enforceable but are nevertheless highly ethically desirable. These are often mentioned in ethical codes.

In the second place, the performance and best practices of the corporate sector are themselves to be measured by the extent to which they *ultimately* contribute to an ethical *end*, namely, the material well-being of the whole community. As Adam Smith has taught us, this point is quite consistent with the fact that individual corporate actors and companies will need to focus most of their energies on subsidiary ends, such as product creation and distribution, profit maximization, and so on.

In the third place, the very concept of a good businessman or businesswoman—as opposed to someone who merely happens to be in business—is an ethical concept involving a particular array of ethical *virtues,* including shrewdness, prudence, tough-mindedness, a competitive instinct, as well as honesty, a willingness to work hard, the capacity to envisage and build genuinely economically beneficial business enterprises, and so on. These virtues may not be necessary in other walks of life, and some of them may very well constitute vices in other contexts, such as the family home. However, these virtues are definitive of the notion of a good businessman or businesswoman, and since the corporate cowboys evidently were lacking in many of them, they were simply not good businesspersons.

In the fourth place, corporations and their constitutive practices are, like any other human organization, objects of a wide array of different kinds of ethical evaluation, many of which are not simply to do with conformity to rules or minimal standards. For example, many have argued that the constitutive activities of corporations are routine and unfulfilling; that their products do not for the most part satisfy genuine needs but rather irrational impulses to consume; that their organizational structures are bureaucratic and inimical to individual enterprise; and that their systems of remuneration and promotion assist those who curry favor with their superiors and never rock the boat, rather than those who work hard and are genuinely productive. Naturally, these claims are open to dispute, but our point is that both the people who make these claims and their disputants are making ethical evaluations of a sort that go well beyond issues of conformity to rules and minimal standards.

Moreover, not all of the ethical virtues, obligations, and principles involved in business activity are timelessly valid. Ethical principles and obligations may undergo change as business and its cognate professions respond to a new business environment. This is perhaps most obvious in relation to new technologies, such as genetic engineering, and in increased interaction with different cultures with divergent business practices, wage structures, and so on. But they also arise in the context of institutional change, including regulatory changes, and evolving corporate structures.

For example, the coming into existence of huge corporations has increased the ethical responsibilities of corporate executives just in virtue of the sheer magnitude of good or evil that such institutions can do. Consider the damage done to the health of hundreds of thousands of innocent human beings by Union Carbide's Bhopal disaster in India (see Chapter 5). By contrast, consider the process of economic liberalization in India and the possibilities that corporations now hold out to millions of Indians for an improvement in their standard of living.

Moreover, many of these corporations are so large and complex that the lines of ethical responsibility are either no longer appropriate or else very unclear. It may well be that institutional designers ought to pursue less hierarchical models, where CEOs have less power, or ones where there is a clearer demarcation of responsibilities between, say, boards of directors and day-to-day management. At any rate, our point here is simply that institutional change, whether by design or not, has generated new configurations of ethical responsibility and given rise to new ethical problems, including in relation to the ascription of ethical responsibility.

If structural changes in corporations can have ethical implications, obviously so can changes in the regulations governing corporate activity. For example, regulatory change, including deregulation, ought to proceed in such a way as to secure appropriate ethical ends, including the elimination of fraud, theft, unfair practices, and so on, as well as an efficient, competitive corporate sector. Moreover, in contriving or eliminating regulations, account must be taken not simply of the self-interested motivations of corporate players, but also of their ethical motivations, including not only their sense of fairness and susceptibility to feelings of shame, but also their desire for the respect that goes with achievement.

Here it is worth bearing in mind that regulations, and the law more generally, are conformed to not only because they have sanctions attached but also because they are perceived to be fair and also rational in terms of the ends of the activity regulated. Compliance with unfair or irrational regulations can be very hard to achieve, even if heavy penalties attach to noncompliance. Indeed, it may be that the best regulatory strategies—including that of Ayres and Braithwaite, involving a sequence of interventions beginning with persuasion and escalating into heavy penalties for continued noncompliance—are ones in which the fairness and reasonableness of a regulation and the sanctions attaching to it mutually reinforce one another.[87]

Contriving and framing regulations gives rise to a wide array of quite specific ethical problems concerning the fairness of particular practices or reward systems, the ethical unacceptability of some conflicts of interest, and so on. Many of these are complex intellectual problems, and solving them involves not simply the identification of (often competing) ethical considerations but also the elaboration of new principles that give due weight to these ethical considerations.

Regulations may be too few and too simple, or conversely, too many and too complex. If the former, they might fail to regulate ethically undesirable practices; if the latter, businesspeople might be unduly hamstrung and have to face the consequent moral dilemma of either ignoring regulations or of failing to operate an efficient, profitable business. Indeed, if regulations are incomprehensible, then businesspeople may not be able to discharge their moral obligations to obey the law even if they want to. In this connection, the simplification process is to be welcomed, though taking this process to the point of enacting so-called "fuzzy law" may bring with it the same old problem of uncertainty in respect of legal obligations, albeit in a new form.[88]

An important aspect of regulatory activity with ethical implications is that of fixing responsibility, and ultimately liability, for harm done. For example, in the context of an increase in corporate crime and the tendency for corporations to simply treat fines as a business cost, Fisse and Braithwaite have advocated the strategy of so-called "enforced accountability." Enforced accountability consists of strengthening and restructuring corporate criminal liability in such a way as to enforce internal disciplinary measures against offending individuals.[89] A second example is Tomasic and Bottomley's suggestion that partnership-like liability rules be placed on the boards of public companies, so that members of boards become jointly and severally liable for the actions of any particular director.[90] A third example is the strategy whereby third parties, such as legal and accountancy firms, are held liable for managerial impropriety in virtue of the fact that they assisted the impropriety and, more importantly, the fact that they have deep pockets.[91] Such strategies raise important ethical questions in relation to the collective moral responsibility of corporations and subgroups of corporations, as distinct from the individual moral responsibility of particular human beings.

Thus far, we have spoken in very general terms about ethics in business and the excesses of the 1980s and in more recent times. In so doing, we have emphasized the centrality of the ethical dimension. However, it also needs to be stressed that, typically, ethical problems cannot be solved in advance of empirical knowledge of the workings of corporations, the consequences of particular regulations, and so on. Here as elsewhere, philosophers must rely on the work of other specialists. In the second part of this chapter, we focus on a particular notion of moral responsibility that is quite central to the ethical problems that arose out of the corporate collapses and that may well have implications for subsequent attempts at regulatory reform, including the aforementioned strategies of holding corporations criminally liable, directors jointly and severally liable, and so on. We are speaking of the notion of collective responsibility.

COLLECTIVE MORAL RESPONSIBILITY

Here we need first to distinguish some different senses of responsibility.[92] Sometimes to say that someone is responsible for an action is to say that the person had a reason, or reasons, to perform some action, then formed an intention to perform that action (or not to perform it), and finally acted (or refrained from acting) on that intention, and did so on the basis of that reason(s). Note that an important category of reasons for actions are ends, goals, or purposes; an agent's reason for performing an action is often that the action realizes a goal the agent has. Moreover, it is assumed that in the course of all this, the agent brought about or caused the action, at least in the sense that the mental state or states that constituted the agent's reason for performing the action was causally efficacious (in the right way) and that the agent's resulting intention was causally efficacious (in the right way).[93]

This sense of being responsible for an action is different from other well-known cognate senses of responsibility. These latter include what might be termed "bare responsibility." An agent has bare responsibility for an action if and only if the agent intentionally performs the action (and the intention causes the action). These latter cognate senses also include the notion of a responsible agent—as distinct from someone's being responsible for an action. An agent is a responsible agent if he or she is not insane, is not under the influence of drugs, and so on. Finally, there is being responsible for an action in the sense of freely performing the action. This notion of a freely performed action is notoriously difficult to pin down. According to one popular line of thought, a freely performed action is an action such that the agent could have done otherwise. But this line of thought has been heavily criticized.[94] At any rate, we will dub the very first of these just-mentioned senses of being responsible for an action "natural responsibility," namely, intentionally performing an action and doing so for a reason.[95]

On other occasions, what is meant by "being responsible for an action" is that the person in question occupies a certain institutional role and that the occupant of that role is the person who has the institutionally determined duty to decide what is to be done in relation to certain matters. For example, the mechanic has the responsibility to fix the brakes on my car when it goes in for a service, irrespective of whether or not the mechanic does so, or even contemplates doing so.

A third sense of "being responsible" for an action is a species of our second sense. If the matters in respect of which the occupant of an institutional role has an institutionally determined duty to decide what is to be done, include ordering other agents to perform or not to perform certain actions, then the occupant of the role is responsible for those actions performed by those other agents. We say of such a person that he or she is responsible for the actions of other persons by virtue of being in charge of them or of being the person with authority over them.

The fourth sense of responsibility is, in fact, the sense with which we are principally concerned, namely moral responsibility. Roughly speaking, an agent is held to be morally responsible for an action if the agent was responsible for that action in one of our first three senses of responsibility and if that action is morally significant.[96] The ways in which an action can be morally significant are too many and varied to be detailed here. They include instances of infringing on or conforming to a moral principle or right, causing great good or evil, and being motivated by a moral emotion.

Let us now turn to collective moral responsibility. Our suggestion here is that collective moral responsibility can be regarded as a species of joint responsibility, or at least one central kind of collective moral responsibility can be so regarded. Here we need to distinguish four senses of collective responsibility. In the first instance, we will do so in relation to joint actions.

What is a joint action?[97] Roughly speaking, two or more individuals perform a joint action if each of them intentionally performs an individual action but does so in the true belief that in so doing, they will jointly realize an end that each of them has. Having an end in this sense is a mental state in the head of one or more individuals, but it is neither a desire nor an intention. However, it is an end that is not realized by one individual's acting alone. So we have called such ends "collective" ends. For example, the members of a corrupt cartel might perform the joint action of setting a fixed, exorbitantly high price in violation of laws in relation to fair competition. One member of the cartel sets his or her goods at a certain agreed-on price, as does another member of the cartel, and so on. So each performs a contributory action in the service of the collective end of ensuring high profit margins for all.

Agents who perform a joint action are responsible for that action in the first sense of collective responsibility. Accordingly, to say that they are collectively responsible for the action is just to say that they performed the joint action. That is, they each had a collective end, each intentionally performed their contributory action, and each did so because each believed that the other would perform his or her contributory action, and that therefore the collective end would be realized.

Here it is important to note that each agent is individually (naturally) responsible for performing his or her contributory action, and responsible by virtue of the fact that the agent intentionally performed this action and that the action was not intentionally performed by anyone else. Of course, the other agents (or agent) *believe* that the first agent is performing, or is going to perform, the contributory action in question. But mere possession of such a belief is not sufficient for the ascription of responsibility to *the believer* for performing the individual action in question. So what are the agents *collectively* (naturally) responsible for? The agents are *collectively* (naturally) responsible for the realization of the (collective) *end* that results from their contributory actions.

Furthermore, on this account, to say that they are collectively (naturally) responsible for the realization of the collective end of a joint action is to say that they are *jointly* responsible for the realization of that end. They are jointly responsible because (1) each relied on the other to bring about the state of affairs aimed at by both (the collective end), and (2) each performed his or her contributory action on the condition, and only on the condition, that the other(s) performed theirs. Here condition (2) expresses the *interdependence* involved in joint action.

Again, if the occupants of an institutional role (or roles) have an institutionally determined obligation to perform some joint action, then those individuals are collectively responsible for its performance, in our second sense of collective responsibility. Consider the collective institutional responsibility of the members of a team of auditors to ensure that the financial reports of a large company are true and fair. Here there is a *joint* institutional obligation to realize the collective end of the joint action in question. In addition, there is a set of derived *individual* obligations; each of the participating individuals has an individual obligation to perform his or her contributory action. (The derivation of these individual obligations relies on the fact that if each performs his or her contributory action, then it is probable that the collective end will be realized.)

The *joint* institutional obligation is a composite obligation consisting of the obligation that each of us has to perform a certain specified action in order to realize that end. More precisely, Agent A has the obligation to realize a collective end by means of doing some action, believing Agent B to have performed some other action for that self-same end. The point about joint obligations is that they are not discharged by one person acting alone.

Notice that, typically, agents involved in an institutional joint action will discharge their respective individual institutional obligations and their joint institutional obligation by the performance of one and the same set of individual actions. For example, if each of the members of an anti-corruption task force performs his or her individual duties, having as an end the exposure and conviction of the members of a money-laundering operation, then given favorable conditions, the task force will achieve its end. But one can imagine an investigating agent who recognizes his individual institutional obligation, but not his jointly held obligation, to realize the collective end in question. This investigator might have an overriding individual end to get himself promoted, but the head of the task force might be ahead of him in the queue of those to be promoted. So the investigator does not have exposing and convicting the members of the money-laundering operation as a collective end. Accordingly, although he ensures that he discharges his individual obligation to, say, interview a particular suspect, the investigator is less assiduous than he might otherwise be because he wants the task force to fail in its overall enterprise.

There is a third putative sense of collective responsibility. This third sense concerns those in authority. Here we need to distinguish two kinds of case. If the occupant of an institutional role has an institutionally determined right or obligation to order other agents to perform certain actions, and if the actions in question are joint actions, then the occupant of the role is *individually* (institutionally) responsible for those joint actions performed by those other agents. This is our first kind of case; but it should be set aside, since it is not an instance of *collective* responsibility.

In the second kind of case, it is of no consequence whether the actions performed by those under the direction of the person in authority were joint actions or not. Rather, the issue concerns the actions of the ones in authority. In what sense are they collective? Suppose the members of the Cabinet of the U.K. government (consisting of the Prime Minister and his cabinet ministers) collectively decide to exercise their institutionally determined right to embark on an anti-corruption program. (For purposes of simplification, we will not refer to the role of Parliament in this.) Accordingly, a budget is allocated, an anti-corruption agency is established, law-enforcement agencies are briefed, and so on. The anti-corruption agency, relevant law-enforcement agencies, and others do what they have been instructed to do, and the Cabinet is collectively responsible for embarking on its anti-corruption program, in some sense of collective responsibility. Moreover, depending on the precise nature of the institutional arrangement, it might be that the Prime Minister instructs the newly appointed head of this anti-corruption agency, or perhaps her superior, to give priority to a particular form of corruption that is salient at the time, and does so as the representative of, or under instructions from, the Cabinet of which the Prime Minister is the head. If the decision is the Cabinet's to make, then there is full-blown collective responsibility. If the decision is the Prime Minister's to make, albeit acting on the advice of the Cabinet, or even subject to the veto of the Cabinet, then matters are more complex; the prime minister has individual responsibility, albeit individual responsibility that is tempered or constrained by a layer of collective responsibility.

There are a couple of things to keep in mind here. First, the notion of responsibility in question here is, at least in the first instance, institutional—as opposed to moral—responsibility. Second, the "decisions" of committees, as opposed to the individual decisions of the members of committees, need to be analyzed in terms of the notion of a joint institutional mechanism.[98] So the "decision" of the Cabinet—supposing it to be the Cabinet's decision, and not simply the Prime Minister's—can be analyzed as follows. At one level, each member of the Cabinet voted for or against the anti-corruption program; and let us assume that some voted in the affirmative, and others in the negative. But at another level, each member of the Cabinet agreed to abide by the outcome of the vote; that is, each voted having as a (collective) end that the outcome with a majority of the votes in its favor would be the one adopted. Accordingly, the members of the Cabinet were jointly institutionally responsible for the decision to instruct the relevant agencies to embark on this anti-corruption program. So the Cabinet was collectively institutionally responsible for starting the program, and the sense of collective responsibility in question is *joint* (institutional) responsibility.[99]

What of the fourth sense of collective responsibility, collective *moral* responsibility? Collective moral responsibility is a species of joint responsibility. Accordingly, each agent is individually morally responsible, but conditionally on the others' being individually morally responsible; there is interdependence in respect to moral responsibility. This account of collective moral responsibility arises naturally out of the account of joint actions. It also parallels the account given of individual moral responsibility.

Thus, we can make the following claim about moral responsibility. If agents are collectively responsible for the realization of an outcome, in the first or second or third senses of collective responsibility, and if the outcome is morally significant, then—other things being equal—the agents are collectively morally responsible for that outcome and can reasonably attract moral praise or blame, and (possibly) punishment or reward for bringing about the outcome.

Here we need to be more precise about what agents who perform morally significant joint actions are collectively morally responsible for. Other things being equal, each agent who intentionally performs a morally significant *individual* action has *individual* moral responsibility for the action. So in the case of a morally significant joint action, each agent is *individually* morally responsible for performing *his or her contributory* action, and the *other* agents are *not* morally responsible for his or her individual contributory action. But, in addition, the contributing agents are *collectively* morally responsible for the outcome or *collective end* of their various contributory actions. To say that they are collectively morally responsible for bringing about this (collective) end is just to say that they are *jointly* morally responsible for it. So each agent is individually morally responsible for realizing this (collective) end, but conditionally on the others' being individually morally responsible for realizing it as well.

Note the following residual points. First, it is not definitive of joint action that each performs his or her contributory action on the condition, and only on the condition, that *all* of the others perform theirs. Rather, it is sufficient that each performs his or her contributory action on the condition, and only on the condition, that *most* of the others perform theirs. So the interdependence involved in joint action is not necessarily *complete* interdependence. Second, an agent has moral responsibility if his or her action was intentionally performed in order to realize a morally significant collective end and if the action causally contributed to the end. The action does not have to be a necessary condition, or even a necessary part of a sufficient condition, for the realization of the end. Third, agents who intentionally make a causal contribution in order to realize a morally significant collective end are not necessarily fully morally responsible for the end realized.

A problem in relation to collective moral responsibility for actions arises in the context of the actions of large groups and organizations. Consider the Mafia organization. The actions of the members of the Mafia are interdependent in virtue of the collective end—say, to profit from the sale of heroin in southern Italy. Naturally, this interdependence is far more complex than simple cases of joint action, given the existence of a hierarchical organization and its more loosely structured extensions. Moreover, the contribution of each individual to the outcome is far more various and in general quite insignificant, given the large numbers of people involved.

At this point the notion of what has elsewhere been termed a "layered structure of joint actions" needs to be introduced.[100] Suppose that a number of "actions" are performed in order to realize some collective end. Call the resulting joint action a *level two* joint action. Suppose, in addition, that each of the component individual "actions" of this level two joint "action" is itself—at least in part—a joint action with a second set of component individual actions. And suppose that the member actions of this second set have the performance of this level two "action" as their collective end. Call the joint action composed of the members of this second set of actions a *level one* joint action. An illustration of the notion of a layered structure of joint actions is, in fact, a Mafia organization involved in illicit drugs. At level one, we have a number of joint actions. The team of Mafia "soldiers," drivers, and others ensures that a given heroin shipment is procured and transported safely to the distribution point in a large city—this is a level one joint action; a Mafia "sales" team distributes smaller quantities of the heroin to individual dealers—this is a level one joint action; and finally, the money received back from individual dealers is laundered by members of the organization's money-laundering arm, for example, by being deposited in small amounts in numerous bank accounts—this is a level one joint action. So there are at least three level one joint actions. Now, each of these three (level one) joint actions is itself describable as an *individual* action performed (respectively) by the different groups, namely, the action of procuring a given heroin load, the action of selling the load, and the action of laundering the profits made from selling the heroin load. However, each of these "individual" actions is part of a larger joint action directed to the collective end of making money from the sale of heroin, that is, running a heroin business, because each of these individual actions—procuring, selling, and laundering—is part of the larger "business" plan of the Mafia leadership. So these "individual" actions constitute a *level two* joint action directed to the collective end of making money from heroin.

Accordingly, if all, or most, of the individual actions of the members of the Mafia organization were performed in accordance with collective ends and if the performance of all of the resulting level one joint actions were themselves performed in accordance with the collective end of making money for the Mafia organization from the sale of heroin, then, at least in principle, we could ascribe joint moral responsibility for the realization of this collective end to the individual members of the Mafia organization.

At any rate, we are now entitled to conclude that agents involved in complex cooperative enterprises can, *at least in principle,* be ascribed collective or *joint natural* responsibility for the outcomes aimed at by those enterprises; and that in cases of morally significant enterprises, they can be ascribed collective or *joint moral* responsibility for those outcomes. This conclusion depends on the possibility of analyzing these enterprises in terms of layered structures of joint action. Such structures involve (1) a possibly indirect and minor causal contribution from each of the individuals jointly being ascribed responsibility; (2) each individual's having an intention to perform his or her contributory (causally efficacious) action; and (3) each individual's having as an ultimate end or goal the outcome causally produced by their jointly performed actions.

The upshot of the discussion in this section is that the undoubted existence of the phenomenon of collective moral responsibility for actions is entirely consistent with individualism in relation to moral responsibility, because an acceptable individualist account of collective moral responsibility is available.

CORPORATIONS AND COLLECTIVE RESPONSIBILITY

A number of things should be kept in mind in what follows. First, we are concerned with ethical or moral responsibility, and not legal responsibility, and we are concerned with ethical responsibility for doing good, as well as for doing evil. We say this notwithstanding the fact that we pay a disproportionate amount of attention to moral responsibility for serious forms of corruption. (We do this because serious wrongdoing has more obvious implications for institutional accountability systems, including regulatory regimes.)

Second, the account we offer of collective or joint responsibility necessarily relies on a particular conception of a corporation. It is impossible to do broad-brush institutional ethics without operating with some explicit or implicit model of the institution in question. Moreover, the particular conception we put forward is in part an idealized or prescriptive model of corporations. By that we do not mean that it is a completely unrealistic model—there is little point in ethical ruminations that can have no impact on our everyday world. Rather, we are tentatively putting forward a model that we believe may be an ethically desirable one for corporations to aim at.

Third, we are of the view that although it may be entirely legitimate to ascribe *legal* liability to nonhuman entities such as corporations, it is only human beings that are, properly speaking, *moral* agents. So, our starting position in relation to the notion of collective or joint responsibility is that whereas individual human beings have moral agency, and therefore moral responsibility, corporations and other institutions do not. This position has been argued for in detail elsewhere.[101] Suffice it to say here that corporations are not agents because they do not possess mental states, such as intentions and beliefs. But if they are not agents, then they are not moral agents, and therefore they cannot be held morally responsible. We say all this notwithstanding the fact that *in law* they can be held to be agents, to perform actions, and to be liable. It simply does not follow from the fact that corporations can be held legally liable, that they have moral responsibility. Accordingly, our rejection of the notion of corporate moral responsibility is consistent with embracing, for example, Fisse and Braithwaite's previously mentioned strategy of enforced accountability. At any rate, our concern is to identify moral responsibility, and joint moral responsibility in particular.

Given that individuals but not corporations are the bearers of moral responsibility, we need to focus (at least) on the individual members of the board of directors, the day-to-day managers, and the other employees of the corporation. We will refer to board members, including nonexecutive members and senior and middle managers, as officers, thereby distinguishing the officers of a corporation from its employees in the lower echelons, on the one hand, and from its ownership—which is to say from its shareholders—on the other. Note that we will have little to say about the ethical responsibilities of shareholders. We do this largely in order to simplify matters in an already ethically complex area. But we also take the view that corporations as organizations fundamentally consist of managers and lower-echelon employees. In our view, incorporation consists of an act whereby an institutional mechanism is grafted onto something more basic—namely, an organization of managers and workers who cooperate to produce some economic good or service. That said, we certainly endorse the importance of the role of shareholders as owners, and we recognize the moral responsibilities of investors in relation to, for example, boycotting companies that pollute or make use of child labor and so on.

Our general concern in what follows is to emphasize the point that when it comes to ascribing ethical responsibility—whether it be responsibility for bringing about some good or some evil—corporate officers and other employees should not principally be regarded as isolated individuals, because their actions, and indeed spheres of activity, are for the most part interdependent, and thus give rise to a complex network of joint moral responsibilities, and indeed joint moral rights, though our focus in what follows is on responsibilities. In short, the key notion of responsibility at issue here is collective moral responsibility.

We now need to make a number of more specific points. First, at any one time the officers and employees are involved in a joint economic enterprise that has as a collective end the production of goods for consumption by the wider society. Moreover, this joint enterprise consists in part of a number of interlocking, constituent joint activities—for example, the designing of a particular new car and the marketing and distribution of that car. In short, we have a layered structure of joint actions.

That is, we suggest that we can conceive of corporations as consisting of a set of jointly participating individual agents. It follows that the officers and employees of a corporation can be held jointly morally responsible for many of their actions, namely their joint actions. For example, all the members of a production team could be held jointly responsible for the existence of the new car that their individual actions jointly produced. Moreover, fairness dictates that the members of that production team be rewarded, at least in part, on the basis of the economic success of this new car, and conversely, penalized if it should turn out to be defective in some way. Naturally, officers and employees can in addition be held individually morally responsible for their individual actions. So Fred can be held individually responsible for, say, designing the steering mechanism of this car.

Second, individual participants in the joint enterprise come and go. In doing so, they take over, and ideally further, the long-term collective ends of the corporation. For example, South African Breweries had the long-term goal of becoming the fifth largest distributor of beer in the world by the year 2000. Here, the first generation of officers and employees has joint responsibility with the generations that follow it. Each generation contributes in an analogous way to that in which each member of a relay team contributes to the success of the team. Moreover, each new generation of officers and employees benefits from the efforts of previous generations. For example, without the efforts of previous generations, there may not in fact be any managerial or other job.

Furthermore, each new generation is rightly expected to shoulder burdens, including moral responsibilities, incurred by earlier generations. For example, if past company profits depended heavily on dumping hazardous wastes, the current generation of officers and employees of the company in question may have moral obligations to clean up the environment in virtue of the benefits accruing to them from that past policy.

Third, the fact that a corporation is hierarchically structured and consists of specialized spheres of individual, as well as joint, activity has implications for ascriptions of ethical responsibility. On the one hand, directors and other managers—the so-called "directing mind and will" of a corporation—are morally responsible for the actions of their subordinates, insofar as those subordinates are acting under the instructions of these managers. Correspondingly, employees in the lower echelons have diminished individual and collective responsibility for corporate policies and procedures.

On the other hand, employees involved in a certain form of activity in one part of the corporation are not morally responsible, or have only diminished responsibility, for the interlocking activity of employees in another area. Nevertheless, all employees may share responsibility in some measure for the fundamental activity of the corporation, since as participants they knowingly contribute to the realization of the collective end(s) of the joint enterprise. For example, the managers of a German firm that manufactured gas chambers for Hitler are in part responsible for the existence of those chambers and cannot escape all blame for the deaths that resulted from their use. In our view, the managers and the employees are jointly morally responsible (with others)—that is, collectively morally responsible—for the construction of those chambers and for the realization of the end for which they were produced, namely the killing of Jews.

Fourth, individuals can be held collectively morally responsible if they could have jointly acted in such a way as to avoid the wrongdoing. Whether or not they could have jointly avoided such wrongdoing is partly a matter of their mutual knowledge of one another's willingness to avoid such wrong-doing and of the organizational possibilities open to them—including those provided by trade unions—for collectively avoiding that wrongdoing. It is also partly a matter of the nature and extent of the wrongdoing in question. Individuals working in corporations are subject to a complex array of poli-cies and procedures. It may be too much to expect that employees, whether acting individually or jointly, could ensure that all of the procedures and policies that they follow are as they ideally ought to be. It may be that this could be ensured only if every individual policy and procedure were to be subjected to detailed scrutiny. But perhaps such a process is prohibitively expensive in terms of time and resources.

Fifth, *in general* if an individual did all that he or she could in the circum-stances to avoid performing a wrongful individual action, or contributing to a wrongful joint action, or contributing to abandoning a wrongful policy or procedure, then that individual should not be held responsible or penalized for such actions, procedures, and policies. There are some exceptions to this general moral rule. For example, there are cases in which we hold agents legally liable for outcomes that they cause, even though the agents acted un-intentionally, unknowingly, nonnegligently, and so on. The moral basis for this view is in part the fact that the agents in such cases fulfill one of the stan-dard conditions for ethical responsibility, namely causal responsibility.

Finally, it may be that certain individuals cannot even be held morally responsible for willingly performing or participating in such wrongful actions, procedures, and policies. It may be that they have been inducted into ways of thinking and behaving, and have internalized certain values, as a result of which they do not know and could not have known that what they were doing was morally wrong. There are limitations on the extent to which individuals are morally responsible for being the kinds of persons they are.

Thus far we have focused in general terms on the individual and col-lective ethical responsibility of the officers and employees of a corporation, and have sought to identify salient dimensions of ethical responsibility in corporate activity, including especially responsibility for wrongdoing. Before proceeding with a number of specific problems and regulatory implications for this account, we must once again emphasize that the collective ethical responsibilities of officers and employees go well beyond simply avoiding unlawful and/or corrupt activity. Corporate officers and employees are re-warded financially, and in other ways, in order that they collectively pursue collective ends, such as efficiency and profitability, and they have ethical responsibilities to pursue those ends.

On the preceding account, a corporation is not just a legal entity, it is also a joint enterprise, and the activity of the corporation consists in large part of a layered structure of joint actions. Moreover, the corporation's offi-cers and employees conduct themselves in accordance with the corporation's internal decision procedure—which is to say, in accordance with the general policies, procedures, and chain of command of the corporation.[102] Accordingly, corporate penalties, such as fines, and ultimately the shutting down of a corporation, are necessarily costs borne (in part) by officers and employees. But this being so, it is *in principle* morally legitimate to impose legal penalties on a corporation for the *collective* wrongdoing of its officers and employees, just as it is in principle morally legitimate to distribute rewards and privileges to a corporation for the goods that it collectively produces.

Furthermore, *in some cases,* it may even be justified—on grounds of ethical responsibility—to hold the corporation legally liable for the collective wrongdoing of its *past* directors, managers, and/or other employees. For, as we indicated earlier, the current generation of officers and employees of a given corporation can legitimately be expected to shoulder some of the ethical responsibilities (initially) incurred by past members.

Consider a corporation with a particular defective safety procedure. Past and present officers and employees are typically jointly responsible for a corporation's internal decision structure being what it is, including its safety procedures. But present officers joined the corporation knowing that it had an internal decision structure, and in some cases also knowing that they could not initially have a comprehensive knowledge of that structure. So they know that there might be a defective safety procedure that they are unaware of. On the other hand, it is obvious that only present officers can effect changes to that structure. Accordingly, present officers of a corporation could legitimately be held jointly responsible for the corporate procedures, including safety procedures, and also for some of the morally unacceptable outcomes of those procedures. After all, it is not as if new management will reject the *benefits* of some procedure that, unknown to them, was put in place by their predecessors. Can one imagine a new management team giving part of their bonus to a now-retired management team on the grounds that the increased profits that justified this bonus were substantially due to policies put in place by the retired managers when they were in charge?

Needless to say, the ascription of joint ethical responsibility to a corporation's officers and employees needs to be qualified in any particular case by considerations of the diminished responsibility of subordinates, the kind of responsibility it is, and so on.

Moreover, the ascription of joint ethical responsibility to a corporation's entire cohort of officers and employees is in some cases consistent with the ascription of selective joint responsibility to, say, the board of directors in other cases. Furthermore, legal liabilities and penalties *could* reflect such differential ascriptions of joint ethical responsibility. For example, the shutting down of a corporation would impact on all officers and employees, whereas fining the board of directors might not.

Corporate crimes, including acts of corporate corruption, are obviously not always joint actions per se or the outcomes of joint actions. They are often crimes committed by individual officers and employees of the corporation acting on their own. Such individual actions might not be the actions of the corporation in any sense. Thus, a single individual (or even a small number of individuals) who commits fraud without the participation or knowledge of any of the other members of the corporation is not jointly participating in the activity of the corporation. The individual is acting in his or her capacity as an individual and is wholly morally responsible for his or her crime.

But just as members of the public, and not just members of the police force, are morally responsible for the prevention of crime and the capture of criminals—for example, members of the public have a duty to report crimes—so the officers and employees of a corporation are in part morally responsible for the prevention of corruption within that corporation. This is not yet to spell out what their specific duties in this regard ought to be. But if there is moral responsibility here, then one barrier to the ascription of legal liability has been removed. Whistleblowing, for example, *could* be made a legal obligation (see Chapter 8). Moreover, a corporation could be required by law to have in place various measures to lessen the possibility of corruption, including internal disciplinary measures, in the same way that they are typically now required to put in place various measures for safety. Needless to say, from the fact that there is moral responsibility for an act or omission, it would not follow that there ought to be legal liability. The case for legal liability needs to take account of a whole host of additional considerations, including its economic effects, the possibility of enforcement, and so on.

A third relevant issue is the so-called "problem of many hands."[103] This problem arises in situations in which many individuals contribute to an outcome, though each only in a very small way. Thus, one firm discharging its waste product into a nearby lake may have a negligible effect, but if a thousand firms discharge their waste into the lake, the result might be massive environmental pollution. Other cases might involve boards of directors. Suppose that a particular member of a board of directors votes against a dubious loan proposal or against the practice of using negative pledge,[104] but the member is outvoted. What responsibility, if any, does that member have for that outcome?

In each of these kinds of case, there may be a genuine ethical dilemma. The polluting firm may go out of business if it procures expensive environmental equipment and its competitors do not. Similarly, the resignation of a board member, or the recourse to whistleblowing, may ruin a career, cause financial hardship, and so on. One's individual interest, and the interests of one's family and one's company, must be given some moral weight.

The first thing to determine is whether it is wrong for the firm to discharge its waste. Clearly, an undesirable state of affairs, namely environmental pollution, is brought about if all of, say, 1,000 firms discharge their waste. Equally clearly, although no one firm is responsible for the pollution, each firm is contributing to that pollution. Thus, the act of discharging waste is prima facie morally wrong. On the other hand, merely to stop polluting by oneself may well put one out of business and cause financial hardship to one's family. One has a prima facie duty to avoid causing financial hardship to one's family. One way out of this ethical dilemma would be for the firms to come together and jointly decide that no one will pollute. If so, then there is an obligation on each firm to at least try to convince other firms to come to an arrangement whereby no firm pollutes. Having arrived at that arrangement, any firm that continues to discharge waste—even though in so doing it is now making no substantial difference to pollution levels—is giving itself an unfair advantage and is putting at risk the arrangement whereby the environment is protected. Naturally, regulation and attendant legal sanctions may well be necessary in this sort of case. But the point is that legal liability and acceptance of the ethically justified arrangement would exist side by side and would mutually reinforce one another.

The case of the board of directors is somewhat different in that the board is a formal collective body. Accordingly, each individual member has a moral responsibility to follow established procedures. For example, an individual banker ought not to approve large loans without the appropriate supporting documentation.

Moreover, some formal collective bodies are so constituted that the collective can be held morally responsible for *some* of the individual actions of individual members. If boards of directors are of this sort—and if they are not, bringing it about that they are may be institutionally desirable—it would follow that there is no *in principle* objection to holding a board legally liable for the actions of one of its members. Indeed, as we saw before, Tomasic and Bottomley argue for a form of such liability.

Furthermore, in some formal collective bodies, each individual member is morally responsible for many of the decisions of the collective, whether that member influenced those decisions or not. If boards of directors are collective bodies of this sort—and, once again, if they are not, then they could be redesigned to become so—then the fact that the driving force behind a dubious loan proposal was some individual member of the board would not absolve other members of the moral responsibility for the outcome of the loan's being approved, even if those members voted against the proposal. But if there is this moral responsibility, then it may be legitimate to ascribe legal liability to all members of the board for recommending a dubious loan proposal, including those members who voted against the proposal. Here it should be noted that voters are jointly committed to the outcome of the voting procedure, whatever that outcome is. In this sense, each individual voter supports that outcome, even if he or she voted against it.

Finally, the fact that an individual's action in such situations will make no difference is not necessarily to the point; as we saw in the last section, one's action or inaction does not have to be a necessary condition for some untoward outcome for one to be (at least in part) morally responsible for that outcome. The question is, typically, not whether an individual's action considered alone would make a difference, but rather whether *our* actions would make a difference. For example, if one or two other members of the board are wavering, then the obligation of any given individual is to try and convince them to do other than they would do without the intervention of that individual.

A fourth issue concerns unfairness. We have argued that holding corporations or other collectives, such as boards of directors, legally liable is consistent with the view that since only individual human beings are moral agents, only individuals who are, individually or jointly, morally responsible for an action (or actions) ought to be punished for it. However, as it happens, we are not averse to the imposition of some legal liabilities that are not morally justified on the basis of fairness, but rather on the basis of the desirable consequences that will flow if they are imposed, and the undesirable consequences if they are not. Thus, it may be that the burdens of punishment meted out to a corporation or a board of directors are necessarily unfairly distributed among its members. (It may even be necessary to unfairly, or at least disproportionately, punish those who are not principally responsible but who have assisted and happen to have "deep pockets.") If so, the judgment may well have to be that the avoidance of undesirable consequences overrides considerations of fairness. But we take it that, in this respect, regulatory policy in relation to corporations is no different from many other kinds of social policy. Social policy is, after all, a blunt instrument.

In this connection, we repeat the earlier point that the account of corporations as joint enterprises is an idealized and partly prescriptive model. Joint moral responsibility cannot be ascribed in many cases at this time because corporations are simply not as close to our model of joint enterprises as they would have to be. For one thing, many corporations are really groups of companies, and the individual companies may not have many fundamental activities in common—and very few, if any, collective ends in common.

And for another thing, corporations might be extremely hierarchical; indeed, far from being involved in the decision-making process, workers within a corporation might be the victims of exploitation or coercion. If so, those workers whose tasks contribute to the collective ends of the corporation have not themselves adopted those ends. But—ideally, at least—employees work in order to secure the collective end of a productive enterprise and thereby to receive their reward. Moreover, the existence of corporations in which workers are powerless is presumably in itself morally abhorrent. Accordingly, this circumstance would be an argument for greater democratization of corporations and for greater protection of individual rights, such as autonomy, in workplace settings. Once again, the result of such a process of democratization and increase in individual autonomy would be to drive corporations toward the joint enterprise model that we are putting forward for consideration.

Again, employees often do not understand what is taking place in their corporation even in very general terms. But there can be joint activity and collective ends, notwithstanding the fact that many of the participants do not know or understand in what precise way many of the other participants contribute to the collective ends of the joint activity. (This point has to be distinguished from the fact that often joint activity, and contributory actions to joint activity, have unforeseen consequences, unforeseen, that is, by any of the participants.) It is sufficient that the participants have an overall grasp of the enterprise, of their own contribution to it, and in very general terms, of the way that others contribute. If this minimal requirement is not met, then the concept of joint activity begins to lose purchase.

CONCLUSION

We have provided an analysis of the concept of collective moral responsibility and have argued for its importance in understanding the moral responsibility of business corporations in relation to corruption. Our analysis is an individualist one in that collective responsibility is cashed out in terms of the jointly held individual responsibilities of individual agents. This plan enables us to sheet home blame for corporate corruption to individual managers, directors, and employees, albeit jointly. Moreover, it provides an *in principle* justification for the practice of imposing fines and other punishments on the corporation per se. That said, various moral problems, including unfairness, can arise in some instances; specifically, in the case of corporations whose employees (1) suffer as a consequence of penalties imposed on the corporation and yet (2) are powerless to prevent the corruption. On the other hand, we have suggested that one way to redress some of these moral problems is to (partially) democratize them so as to empower employees. Just as no power implies no responsibility, so collective power implies collective responsibility.

chapter seven

Anti-Corruption Systems

In this chapter, we cover

- Reactive anti-corruption systems
- Preventive anti-corruption systems
- Holistic anti-corruption systems
- Corruption control in the context of developments in public sector administration.

In the last chapter, we considered the notion of *moral responsibility* in relation to corruption, and specifically collective moral responsibility for corruption and for combating it in corporate contexts. In this chapter, we move on to examine *institutional accountability* systems in relation to corruption, and specifically anti-corruption systems.

In looking at options to combat corruption, it is very easy to leap to a particular single "magic bullet" solution, like increasing custodial sentences or giving more powers to police, and doing so without considering the social, economic, and moral implications. As outlined earlier in this book, there is an enormous variety of activities that can be seen as corruption, and the ways of dealing with those activities are correspondingly diverse.

Before looking at the mechanisms that are available for dealing with corruption, there are a number of threshold issues that need to be addressed. The first is whether the corrupt activity is sporadic or continuing. As discussed earlier in the book, corruption typically entails a repeated set of acts; but a single act, although wrongful and unlawful, may not count as corruption because it does not corrupt, or at least not to any serious extent. Therefore, any contemplation of anti-corruption mechanisms that will require the expenditure of energy and resources—and may well impinge on individual freedom—needs to be justified in terms of the seriousness and extent of the corruption to be successfully combated.

In relation to the issue of seriousness, some corruption, although widespread, is relatively trivial in relation to the anti-corruption resources that would be needed to deal with it, for example, price collusion of a kind that sets the price only marginally higher than it otherwise would be. Another reason why formal anti-corruption mechanisms are not established may be the recognition that the corrupt action lies purely in the private domain. For example, in many Western cultures, adultery is regarded primarily as a personal matter. Even though the practice of adultery, if widespread, may corrupt the institution of marriage, and may have far-reaching deleterious effects, it is (rightly or wrongly) left to individuals to grapple with; or at least there is reliance only on indirect and informal social policies—the application of formal anti-corruption mechanisms is eschewed.

Anti-corruption systems can be thought of as being either predominantly reactive or predominantly preventive. Naturally, the distinction is somewhat artificial, since there is a need for both reactive elements, for example, investigation and adjudication, as well as preventive elements, for example, ethics training and transparency, in any adequate anti-corruption system. At any rate, we propose to consider anti-corruption systems under two broad headings, reactive and preventive. We will look at preventive systems under three subheadings: promoting ethical behavior; corporate governance procedures; and transparency.

REACTIVE ANTI-CORRUPTION SYSTEMS

The reactive way of dealing with corruption is the one that first comes to mind. The logic is direct: the corrupt activity is defined as one that is not acceptable; an individual engages in that activity and therefore, as a direct result, should be apprehended, tried, and if found guilty, punished in some way. This approach exists in many spheres of activity. If a Boy Scout who is assigned the task of cooking in fact abuses the trust put in him and steals food from the rest of the troop, the matter would be investigated, he would be asked to explain, and if found guilty, he would suffer the indignity of public admonition; he might be required to undertake extra menial tasks or even, in the case of repeated behavior, be asked to leave the troop.

At the more serious and complex end of the corruption spectrum is the famous case of Vice President Spiro Agnew. Before being Richard Nixon's running mate in 1968, Spiro Agnew was the governor of Maryland. In the early 1970s, the U.S. attorney for Maryland launched an extensive investigation into corruption that uncovered that Spiro Agnew had accepted bribes from contractors while governor of Maryland. Because Agnew was the vice president, there were highly complex constitutional issues about whether he could be indicted, and federal prosecutors offered him a deal whereby he agreed to resign as vice president in return for a plea of no contest, pay a $10,000 fine, and serve three years' probation. Maryland filed a civil suit for recovery of the money he received in bribes, and many years later, Spiro Agnew paid $248,735 in restitution and died in ignominy. Even though he was never convicted, Spiro Agnew felt the punitive effect of the law.

The rationale for the reactive response for dealing with corruption is threefold: offenders are held to account for their actions; offenders get their just deserts; and potential offenders are deterred from future offenses. It cannot be denied that the case of the vice president just mentioned or the image of Andrew Fastow's (Enron's chief financial officer) being led away in handcuffs in his immaculate suit, is a very powerful message for others in the community that corrupt behavior is not tolerated.

Reactive mechanisms for dealing with corruption are fundamentally linear: setting out a series of offenses (usually in legislation), waiting for an individual to transgress, then apprehending, investigating, adjudicating, and finally taking punitive action. The weaknesses of the reactive approach are manifest and have been well explained elsewhere. One obvious weakness is the passivity of the approach; by the time the investigators swing into action, the damage has been already done.

Another problem stems from the fact that—as we saw in Chapter 2— institutional corruption is typically secretive. One consequence of this tendency is that police are inclined to focus upon the highly visible areas of unlawful activity, for example, armed robbery and street violence.

Yet a further problem stems from the inadequacy of the resources to investigate and successfully prosecute (especially) corporate corruption. On the one hand, in the corporate sector, there is a vast multitude of transactions and—as we saw in Chapter 2—the twin processes of globalization and the introduction of the new information and communication technology have increased the opportunities for corruption. On the other hand, the process of investigation and prosecution is resource intensive, and yet investigators and prosecutors are typically poorly resourced.

Finally, because the chances of being caught are relatively slight, the deterrent effect is undermined, an outcome that means that there are an even larger number of offenses and offenders for investigators to deal with.

Since we have considered the general nature of the reactive approach to dealing with corruption, it is now necessary to examine the linear and logical progression that proceeds from the corruption offenses that are set down in legislation, that moves to the detection of the offense and its investigation, and that finally leads to prosecution and the imposition of punishment. In the light of the discussion earlier in this book about the nature of institutional corruption, it is clear that it embraces a wide variety of activities, including fraud. For the purposes of this analysis, we will concentrate upon corruption that is identified in criminal codes; we do so with the understanding that the criminal justice system represents the most salient and sophisticated, reactive institutional response to combating serious forms of corruption.

Legislative Framework

Almost every jurisdiction has criminal laws against self-evident forms of corruption, such as offering or soliciting bribes, or abusing the power of a public office. There are other activities, like pedophilia, which may involve corruption of, say, a person's parental role but which are (1) not defined as forms of corruption within the criminal justice system, but (2) which are defined as crimes and therefore are subject to criminal justice processes. Although it is common for anti-corruption laws and other criminal laws to be consolidated into a criminal code, it is almost universal that legislation dealing with particular areas of activity, like the regulation of companies and corporations, will also contain criminal offense provisions. In essence, these provisions will be dealing with the same issues of abuse of office, bribery, and fraud, but in a more specific context.

At the core of dealing with corruption using reactive mechanisms is the codification of the community's moral attitudes into statutes, regulations, or other such instruments. These are enacted by a legislature and embody a fragment of the basic social norms of the community. By virtue of embodying social norms in a community, anti-corruption laws and the like reflect the moral beliefs of the community; by virtue of being laws passed by the duly elected representatives of the community, anti-corruption laws reflect the will of the community.

The Australian legislative scheme for dealing with corruption, as contained in the Commonwealth Criminal Code Act 1995 (Division 7.6 of the Criminal Code), is indicative of relevant statutes:

- For giving a bribe to a Commonwealth official, maximum penalty of 5 years (section 141.1 (1));
- For a Commonwealth official receiving a bribe, maximum penalty of 5 years (section 141.1 (3));
- For providing a corrupt benefit to a Commonwealth official, maximum penalty of 5 years (section 142.1 (3));
- For a Commonwealth official receiving a corrupt benefit, maximum penalty of 5 years (section 141.1 (3)); and
- For a Commonwealth official using his official position to dishonestly obtain a benefit, maximum penalty of 5 years (section 142.2 (1)).

This Australian legislation is the outcome of an exhaustive process of rationalizing and coordinating the criminal code.

The equivalent statute in the United States can be located in the Bribery and Conflict of Interest Act 1962, which aggregated many of the federal bribery provisions and all of the federal conflict-of-interest provisions at one place in the United States Code. These sorts of legislative cleanups are very useful in that they make it easier for employees and officials to know exactly what laws apply to them.

Frequently, the key provisions that are utilized are not so obvious. Section 1951 of the United States Code (commonly referred to as the Hobbs Act) makes it a violation of federal law for anyone to obstruct, delay, or affect commerce—"or movement of any article or commodity in commerce"—"by robbery or extortion." This provision was enacted in 1946 to stop criminals from extorting money from businesses engaged in interstate commerce. U.S. attorneys and federal prosecutors found these provisions very helpful in their quest to prosecute corrupt officials, arguing that accepting any sort of benefit for agreeing to perform an official act was an offense under the Hobbs Act. Notwithstanding that some recent cases have limited the scope of this use of the Act,[105] it is still used to prosecute corrupt officials. Similarly, prosecutors in the United States used the Mail Fraud Statute as a tool for dealing with corruption. They argued that whenever officials used the mail as a part of their corrupt activities, they then deprived citizens of honest government, on the basis that all citizens had an "intangible" property interest in honest government. The courts accepted this creative argument until it was successfully challenged in the 1980s.[106] However, the legislature quickly moved to reestablish the status quo, so the Hobbs Act, the Mail Fraud Statute, and the False Statements Act (see later) remain important provisions for prosecuting officials for corruption.

The False Statements Accountability Act 1996 is a statute that was originally enacted as a mechanism to prohibit citizens from making fraudulent claims for benefits, and later was extended in its scope. In 1999, Henry Cisneros, former secretary of labor, pleaded guilty to lying to the Federal Bureau of Investigation about payments to his one-time mistress. Cisneros had made the false statement as part of an FBI background check undertaken when he was being considered for a Cabinet post.

The capacity for a legislature to be able to enact effective statutes in relation to corruption requires a commitment to combating corruption. As will be discussed later in this chapter, some members of the legislature lack this requisite level of commitment because corruption is so deeply entrenched that enacting anti-corruption legislation may have adverse political consequences for them.

The creation and maintenance of a legislative regime to deal with corruption involves a number of difficulties. In the sphere of commercial activity there is an ever-present financial incentive to find ways to avoid compliance with laws and regulations. As a consequence, there is a constant need to monitor compliance with the regulatory system in order either to ensure that new forms of corruption have not been found, or if they have, to enable legislative changes to be made to defeat them. In the case of Enron, an array of techniques was used to undermine the regulatory framework existing at that time. It is worth going into some detail on just one of the techniques used by Enron—Special Purpose Entities (SPEs).

CASE STUDY 7.1 Enron and Special Purpose Entities

SPEs, which were a specialty of Andrew Fastow (Enron's chief financial officer), were initially introduced by banks and law firms as "structured finance"—complex financial deals intended to enable companies to generate tax deductions and move assets off a company's books.[107] With names such as Cactus, Braveheart, Whitewing, JEDI, Chewco, Raptors, LJM I and LJM II (named after Fastow's wife Lea and his two children), Enron used SPEs for various purposes. The primary purpose was for financing new projects in Enron's ever-expanding trading business, which continuously needed new injections of cash funds to sustain that expansion, as well as providing insurance hedging for those projects while managing—sometimes legally, but mostly not—to keep debt related to those projects off its balance sheet, while taking up earnings relating to those projects in its income statements. For his role in those SPEs, Andrew Fastow reportedly made more than $45 million. In the wake of the revelations concerning Fastow's key role in the Enron SPEs, especially Chewco and LJM—and just one month prior to Enron's final collapse and bankruptcy on December 2, 2001—the company was forced to restate its earnings from 1997 through 2002. This action required a $1.2 billion equity write-down.

Chewco alone accounted for the inflation of earnings by $405 million from 1997 through 2000, which Enron was not entitled to have on its books, and the concealment of a $600 million debt, which, by contrast, Enron was required to show on its books. Named after Chewbacca, the character from *Star Wars*, Chewco was set up to buy out the share of equity of the California Public Employees' Retirement System (CALPERS) in JEDI I (another allusion to *Star Wars*).

The main problem with Chewco was that Enron did not meet the 3 percent investment rule that required that at least 3 percent of equity in the SPE be held by an independent investor not associated with Enron. Because this rule was not met in the case of Chewco, Enron was not legally allowed to keep the SPE off its balance sheet.

Given the complexity of the Enron SPEs—a complexity that seems now to have been intended as a deliberate ploy to obfuscate and render opaque the real purpose of the SPEs to outsiders—it is difficult to explain in great detail the intricate financial mechanisms of these devices. However, by focusing on one of the SPEs, LJM, which together with Chewco proved to be the catalyst that brought down the Enron empire, this much seems clear: whereas Chewco was at the periphery of financial impropriety, LJM[108] proved to be its very nucleus.

LJM, and its successor LJM II, were set up to finance an array of deals. The original LJM—LJM I—was set up to finance the Rhythms deal in March 1998, a deal that saw Enron invest $10 million for a block of shares in Rhythms NetConnections, a high-speed Internet service provider. As was the case with many dot.com companies, Rhythms both went public (in April 1999) and saw its shares climb rapidly—making Enron's investment worth $300 million. Because Enron's accounting rules, mark-to-market, required Enron to mark the shares to market on a daily basis, it meant that Enron had already booked $290 million of profits on the transaction. Concerned, however, that the profit might be reduced or turn to a loss in the future, which would require Enron to take into account substantial losses, Enron had to cover for that contingency. Not allowed to sell the shares for several months until the end of 1999, Enron wanted to get insurance against a fall in the value of those shares. Traditionally, the way to acquire insurance is through the purchase of a "put option." A put option locks in a specific sale price for the shares for the life of the option. So, for example, with Rhythms trading at $65 per share, Enron might have wanted to purchase a put option until it could sell them at the end of 1999 at a lock-in price of $60. The option would not cover the first $5 of loss, but it would cover any remaining loss that might arise, dollar for dollar.

The problem for Enron, however, was that its block of shares in Rhythms was so large and the company was so risky that no one would be willing to provide insurance at a price that Enron considered reasonable. Fastow's solution was to create a company that he would manage that used Enron stock as its capital to sell the insurance on Rhythms stock to Enron. Essentially, this amounted to Enron's insuring itself! If the insurance was never needed, no one would be the wiser, and Fastow and his partners in the scheme, who were chosen among his subordinates within Enron, could pocket most of the premium that Enron paid, making them quite wealthy. If the Rhythms stock fell dramatically, then the Enron stock that hedged the company would cover the losses. However, if both Rhythms *and* Enron stocks suffered a significant fall, the company would go broke unless someone bailed it out. However, because Enron was in effect insuring itself, there really was no insurance.

What defies understanding was that such a scheme passed Enron's board, Enron's auditors, Arthur Andersen, and Enron's law firm, Vinson and Elkins. According to the Powers Report, the Enron board approved a waiver of its code of ethics to allow Fastow to set up LJM I that covered the Rhythms deal.

The sequel to LJM I, LJM II, took Fastow's ingenuity in coming up with ever more complex and ethically and legally dubious SPEs to new heights. While LJM I was used to provide a faulty hedge in a profitable investment in the Rhythms deal, the deals that LJM II helped finance—and that were named "Raptors" after the cunning dinosaurs in the film *Jurassic Park*—were used to hide the losses of unprofitable projects. In total, LJM II was used to conceal $1.1 billion of Enron losses. Fastow's secret profit from LJM I and the Rhythms deal alone was a staggering $22 million from a $1 million investment in little less than a year!

The Enron collapse highlighted the difficulty that legislatures face in establishing and maintaining a regulatory regime in such a complex and rapidly changing field. In April 2002, the United States House of Representatives—at that time under Republican control—passed a bill to deal with the problems that Enron exposed, and at the same time to meet the interests of the corporate sector to operate without excessive government interference. However, the daily disclosures about corporate malfeasance led lawmakers to toughen the draft legislation and bring it more in line with a version passed by the Democrat-controlled Senate.

The legislation that was finally agreed upon and passed into law in July 2002 made security fraud a criminal offense. Any chief executive officer or chief financial officer who is found guilty of certifying false financial reports could get 20 years in prison and be fined $5 million. Destruction of evidence, like the shredding of documents, could result in a 20-year sentence. The justification for bringing into being such harsh punitive measures is a teleological one. Presumably, there is nothing intrinsically wrong in shredding documents; however, if these documents are a necessary means for the end or purpose of detecting and prosecuting serious fraud and if punitive measures are a necessary means to ensuring the preservation of these documents, then punitive measures have been justified in terms of means/end reasoning—in fact, a chain of means/end reasoning (see Chapter 1). Naturally, if the means do not in fact realize the end, then the means are not justified; so such punitive measure are justified only if they ensure that documents are preserved and that serious fraudsters are prosecuted as a result.

The legislation set up an independent private-sector oversight board to watch over the industry, and it restricted the ability of accounting firms to perform consulting work for companies that they are auditing. Immediate disclosure of stock sales by company executives is now necessary, and the legislation prohibits companies from giving personal loans to top officials.

The Corporate Reform Act of 2002 can be interpreted in a number of ways. In signing it into law, the president hailed it as a quick response to corporate wrongdoing, reflecting the community's desire to have corporate wrongdoers punished. Critics could see it as a knee-jerk reaction to a particular set of problems, which will only result in the unethical seeking more creative ways of circumventing the law. Such critics are in effect rejecting the premises of the teleological argument outlined before; they do not believe that the Act will achieve its end. On the other hand, it might be countered that law enforcement is necessarily, to an extent, an ongoing process of closing loopholes and responding to creative criminality; the solution does not lie in abandoning the process, but in trying to get ahead of the criminals so that one is not playing catch-up.

While looking at legislative schemes to deal with corruption, it is necessary to briefly mention that most jurisdictions have elaborate arrangements to guard the democratic system against political, and particularly electoral, corruption. The United States Federal Electoral Commission exists to monitor compliance with the Federal Campaign Act; the act itself sets out elaborate rules regarding campaign funding and makes it an offense to break these rules.

Investigation

In order to bring corrupt offenders to justice, there needs to be an investigative capacity. Most typically, this is the police service, but in many jurisdictions, bodies with the specific responsibility to deal with corruption have been established. Both types of organizations will employ staff who need to be specifically trained and who have power to question witnesses; subpoena documents; utilize surveillance techniques (including telephone intercepts, and the planting of listening devices and hidden cameras); and prepare evidence for prosecution. The individuals and organizations that undertake these activities are in a very powerful position. They have access to an enormous amount of personal information, which could potentially be used to violate the privacy of citizens (see the discussion of suspects' rights in Chapter 9). They also play a crucial role in the effective handling of corruption. Thus, these individuals are subject to significant pressures to become corrupt themselves (see the discussion of noble cause corruption in Chapter 5). Accordingly, it is very important to have anti-corruption mechanisms to detect and deter corruption on the part of the investigators themselves. These mechanisms should have all the elements of a reactive system: offenses set down in legislation, an independent authority to determine cases, special powers to investigate and detect allegations of corruption, and specific penalties (like the loss of pension entitlements for investigators found to be corrupt).

An example of the sorts of mechanism that are put in place to deal with police corruption is those that apply to the New South Wales Police Service in Australia. This is a police service of some 14,000 officers, which has suffered a number of corruption scandals. Public concern reached its peak in the early 1990s, and a thorough investigation by the Wood Royal Commission made recommendations for sweeping changes in the way allegations of corruption were handled. As a result, an independent body, the Police Integrity Commission, was established under the New South Wales Police Integrity Commission Act 1996. The functions of the Police Integrity Commission, which are to deal with serious misconduct, can be summarized briefly as preventing, detecting, or investigating serious police misconduct; and managing or overseeing other agencies in the detection and investigation of serious police misconduct. The Police Integrity Commission investigates police conduct that falls within any one of the following classes:

- Perverting the course of justice (for example, by giving false evidence);
- Being involved in crimes attracting a minimum of five years imprisonment (for example, assault occasioning grievous bodily harm);
- Soliciting or accepting bribes;
- Improperly interfering in an investigation carried out by another police officer;
- Improperly investigating a complaint against another officer; and
- Being involved in the manufacture, cultivation, or supply of prohibited drugs.

Other kinds of police misconduct, such as abusive behavior, minor assault, negligence, and breaches of police rules and procedures, are matters dealt with by the New South Wales Police Service internally, with the New South Wales Ombudsman monitoring these kinds of complaints.

The Police Integrity Commission is not part of the New South Wales Police Service. Rather, it is an independent body. The commission employs experienced senior investigative staff comprising lawyers, accountants, current and former police investigators, and analysts, and is prevented from having serving or former members of the NSW Police Service on its staff. This emphasis on independence is clearly an attempt to deal with some of the conditions that we identified in Chapters 2 and 3 as being conducive to corruption—namely, the possibility of being influenced by the interests of one's "friends," or those to whom one is beholden, and the potential for corruption arising from conflicts of interest.

Besides internal corruption, another major issue faced by investigators is their independence in the context of their investigation into very senior figures in government. Here the nexus between power on the one hand, and corruption on the other, is salient. The potential for corruption in relation to the investigation of the crimes of the powerful is very great, unless the independence of investigators is protected. In the United States, one of the traditional mechanisms for investigating very senior figures in government was the appointment of a special prosecutor by the Attorney General. The limitations of this arrangement became very painfully obvious during the Watergate scandal. When the investigation by Special Prosecutor Archibald Cox threatened the presidency of Richard Nixon, Nixon ordered Attorney General Richardson to fire Cox. Both Richardson and his deputy resigned in protest, and Nixon appointed another attorney general who then fired Cox. The "Saturday Night Massacre" did not save Nixon's presidency, but it did cause widespread public debate about the capacity of the legal system to deal with high-level corruption.

The Ethics in Government Act 1978 contained provisions that stripped the attorney general of the authority to appoint independent counsel to conduct the preliminary investigations into allegations of corruption involving the president, vice president, Cabinet officers, top White House aides, and top officials of the Department of Justice, the Central Intelligence Agency, the Federal Bureau of Investigation, and certain campaign officials. The legislation established a panel of judges to appoint independent counsel and had a sunset clause of five years. President Reagan extended the independent counsel law in 1987, but by 1992 there was considerable opposition to the scheme, so this courageous experiment lapsed.

Proceeding further along the linear process of reactive action, effective handling of corruption requires that detection mechanisms are available. As has been stressed before, corruption is typically secretive. As argued in Chapter 2, the corrupt have at least two good reasons to fear exposure: first, detection may lead to criminal sanctions, and second, it may lead to moral sanctions emanating from the community and from significant others, for example, friends and relatives. Nevertheless, there are a number of sources of information in relation to most forms of corruption. One of the most important is fellow workers, who may report corrupt or suspicious activity to superiors or even blow the whistle. Chapter 8 will go into detail about whistleblowers, what motivates them, and why they need protection.

There are other sources of information in relation to corruption that investigators can use to assist them in their task. The advent of computers has seen the capacity to record and track virtually all financial transactions. Countries like Australia have stringent and elaborate arrangements controlling the operation of accounts in financial institutions, and requirements for the reporting of cash transactions over a certain limit, identifying and reporting suspicious transactions, and monitoring all overseas money transactions. This ability provides an invaluable source of information that can be used to detect corruption and to assist in its prosecution. As is the case with many of the mechanisms for dealing with corruption, transaction analysis is a very beneficial tool, but it comes at a moral cost: it impinges upon the privacy of members of the community. That is, transaction analysis involves vast amounts of information on citizens' financial activities being recorded and transmitted to enforcement agencies. We examine the rights of suspects and others in Chapter 9.

Courts

The next stage in the process is the prosecution of the corrupt in the courts. In developed countries, this process has the trust of the community, although it is not unknown for judges to be found guilty of corrupt behavior. In this connection, consider the Escobar case study in Chapter 2. In Australia,

Queensland's Chief Justice Vasta was stood down in 1989 for conflict-of-interest reasons; and in New South Wales, Chief Stipendiary Magistrate Murray Farquhar was removed from office in 1983 after a Royal Commission found that he had engaged in corrupt behavior. Fortunately, these have been rare events; nevertheless they serve to highlight the fact that judicial integrity cannot be taken for granted and that corruption of the prosecutorial process constitutes a serious obstacle to combating corruption. If the corrupt are to be prosecuted for their offenses, then there must be procedures in place to ensure that the holders of judicial office act with integrity and also that administrative processes are efficient, effective, and corruption-free, for example, cases are brought before the courts with minimum delay, files are not lost, and court officials act with integrity.

The final element of the criminal justice process is the carrying out of punishments that have been set by the courts. That too requires a series of mechanisms: jail procedures, parole procedures, suitably appointed buildings/cells to house inmates, and appropriately recruited and properly trained custodial staff. It is not unknown for these processes to be corrupted. In 1989, the New South Wales Corrective Services Minister was convicted and jailed for receiving bribes to arrange the early release of prisoners. We will deal with the efficacy and ethics of the punishment of the corrupt in Chapter 10.

PREVENTIVE ANTI-CORRUPTION SYSTEMS

A preventive anti-corruption system will typically embrace, or act in tandem with, a reactive anti-corruption system. However, we can consider preventive mechanisms for dealing with corruption independent of any reactive elements. If we do so, we see that they can be divided into three categories:

- Mechanisms for promoting an environment in which integrity is rewarded and, as a consequence, corrupt behavior is discouraged. This category is an attempt to reduce the desire or motivation to act corruptly, so that opportunities for corruption are not pursued or taken, even when they arise;
- The array of institutional mechanisms that limit (or eliminate) the opportunity for corrupt behavior. We have used the term "corporate governance" to characterize these mechanisms; and
- Those mechanisms that act to expose corrupt acts, so that the organization or community can deal with them. We have used the term "transparency" to characterize these mechanisms.

We accept that this threefold distinction is somewhat artificial and that some institutional mechanisms will in fact come under more than one heading, and indeed that some—for example, regulations—have both a reactive, as well as a preventive, role.

Promoting Ethical Behavior

The first category in our breakdown of prevention mechanisms are those institutional processes that exist to promote ethical behavior. This category is made up of those components of an anti-corruption system that engage with the individual's desire to do what is morally right and avoid what is morally wrong, and to be morally approved of by others for so acting. We will consider some of these institutional instruments under two broad headings, codes of ethics and regulatory frameworks.

Codes of Ethics

An example of an aspirational public sector statement of values is contained in Australia's Commonwealth Public Service Act 1999. Illustrative of the content of this statement is the description of the entity in the following terms:

> The Australian Public Service:
> - is apolitical, performing its functions in an impartial and professional manner;
> - is a public service in which employment decisions are based on merit;
> - provides a workplace that is free from discrimination and recognises and utilises the diversity of the Australian community it serves;
> - has the highest ethical standards;
> - is openly accountable for its actions, within the framework of Ministerial responsibility to the Government, the Parliament and the Australian public;
> - is responsive to the Government in providing frank, honest, comprehensive, accurate and timely advice and implementing the Government's policies and programs;
> - and so on . . .[109]

The United States equivalent is the following segment of Executive Order 12674, made by President Bush (senior) in 1989:

> Section 101. Principles of Ethical Conduct. To ensure that every citizen can have complete confidence in the integrity of the Federal Government, each Federal employee shall respect and adhere to the fundamental principles of ethical service as implemented in regulations promulgated under sections 201 and 301 of this order:
>
> (a) Public service is a public trust, requiring employees to place loyalty to the Constitution, the laws, and ethical principles above private gain.[110]

A corporate sector example of an ethics statement is from the transnational technology producer Motorola:

> Key beliefs define who we are—as individuals and as a company. Our key beliefs have defined us for many years to each other, to our customers, our shareholders, our suppliers, our competitors, and our communities.

Uncompromising integrity means staying true to what we believe. We adhere to honesty, fairness and "doing the right thing" without compromise, even when circumstances make it difficult.

Constant respect for people means we treat others with dignity, as we would like to be treated ourselves. Constant respect applies to every individual we interact with around the world.

Each of us is expected to demonstrate these key beliefs in our work as Motorolans.[111]

Two observations can be made about the nature of these sorts of statement. The first is that they are often couched in aspirational terms—they exhort the recipients to strive to achieve certain goals of exemplary behavior; they do not merely prescribe minimum moral standards. Unfortunately, there are often fundamental divergences between the reality of everyday practice and the behavior being recommended in ethical codes; the codes are "Pollyannaish." In the case of Motorola, the divergence is between the ethical conduct that managers and employees are supposed to aspire to, and the necessity for the organization to be profitable and competitive in the marketplace. Such divergences can engender a sense of skepticism in many recipients toward such instruments. The solution appears to be, first, that codes of ethics cease to be mere window dressing by facing up to real and difficult moral problems and by offering guidance in relation to them; and, second, that where appropriate, employees and others begin to seriously rethink their day-to-day practices in the light of moral principles and ethical concerns.

The second observation is that such codes of ethics necessarily reflect values that are generally accepted in the community. At a very basic level, the terms that they use—like "trust," "ethical," and "honesty"—have meanings that individuals bring to the context in which they are operating. To a large extent, statements of values are reflective of the underlying moral values of the community from which the employees are drawn and serve to remind employees that they are also operative in the work context. However, the point about an effective code of ethics—as opposed to a piece of window dressing—is that it is the result of a process of collective reflection and discussion in which basic community values and moral principles are applied to, and refined in, specific work contexts; the result should be a set of meaningful ethical prescriptions in relation to behavior and attitudes in the workplace.

Effective codes of ethics facilitate the engagement between preexisting moral values on the one hand, and the reality of day-to-day practice on the other. That said, even effective statements of values and codes of conduct alone are obviously not sufficient to create an ethical organizational climate.

Another institutional element necessary for promoting ethical values in the public sector are the institutional entities that have been created to oversee these ethics frameworks. For the statements provided before, they are (respectively) the Australian Public Service Commission and the United States Office of Government Ethics. Both of these have a role of providing institutional leadership in promoting ethics, articulating the detailed procedures, and monitoring compliance with the third element—the regulatory framework.

Regulatory Frameworks

Regulatory frameworks exist to achieve a number of things—including providing the threshold point for reactive responses, such as investigation—but one of the central ones is to promote ethical behavior. One of the most important ways that they do this is not by setting minimum standards and enforcing compliance with the threat of punishment, but rather by regulating practices known to embody some of the conditions that facilitate corruption, for example, conflicts of interest (see Chapters 2 and 3).

The United States has a highly developed and elaborate regulatory framework[112] that applies to public employees, top officials, Cabinet members, and elected representatives. Some of the key elements of this framework are as follows:

- The Appearance of Impropriety Rule, which was authorized by President Johnson in 1965[113] and was aimed specifically at conflict of interest issues. The Rule required all executive branch employees and officials "to avoid any action . . . which might result in, or create the appearance of 1) using public office for private gain, 2) giving preferential treatment to any organization or person, 3) impeding government efficiency or economy, 4) losing complete independence or impartiality, 5) making a government decision outside official channels, or 6) affecting adversely the confidence of the public in the integrity of the Government";
- Blind trusts are mechanisms by which the assets of high-level officials are placed under the control of an independent trustee and the trustee buys, sells, and trades assets without the knowledge or influence of the asset holder. The purpose is to enable the official to protect assets while avoiding conflicts of interest. The Ethics in Government Act 1978 gave the Office of Government Ethics responsibility for blind trusts; however, their use became infrequent. In recognition of the lack of use of blind trusts, the Ethics Reform Act 1989 included provisions for Certificates of Divestiture, which required officials to sell assets, but they were then able to roll over the funds into financial instruments like mutual funds and defer paying capital gains tax from the sale of the asset;
- Conflict of interest prohibitions specifically regulating gifts from outside sources, gifts between employees, conflicting financial interests, outside employment activities, misuse of position and restrictions on former employees. These prohibitions have been brought together under the Bribery and Conflict of Interest Act 1978;
- Rules governing honorariums prohibit the acceptance of fees for the giving of speeches, and the attending of conferences and other special events. They specifically target elected representatives and senior officials, and over time

have become more and more restrictive, with the current austere prohibitions enacted as part of the Ethics Reform Act 1989; and

- "Revolving door" restrictions address the long-standing community concerns that elected representatives and senior officials leave their positions to work for companies whose business it is to lobby government or that have significant business dealings with government. The concern arises from the suspicion that prior to leaving, the officials will set up (in secret) highly lucrative deals so as to attract high salaries from their future employers, and/or use their extensive social contacts within government to give their new employer an unfair advantage. Over time, the "revolving door" restrictions have become more specific and wider in scope. The Ethics in Government Act 1978 mandated a one-year "cooling off" period, delaying the take-up of the new position, and prohibited former officials from contacting anyone in their former government agencies on behalf of their new employers. The Ethics Reform Act 1989 subjected members of Congress to the regime.

It is clear from the descriptions of the preceding mechanisms that the processes for regulating ethical behavior have, over time, become more and more complex. In a spirited attack upon this trend, Frank Anechiarico and James B. Jacobs, in their book *The Pursuit of Absolute Integrity: How Corruption Control Makes Government Ineffective,* have pointed to this complexity, and they argue that the elaborateness of these mechanisms is such that they adversely impact upon the capacity of public sector organizations to do their job.[114] They advocate a greater emphasis on promoting ethical values, rather than relying on regulatory mechanisms.

The U.S. regulatory framework includes institutions with investigatory and enforcement functions. Legislators are dealt with by ethics committees (for the House, the Committee on Standards of Official Conduct, and for the Senate, the Senate Select Committee on Ethics). The executive level of government is subject to the Office of Government Ethics.

Before leaving the notion of a regulatory framework, it is worth considering briefly a very important aspect of the regulatory framework that protects the political system from corruption. These are the mechanisms to ensure that free and fair elections are not compromised by the payment of money to particular political parties without the knowledge of the electors.

In modern democracies, advertising plays a very significant role in political campaigns. Candidates for political office can spend many millions of dollars in slick, expensive advertising campaigns. It is generally accepted that a political grouping without access to funds is very unlikely to be elected. Moreover, it is very important for the citizens of the country to know where the money to pay for the political advertisements is coming from. As was said in the debate introducing legislation to regulate campaign donations in Australia: "It is simply naive to believe that no big donor is ever likely to want his cut sometime. Australians deserve to know who is giving money to political parties and how much."

The United States has an elaborate framework, the basis of which is the Federal Election Campaign Act 1971. The core of this system, and of systems like it in other democracies, is a framework for the public disclosure of campaign donations and campaign spending. It is not surprising that with the stakes so high, political parties will use every ruse possible to circumvent the framework. Typical of the inexorable search for loopholes were the "soft money" scandals in the 1996 presidential elections in which both the Republican and the Democratic parties took advantage of a Federal Election Committee ruling on "issue ads." Funding for ads on particular issues that benefited one party or disadvantaged the other skyrocketed—the Democrats were reported as spending over $40 million to assist in President Clinton's reelection. This event created a controversy that led to tightening of the rules.

A similar exploitation of loopholes in Australia enabled one political party to evade the restrictions on campaign donations by running up a large debt during the campaign and then creating a corporate entity that lent the party the money to pay off the debt with a very long-term interest-free loan. The political donors subsidized the company rather than making direct donations and thus fell outside the disclosure provisions of the Australian Electoral Act. As in the preceding U.S. case, the Australian Parliament moved quickly to close the loophole.

As well as the disclosure regime, Australia has adopted another mechanism for limiting the potential for corruption in the electoral system. The electoral legislation also contains provisions for the public funding of political parties to run their electoral campaigns. These provisions were introduced in 1983.

The purpose of public funding of political parties was to avoid the problems of political parties having to raise large amounts of money to run campaigns. Registered political parties, independent candidates, and Senate groupings that receive more than 4 percent of the total, formal, first preference vote are entitled to funding. Currently, the rate of funding is $1.84 (Australian) per vote. Some 33 million Australian dollars of public funding was paid to the political parties for the 1998 federal election.

There has been some criticism of the scheme in that it tends to favor the larger, existing political entities at the expense of the smaller parties that are struggling to gain recognition. A right-wing, populist political movement (One Nation) went against this trend by obtaining enough support at its first entry into the federal political arena in the 1998 election and qualifying for public election funding. That short-lived political movement has been the focus of investigation for providing misleading information about its status as a political party and for the diversion of funds by its leader, Pauline Hanson, for her personal use.

Turning back to the private sector, Enron provides a spectacular example of an organization in which the integrity processes broke down—to the extent that organizational integrity was replaced with organizational deviance (see Chapter 2):

- There were excessive payments to Enron management. Enron is credited with creating 2,000 millionaires—the CEO earned $140 million in one year. Executives who negotiated the power deal in India got $50 million bonuses even though the deal failed.
- There were executive stock options, so that executives had an interest in not looking too hard at the suspect deals because they would be personally disadvantaged if the share price stopped rising.
- There were straddling entities. Andrew Fastow was also managing director of companies set up to buy Enron assets that no one else would buy. Fastow pocketed $30 million—basically stolen from Enron.
- Enron executives sold out all their stock options when they saw that the share price was falling rapidly. They did this secretly, so that other shareholders suffered, particularly staff who had share options in lieu of superannuation. This practice was made even more offensive by the CEO, Kenneth Lay, who sent e-mails to his staff urging them to buy more Enron shares.
- Complicit in the deviance just outlined was Arthur Andersen (AA). That company earned $52 million in fees in 2000 from Enron—indeed, Enron was AA's largest client and acted as Enron's management consultant. The situation was exacerbated by a "revolving door" of AA staff working for Enron. One AA auditor who questioned Enron's business practices was reassigned to another client at Enron's request.

Recall that our first category of mechanisms for dealing with corruption was reactive mechanisms. Attached to the procedures for promoting ethical behavior—a preventive mechanism—there are frequently disciplinary processes that come into play when there are breaches of ethical behavior. These processes are usually in-house, involve some form of formal process for investigating the facts of the issue, and then a scale of penalties that range from a reprimand through to dismissal.

Corporate Governance

At a general level, corporate governance describes the elements of organizational control and accountability necessary for the good management of any organization. The processes that are involved in corporate governance also play a crucial role in controlling corruption. Reactive anti-corruption systems involve elements, such as investigation, adjudication, and punishment, that are specifically concerned with combating corruption. By contrast, preventive anti-corruption systems involve elements, such as promoting ethical behavior, that have a broader purpose than just combating corruption; clearly, a good ethical climate in an organization provides benefits above and beyond reducing corruption, for example, it enhances good relations with customers and clients. At any rate, the point to be made here is that although good corporate governance is central to combating corruption, it also has other and wider purposes. Moreover, given the nexus between corruption and, for example, incompetence, good corporate governance often reduces corruption by way of an indirect route, for example, by enhancing competence.

Corporate governance mechanisms operate at an organizational level, rather than at the broader community level. In this respect, corporate governance mechanisms are unlike the criminal justice mechanisms we looked at in our consideration of reactive systems. That said, corporate governance mechanisms rely on reactive systems, including the criminal justice system. It is now widely believed that properly designed corporate governance mechanisms can effectively limit the opportunities for corruption and thereby reduce corruption. The thought behind this line of argument is that corruption prevention is a better option than attempting to deal with the problem after it has occurred.

The notion of corporate governance is sometimes thought of in narrow and strict terms as being the elaborate system of relevant statute law, case law, guidelines, boards, committees, and administrative infrastructure that exist in the private sector.[115]

Looking for the moment at what is (traditionally) thought of as corporate governance in the private sector, the Australian Stock Exchange Listing Rules[116] set down what is effectively a definition of what is corporate governance for a private sector body. These rules are as follows:

- Policies and procedures for appointing members of the governing body, removing them, and having nonexecutive directors;
- Capacity for the governing body to seek independent advice;
- Robust audit procedures;
- Procedures for managing business risk; and
- Policies and procedures for promoting ethical standards and conduct.

Having looked at the menu, it is useful for us to look briefly at the structures that are designed to ensure that all the items on the menu are properly dealt with. The most important is the Board of Directors. Its functions can be summarized as being responsible for the following:

- Establishing the company's strategic direction;
- Providing the leadership to effect those strategies;
- Supervising the management of the business;
- Monitoring financial performance;
- Being responsible for senior management appointments; and
- Reporting to shareholders on their stewardship.

Directors have specific duties: to act in good faith and for proper purposes; to exercise duty of care, skill, and diligence; and to act honestly and refrain from making improper use of position. Most large companies have a number of committees that work with the Board of Directors. They include the Audit Committee, the Compensation (Remuneration) Committee, the Nomination Committee, the Finance Committee, and the Business Risk Committee.

Very relevant to the issue of corruption has been the extension of the structures of corporate governance to the public sector. An indication of the extent of this change is the publication in 1997 of the *Better Practice Guide: Applying Principles and Practice of Corporate Governance in Budget Funded Agencies* by the Australian National Audit Office (ANAO). One of the things that is most interesting about this document is that it would never have even been contemplated in Australia twenty years ago. The reason for this change is that two decades ago, a permanent head (they were not called CEOs then) of a public service department, or authority, had relatively little authority to undertake what we now define as corporate governance functions. Everything that the permanent head needed to know about these functions was directed by the relevant central agency. For example, the Commonwealth and states all had a Public Service Board that ran recruitment, appointed all staff, classified and created positions, set salaries and terms of employment, managed industrial disputes, and so on. Today, that centrally managed system has been largely devolved.

The ANAO document described above sets forth the key elements of corporate governance in the Australian public sector as the following:

- Ethical structures;
- Internal accountability structures;
- External accountability and reporting structures;
- External management structures; and
- Resource management structures.

In looking at these elements, it is useful to consider the key difference between the public sector and the private sector. The difference is that in relation to every action they take, public sector agencies are accountable to the government, to the Parliament and—ultimately—to the citizens.

Even after the changes that have taken place over the last two decades, there remain significant elements of external control in public sector agencies. Very briefly, these are: direct scrutiny from Parliament (in Australia) or Congress (in the United States); operating within a complex and demanding legal framework (covering fields like privacy, administrative review, archives, sexual discrimination, freedom of information, protection of witnesses, reporting of fraud and corruption); operating within a comprehensive set of financial processes, whereby all monies expended are appropriated through statute, and the resource processes are governed by legislative regimes; and being subject to an array of external governance mechanisms (Ombudsman's offices, anti-corruption agencies).

Central agencies, notwithstanding their much more limited role, still exercise authority over public sector agencies. Although this authority is often less prescriptive than it has been in the past, there is a plethora of guidelines, policies, standards, and procedures for the agency to follow—occupational health and safety, workplace bargaining, computer security, anti-fraud/anti-corruption policies, protective security, and so on. Therefore, we can see that although the corporate governance mechanisms that apply to the private sector may be different from those in the public sector, they share a common element of being internal organizational administrative processes designed to promote accountability to an external authority.

The following paragraphs outline some of the more important types of corporate governance mechanisms that have a corruption control function. Note that a number of these mechanisms directly address some of the causes of, and conditions conducive to, corruption that we identified in Chapters 2 and 3, for example, power imbalances between superiors and subordinates in relation to, for example, promotion within an organization.

Processes for Recruitment and Promotion

In the public sector, a major form of corruption has been the awarding of public service (civil service in the United Kingdom) positions on the basis of nepotism, cronyism, or political affiliation. In the United Kingdom, these practices were so widespread that in the mid–nineteenth century a wide-ranging inquiry was held. The subsequent Northcote-Trevelyon Report established in the British civil service statutory independence for the promotion and appointment of civil servants. This system was adopted in Australia and had added to it processes for selection purely on the basis of merit, with promotion processes given a legislative backing. In the United States, a similar system operated—called the "spoils system"—which was dealt with by the Pendleton Act of 1883. Over time, the procedures have been refined so that they are much more wide-ranging in scope and have a comprehensive merit protection system based upon presidential directives and legislation.

Typically, modern recruitment systems rely upon open advertisement of positions, precise job descriptions and selection criteria, interview panels sensitive to minority interests, and procedures for the provision of reasons as to why unsuccessful candidates were not selected. Procedures such as these are now commonplace in the public sector and in large private-sector organizations, and they play an important role in limiting nepotism. Also, such requirements discourage the formation of closed groups of employees able to exercise power corruptly.

Independent Auditing

Procedures for the independent auditing of public sector, private sector, and community organizations are a key element in dealing with corruption. The knowledge that an independent body will be examining the financial records of an organization should act to inhibit corrupt activity. The Enron case illustrates this point; Enron staff deliberately ignored accepted accounting practice in the valuing of assets when they conspired with the banks to represent loans as profits.

Tendering and Contracting

Procedures for tendering and contracting also play a role in inhibiting corruption. Experience in many countries has shown that these activities are often subject to corruption. Over time a variety of procedures have been developed to eliminate or inhibit corruption of the tendering process. These procedures include requirements to advertise tenders, to make clear specification of the work to be done and of the criteria for success in the tender process, to establish systems to guarantee that tenders are not accessed by persons other than the designated authorities, and so on.

In the mid-1980s, the Federal Bureau of Investigation conducted a wide-ranging investigation (known as "ill-wind") into the selling of confidential procurement information from within the Department of Defense to major defense contractors. These contractors were thus able to bid for defense contracts with an unfair advantage. The investigation resulted in 64 convictions of individuals implicated in the fraud, and some defense contractors were required to pay $250 million in fines. The response to this scandal was the Federal Procurement Policy Act Amendments of 1988, more popularly known as the Procurement Integrity Act. This legislation put in place restrictions on current and former federal officials who handled procurement for the purpose of ensuring ethical behavior. In particular, the statute prohibited contractors from providing gifts and gratuities, jobs, and buying or obtaining information on government procurement contracts. This goal was accompanied by provisions for severe penalties of up to five years imprisonment for offending individuals, and fines of up to $1 million for offending companies. In the face of concerns that these stringent restrictions would deter individuals from working in government procurement jobs, these provisions were subsequently watered down in 1996.

Risk Management

Risk management was a part of the package of measures that was introduced into the corporate governance framework as a result of the

Treadway Commission, and the work of the Council of Sponsoring Organizations, to deal with what were seen as the corporate excesses of the 1980s. Very briefly, risk management is a technique for rationally identifying and prioritizing risks, and then developing and implementing treatment options.[117] Risk management can be a very powerful tool for dealing with corruption. When undertaken with expertise and broad participation, risk management can identify inadequacies in corruption controls and can assist in the development and implementation of treatments for those inadequacies.

The Australian Public Service has adopted a policy[118] that specifically recommends adopting risk management techniques as the basis for fraud and corruption prevention. Agencies are required by legislation to undertake a fraud and corruption risk assessment at least every two years and to produce a fraud and corruption control plan. The guideline sets down very broad requirements for undertaking the risk assessment, identifying fraud and corruption vulnerabilities, and preparing a detailed plan to treat fraud and corruption risks.

Although producing some very positive results, the Australian government's policy of mandatory risk management for fraud and corruption control arrangements has not been totally successful. A survey of the arrangements undertaken by the Australian Auditor-General in 2000 found the following:

- That 36 percent of responding agencies had not undertaken a fraud and corruption risk assessment within the last two years as required by the policy;
- That 15 percent of agencies had not prepared a fraud and corruption control plan; and
- That of the agencies that had prepared a fraud and corruption control plan, 13 percent had not undertaken a fraud and corruption risk assessment.[119]

As a part of that process, the Office of the Auditor-General reviewed a sample of fraud and corruption control plans, and found that few met all the criteria set out in the policy; some did not address fraud and corruption risks that were identified; and a significant proportion did not include an adequate timetable for implementation, and mechanisms to monitor implementation were absent.

Before leaving fraud and corruption prevention, there is one very difficult problem that stems from the application of risk management techniques. In many enterprises (flying a plane, building a dam), there is a point at which risks have been reduced to such a degree that it is deemed prudent to proceed with the activity, on the understanding that the residual risk is an "acceptable risk." In a public sector organizational setting, even the most trivial or unlikely fraud and/or corruption incident can create a considerable amount of public criticism. This potential leaves decision-makers in a difficult position. On the one hand, adopting a risk management approach might be the most rational response to corruption reduction, considered independently of the consequences of adverse public opinion to corruption disclosures. On the other hand, given the adverse public reaction to even trivial instances of corruption, adopting a risk management approach might not be the most rational course of action.

Transparency

Let us now turn to the last of the three types of preventive mechanisms for combating corruption, namely transparency mechanisms.

As has been noted a number of times already in this book, one of the most important conditions conducive to corruption is secretiveness. Hence, the importance of transparency mechanisms—mechanisms that ensure that transactions are conducted openly and/or are subject to appropriate scrutiny—is therefore a key element in combating corruption.

A fully functioning parliamentary system plays a central role in deterring public sector corruption, because public sector officials are required to go through a detailed and rigorous process in relation to their expenditure of public monies and their exercise of the powers vested in the public offices that they occupy. Congressional committees in the United States, and Parliamentary committees in the United Kingdom and Australia, play a crucial role in making officials accountable for their actions by using powers to require those officials to explain their actions. At a less dramatic level, there are a variety of public institutions that operate to enable the community to be assured that officials are acting in accordance with the detailed accounting requirements that are in place in the public sector. One of these is the Auditor-General (or the General Accounting Office in the United States). Reports of these bodies make transparent the details of expenditure of public monies.

Operating at yet another level are those mechanisms of transparency that enable citizens to access reasons for decisions that affect them (Administrative Appeals Tribunal Act, Administrative Decisions [Judicial Review] Act), and information (Freedom of Information Act, Privacy Act, Archives Act). All the mechanisms previously described operate to open the workings of government to scrutiny and therefore enable the community to assess whether they are being governed in a way that meets their expectations of integrity.

A parallel, though typically less onerous, set of transparency mechanisms operates in the commercial sphere. Companies are required to file certain reports about their activities, and these are made public. The intent behind these processes is to make key decisions transparent and to assist the community in making judgments about investments. These transparency mechanisms have the force of law, and failure to comply with them is a criminal offense.

Before leaving the role of transparency, it is necessary to mention the crucial role that the media plays in the exposure of corruption, and therefore, if the other mechanisms are operating effectively, in combating corruption. A vibrant and free media is essential in bringing to the community's attention corrupt acts—whether they occur in the corporate sector, like Enron, or in the public sector.

HOLISTIC ANTI-CORRUPTION SYSTEMS

Thus far in our analysis of anti-corruption systems, we have looked at anti-corruption systems and mechanisms under the headings of reactive systems and preventive systems, and in relation to preventive systems, we have considered the issues under the subheadings of promoting ethical behavior, corporate governance, and transparency. It is evident that in most societies, jurisdictions, and indeed organizations, the attempt to combat corruption involves all of these. That is, anti-corruption strategies involve reactive systems as well as preventive systems, and within preventive systems there are mechanisms that promote ethical behavior, there are corporate governance mechanisms with an anti-corruption function, and there are various transparency mechanisms. Moreover, it seems clear that an adequate anti-corruption strategy cannot afford to do without reactive as well as preventive systems, and that preventive systems need to have all the elements just detailed. This consideration suggests that there are two important issues. The first is the adequacy of each of the elements of the preceding systems, for example, how adequate is the investigative capacity or the mechanisms of transparency? The second issue pertains to the level of integration and complementarity between the reactive and the preventive systems; to what extent do they act together to mutually reinforce one another?

In this connection, it is worth noting that many jurisdictions have corruption "watch-dog" agencies, like the Independent Commissions Against Corruption in Hong Kong and in the state of New South Wales in Australia. These bodies are established by statutes that also define a range of offenses, and have powers to investigate and to refer matters to the courts for prosecution. However, it is noticeable that these watch-dog agencies involve themselves in corruption prevention programs that involve the development of preventive mechanisms; they no longer see their role as merely that of a reactive agency.

In the past, there has been a tendency to advocate some specific remedy to deal with a corruption problem that has been identified. Of course, in some situations, it is possible to identify some clear administrative or legal shortcoming that can resolve the particular corruption problem. However, it is far more likely that the corruption problem requires recourse to a wide range of integrated anti-corruption mechanisms. More generally, it is likely that the best anti-corruption systems are holistic in character. In short, it is best to conceive of specific anti-corruption mechanisms as elements of a holistic anti-corruption system.

In looking at the set of anti-corruption processes as a holistic system, we need first to remind ourselves what is presupposed by an anti-corruption system. First, and most obviously, there must be some shared moral values in relation to the moral unacceptability of specific forms of corruption, and a disapproval of those who engage in such corruption. That is, there needs to be a framework of social norms. Second, there needs to be a broadly shared conception in relation to what needs to be done to minimize it, for example, should it be criminalized? Third, there needs to be present some capacity to create and implement mechanisms that deal with the issue of corruption, and this requirement presumes some form of legal system and organizational structure. Finally, there needs to be some source of authority whereby sanctions can be applied to individuals who commit corrupt acts.

Anti-corruption systems exist at different levels, and in any particular jurisdiction they are likely to be interrelated. The peak level of anti-corruption systems will be at the level of the nation-state. Governments will pass laws creating offenses that will apply universally to all persons acting within the nation's borders. Nested within that national system will be a number of anti-corruption systems that apply to a collective of organizations.[120] Industries, groups of sporting clubs, and groups of public service agencies can operate collectively to develop anti-corruption mechanisms that apply to all organizations within that collective. Finally, at the lowest level are the local anti-corruption systems that apply to individual organizations.

Let us see how the different levels of anti-corruption systems might operate in practice. Let us take the case of corruption in the sporting arena. In a recent Australian sporting scandal, the Canterbury Rugby League team in Sydney made payments to players over the agreed salary cap set by the National Rugby League. Those monies were allegedly dishonestly obtained from a major project for building a sports arena. The obtaining of the monies was investigated by the Independent Commission Against Corruption, although no charges were ultimately laid. Thus, the New South Wales state anti-corruption system came into play, and the individuals involved confronted the possibility of being investigated, being charged, and facing a jail sentence. At the collective level, the national association of football clubs, the National Rugby League, stripped competition points from the club, thus exacting a penalty against the club and its fans. At the club level, the offending officials have been stood down. In this example, all three levels took punitive action—of varying degrees of seriousness.

Having discussed what an anti-corruption system looks like, we can now identify some of the key properties of an effective and vibrant anti-corruption system.

One of these factors is leadership. Whether the anti-corruption message is coming from the president of the United States, the company management, or the school principal, an effective anti-corruption campaign requires clear articulation and a strong and visible commitment on the part of the leadership. That said, there is a danger—particularly in organizations or countries in which the governing bodies are weak—that the function of leadership is overestimated. Moreover, even when an individual leader is strong and committed to an anti-corruption program, problems can arise. Specifically, if the necessary institutional mechanisms are not established and entrenched, then the result can be disastrous when the charismatic corruption fighter moves on; the anti-corruption program withers in the absence of the strong and committed leader.

Another feature of a good anti-corruption system is impartiality, and the capacity to deal with the powerful in particular. Put simply, the real test of an effective anti-corruption system is its capacity to deal with corruption cases in which the perpetrators are powerful. It is relatively easy to establish systems that act disproportionately against the least powerful, like junior customs officials who extort small bribes from visitors arriving or leaving the country. The test of the system is whether it can act against the head of the customs service, or the prime minister, who profit from corruption. This issue is critical because if the aim is to eliminate corruption, then it follows that the system must be capable of dealing with the most serious forms of corruption. Moreover, nothing undermines the legitimacy of an anti-corruption system more than the perception that persons involved in petty corruption pay a heavy price, whereas their leaders who are engaged in far more serious acts of corruption are left alone.

A good anti-corruption system maintains a balance between its component parts. Effective operation not only requires that all of these components be present but also that there be a reasonable balance between them. The most obvious example of an anti-corruption system out of balance is one that relies totally on harsh and vigorous enforcement to the exclusion of all other mechanisms. Such systems tend to create a secretive and punitive culture. Secretiveness is generated because if mistakes or minor misdemeanors are disclosed, they are harshly treated. But, as we have seen, secretiveness facilitates corruption. On the other hand, the power of those in authority is greatly increased by virtue of their capacity and tendency to mete out harsh punishment. But, as we have seen, power facilitates corruption.

A final, and related, indicator of the effectiveness of an anti-corruption system is transparency. As we know, corruption thrives in environments in which the members of a community or organization are unable to obtain key information, whether it be through an effective news media, elected representatives, or individuals who wish to come forward and bring corrupt practices to light.

Systemic Corruption

In Chapter 1, the various types of corruption were identified—individual, organizational, organized, grand, and systemic. So far we have looked at anti-corruption mechanisms in the context of individual and (especially) organizational corruption. However, when there is corruption that is pervasive (systemic) and/or engaged in by crime organizations (organized), and it exists at the very highest level of a society (grand)—for example, in the judiciary, the police, the legislature, and the electoral system—the anti-corruption system may need special features or may need to be bolstered in various ways. The difficulty that the United States has had with the independent counsel processes described before are indicative of the complexities involved in creating effective mechanisms that deal with those in positions of power. In these situations, the impetus for dealing with corruption may need to come from outside the political process itself.

Many states in the world are teetering on the edge of collapse through the weight of poverty, corruption, and mismanagement. In a globalized economy, there are a number of leverage points that can be utilized in relation to states in this condition. Aid bodies, and international lending bodies like the World Bank, the OECD, and the Asia Development Bank, are reluctant to put funds into countries where the corruption is at such a level that there is an expectation that a significant proportion will be diverted into the pockets of the powerful. However, there is an increasing awareness in these bodies that for the aid to be effective, it is necessary to invest in targeted programs to enhance governance, particularly anti-corruption programs. All over the developing world, there are teams of experts—usually from the West—who are undertaking this detailed process. This is part of what is called "capacity building," and an example is the work that the Australian Ombudsman's Office and the Australian Electoral Commission undertake in the Pacific region, providing specific advice and training—sometimes down to the level of establishing and maintaining a workable registry system.

Nongovernment bodies like Transparency International play a crucial role in exposing corruption to the international community through tools like the Corruption Perception Index, which ranks most countries in the world upon their propensity to be corrupt. Exposure of this nature has the effect of mobilizing those elements within the country to push for a strengthening of anti-corruption mechanisms. It also alerts the international community to the internal problems of a given country, and this alert can have the effect of encouraging investors, lenders, and aid providers to make their contributions contingent upon the development and maintenance of effective anti-corruption strategies.

There is no template for what action is best for failing states. In Papua New Guinea to Australia's north, the problems with politicians appropriating public monies for buying off votes are endemic. AUSAID, the Australian aid agency, is providing modest funding for women's groups that are campaigning actively against corruption of the political system. This aid is paying dividends, as these groups can now travel out to villages and explain to villagers that the funds used for buying their votes mean that schools and public health clinics are not being provided. In a country with very limited television and radio coverage and a high rate of illiteracy, this direct approach to enhancing civil society is having immediate effects upon the corrupt politicians.

IMPACT OF DEVELOPMENTS IN PUBLIC SECTOR ADMINISTRATION ON DEALING WITH CORRUPTION

Before leaving the issue of anti-corruption systems, we will describe one of the emerging issues in this area. Public sectors throughout the world have been in a state of transformation in the last two decades. What has been advocated, and in large part adopted, is the provision of public services by private sector providers on a contractual basis. Many countries have adopted this purchaser/provider model for the delivery of public services. At its best, this model can bypass inefficient and unresponsive public sector bureaucracies with skilled and dynamic private sector providers keen to fulfill their contractual obligations. This fundamental change that is sweeping through public sector administration and that is being advocated by bodies like the World Bank, has various implications for corruption control.

Rhodes provides an analysis of trends in public sector management in the United Kingdom.[121] He lists the key changes to the U.K. public sector as being the following: privatization; marketization; corporate management; regulation (as the state has pulled back from doing things, it has moved to influence the outcomes by regulatory frameworks and audit regimes); and political control. With regard to the final factor, Rhodes identifies the assertion of authority by ministers (but not necessarily Parliament) over senior public servants by making them more responsive to their direct political instructions. Rhodes goes on to identify a number of what he calls "unintended consequences" of the new public sector management:

- Fragmentation—services formerly delivered by government are now delivered by a variety of bodies;
- Steering—there is a dilution of government control;
- Accountability—the complexity of the arrangements, particularly where they involve commercial contractual relationships, make governments less answerable to the electorate;

- Coordination—the diversity of players makes coordination difficult; and
- Public service ethics—there is an erosion of the traditional standards of ethical behavior in the public sector (a species of moral confusion, in our terms: see Chapter 2).

The set of issues that faces implementing effective anti-corruption systems in this new administrative environment starts with attempting to operate a compliance regime when the mechanisms for ensuring compliance have been removed or decentralized. As central coordination bodies lose influence, the capacity to run anti-corruption campaigns that impact upon all elements of the public sector wanes.

Outsourcing brings another range of issues to anti-corruption campaigns. In Australia, the Australian National Audit Office iterates the "good housekeeping" list of ways in which agencies can control fraud and corruption, when services are being provided by the private sector. These include the following:

- Supplying third-party providers with their anti-corruption policy;
- Conducting robust tendering processes;
- Establishing appropriate contract conditions and access provisions to ensure that performance and financial requirements are met;
- Keeping adequate records; and
- Maintaining, monitoring, and reporting arrangements to provide an adequate flow of information to assess performance against the contracted requirement.

In a purchaser-provider model, large bureaucratic structures, with their multiple levels of control and complex operating procedures, are replaced with a contractual agreement. To be effective, that contractual agreement has to be very carefully structured to ensure that the roles and obligations of all parties are spelled out. Comprehensive costing of the service and examination of all contingencies need to be undertaken. Otherwise, the savings may turn out to be illusory.

From a corruption control perspective, the key element of these purchaser/provider arrangements is the tendering process itself. Large amounts of public monies are involved, and the potential for corruption is inevitably high.

The purchaser-provider model raises other issues for anti-corruption—including fraud control—programs. The contractual basis of the arrangement is almost inevitably regarded as commercial-in-confidence. This feature makes review by external bodies, and by the public, problematic. Also, one of the underpinnings of all anti-corruption programs is that the participants have an agreed set of ethical values and principles. But private sector organizations do not necessarily have an adequate appreciation of public sector ethics, even public sector ethics relativized to the new forms of public sector management.

The move toward providing services online and electronic financial transactions raises another set of issues for effective anti-corruption programs. The technology provides the capacity for sophisticated security and audit functions. However, it also raises a whole new set of risks. One of the more obvious is the capacity to investigate suspect transactions in a complex information technology system. The number of investigators skilled in these techniques is still relatively small, and police services are finding it very difficult to hold onto them in the face of lucrative job offers in the private sector.

CONCLUSION

In this chapter, we have set out and analyzed a large array of institutional mechanisms that have been put into place in an attempt to combat corruption. We have sought to highlight some of the key problem areas—areas that appear most resistant to systematic solutions. It is most important to realize that although corruption has universal elements that transcend cultural boundaries, different technological environments, and so on, the anti-corruption mechanisms that may be the most effective need to be sensitive to cultural and technological context. In a highly religious society, appeals to individuals to act in accord with the ethical principles enshrined in religious texts is likely to have greater effect than in a secular society, notwithstanding the fact that the ethical principles in question may be substantially the same in the two societies.

Most important, we have emphasized the superiority of what we have termed "holistic anti-corruption systems" over alternative methods of combating corruption. First, the elements of such systems, for example, the investigatory agency and processes, are adequate to their role. Second, such systems have both reactive and preventive component systems. Third, and crucially, the reactive and preventive components (and the subelements of each of these) have a high level of complementarity and integration—accordingly, they mutually reinforce one another.

chapter eight

Whistleblowing

In this chapter, we cover

- What whistleblowing is
- The relationship between whistleblowing and corruption
- Some theories as to why whistleblowing might occur
- What can be done to deal with whistleblowing
- Some of the shortcomings of whistleblower schemes.

In the early days of coal mining, miners used to take a canary in a cage down into the mine. If lethal gases were present, the canary would die, and the miners would be alerted to the danger before it was too late for them. In some ways, the position of the whistleblower is analogous to that of those unfortunate canaries. The whistleblower is sensitive to wrongdoing before its existence percolates through to management. And like the canary, the whistleblower is often sacrificed for the greater good of the community.

On the face of it, the notion of whistleblowing is fairly straightforward. We all know of famous cases in which courageous individuals fought against the odds to expose wrongdoing in the organization that they worked for. These individuals suffered derision, harassment, loss of employment, and sometimes threats to their physical safety. Some famous names immediately spring to mind: Karen Silkwood, who exposed the unsafe practices in Kerr McGee's plutonium-processing plant in which she worked; Clive Ponting, the British civil servant who exposed the government cover-up of the sinking of the Argentinian warship *General Belgrano* during the Falklands War; Elsie Elliott, the Hong Kong resident whose tireless exposure of fraud and corruption assisted in creating the climate in which the Independent Commission Against Corruption could be established; and Ernest Fitzgerald, an employee of the U.S. Department of Defense, who testified before a Congressional committee about a $2 billion cost overrun on a Lockheed contract for the supply of military transport aircraft. Many of these identities have entered the popular culture. Almost certainly each of us will know about whistleblowers in our own workplace or, more likely, in our professional area.

For purposes of illustration, it is useful to look in some detail at an actual case of whistleblowing.

CASE STUDY 8.1   Pentagon Papers

Daniel Ellsberg was a brilliant career civil servant with a Ph.D. in economics from Harvard University. He started out as a supporter of the U.S. military involvement in Vietnam—he served as a Marine after he had left Harvard. In the 1960s, Daniel Ellsberg worked as policy adviser in the Pentagon. Robert McNamara, the former Secretary of Defense (who many years later expressed his opposition to the Vietnam War) had requested that a comprehensive analysis of the background to the U.S. involvement be undertaken. Daniel Ellsberg worked on the project and had access to the vast archive of highly confidential documents. In 1969, he developed a deep moral belief that successive administrations had lied to the American public about the prospect of success in Vietnam and that the war had cost immense unnecessary suffering. He decided that the American public had a right to know the details of the documents that he had been working on, later dubbed the "Pentagon Papers." He secretly copied over 7,000 pages of the documents and released them to the *New York Times* newspaper, which then proceeded to publish them in 1971.

The Nixon administration reacted with great ferocity to the disclosures, seeking an injunction to stop their publication. A shady group of former FBI and CIA agents was assembled to counter the perceived threat to the government. That group—called "the plumbers" because its purpose was to stop leaks—in an attempt to smear Ellsberg, stole medical records from a psychoanalyst who had treated him. They even planned to have him bashed. This misconduct totally undermined the legal action that the Nixon administration was taking to punish Ellsberg. The "plumbers" later went on to far greater notoriety when they broke into Democratic Party offices, thus starting the political scandal of Watergate, which saw Richard Nixon removed from the presidency.

Since the 1960s, the term "whistleblowing" has come into common use. However, its precise meaning is somewhat unclear. A common definition is "reporting by a current or former employee of illegal, inefficient or unethical practices in an organization to persons who have the power and resources to take action."[122] However, as we shall see, this definition is inadequate in various respects.

To assist us in our attempt to provide an adequate definition, let us consider that paradigm of a whistleblower, Daniel Ellsberg, and try to pinpoint the key features of his activity as a whistleblower. Proceeding in this way, the first and most obvious feature of whistleblowing is that it involves making some alleged immoral, corrupt, and/or criminal activity a matter of public knowledge. This means much more than voicing one's concerns to one or two individuals. Frequently we tell spouses, friends, and members of our families about disturbing things that happen in the workplace, because we wish them to understand and empathize with our feelings. Whistleblowing involves much more than this. It involves putting information on the public record in such a way that "the world," even if only potentially, can access it, and indeed, is likely to access it. The methods of achieving this goal are quite diverse and consist of such communications as reports to a media outlet, book publications, revelations before a parliamentary or congressional committee, and, more recently, material placed on a website.

A further question that now arises concerns the position of the whistleblower in relation to the organization in which the corruption or wrongdoing is allegedly taking place. The whistleblower is most commonly a current or former employee of the organization whose activities are being exposed. All the cases previously described fall into this category. Using this criterion, Ralph Nader, who exposed unsafe engineering practices in the U.S. automotive industry, is not a whistleblower because he was not an employee of the companies he criticized. Nor was Erin Brockovich a whistleblower by this criterion. Although she performed a remarkable community service by fighting a successful legal battle against the huge utility Pacific Gas and Electric, which had contaminated large areas of the Mojave Desert in California with a chemical (hexavalent chromium), Erin Brockovich was an employee of a small law firm and had the full backing of her superior.

Let us now turn to the question of where the complaint is raised. In cases in which the information is published in the media, it is quite clear that the whistleblower is "going public." However, should an individual raise his or her concerns entirely within the organization, it is far from evident that this step is whistleblowing. In fact, it would seem merely to be part of the normal practice within any organization whereby an individual raises concerns and the management deals with them. This distinction becomes important when organizations ostensibly create mechanisms to accommodate whistleblowing, but then put limits upon the public disclosure by individuals of their concerns. In these cases, it seems that the individuals involved are not whistleblowing, at all but rather are engaging in a formalized staff suggestion scheme, or the like.

Sherron Watkins, vice president for corporate development at Enron, wrote a letter to Kenneth Lay in August 2000, setting down her concerns about some of the more dubious financial transactions, and she met with him that same month to hand over the letter. She was widely hailed as a whistleblower—*Time* magazine saying, "Watkins is the closest thing to a hero in sight. When she goes out for coffee, strangers stop to give her 'attagirls' and ask for her autograph."[123] However, rather than seeing her as a heroic figure, other commentators have questioned her role as a whistleblower. *Forbes* magazine described her status in the following terms:

> A whistleblower, literally speaking, is someone who spots a criminal robbing a bank and blows a whistle alerting the police. That's not Sherron Watkins. What the Enron Vice President did was write a memo to the bank robber, suggesting he stop robbing the bank and offering ways to avoid getting caught. Then she met with the robber who said he didn't believe he was robbing the bank, but said he'd investigate to find out for sure. Then, for all we know, Watkins did nothing, and her memo was not made public until congressional investigators released it six weeks after Enron filed for bankruptcy.[124]

There are various reasons for thinking that Sherron Watkins was not a whistleblower, but the most obvious is that she did not make a public disclosure; accordingly, she did not "blow the whistle" on any corruption or other wrongdoing at Enron.

This distinction between internal and external disclosure can cause confusion, particularly in public sector institutions. When an individual raises his or her concerns with another public sector body—such as the auditor-general or ombudsman—in one sense the complaint has gone beyond being an internal management matter. However, if we conceive the agency to whom the individual belongs, and the external public sector agency to whom the complaint has been referred, as constituting parts of the same public sector organizational entity, then the individual is not engaged in whistleblowing. Specifically, the individual has not made public the alleged corrupt activity.

Implicit in the preceding discussion is that whistleblowing, properly understood, is restricted to corrupt, immoral, and/or criminal activity that is taking place in an organizational context. It is difficult to conceive of the act of "blowing the whistle" on behavior that is taking place in the family home or on the streets, such as a burglary or an assault.

A further crucial feature of whistleblowing is that the making public of the information is an intentional, indeed a deliberate, act. Were the information to be revealed because an individual inadvertently left sensitive documents in a taxi, then no matter what effect the information was to have, the act could not be called whistleblowing, because it was not done with the appropriate *intention.* For an action to count as whistleblowing, it would normally need to be intended, and indeed deliberate, that is, involving some form of prior reason-based decision.

The issue of voluntariness can become quite problematic, as the following case demonstrates.

CASE STUDY 8.2   Mal Colston

In 1997, an Australian senator, Mal Colston, defected from the opposition Labor Party and as payback became embroiled in a scandal over his misuse of travel and accommodation allowances. The scandal grew to engulf some government ministers, and, in the process, the inadequacies of the controls on the allowance system became the subject of public debate.

In the course of this public scandal, John Mellors, head of the Department of Administrative Services, the organization responsible for the parliamentary travel allowance scheme, advised the government of the necessity of a review of the whole scheme of entitlements for members of Parliament. That information became public through documents being leaked to a newspaper. The Prime Minister then came under political questioning as to why he had not adopted the department's recommendations. Several months later, the government abolished the Department of Administration, and John Mellors and many other officials were made redundant.

(Based upon P. Daley, "Government pulled plug on rorts review," *The Sunday Age,* November 23, 1997, p. 5)

The Mellors case has a number of the features of whistleblowing, for example, the information that the government had not acted upon advice to close down an obvious loophole that allowed fraud and corruption was publicly disclosed. Moreover, John Mellors suffered adverse consequences. However, as far as we know, his revelation was not made voluntarily. In our analysis of what constitutes whistleblowing, the act of making the information public needs to be not only deliberate, but also done without compulsion.

An associated issue is whether disclosure as a form of preemptive defense constitutes whistleblowing. The Sherron Watkins case highlights this dilemma. As vice president for corporate development at Enron, she was working directly under the chief financial officer, Andrew Fastow, who has since been indicted for fraud. In August 2000, the wheels were starting to fall off the Enron enterprise, with the share price tumbling and CEO Jeffrey Skilling resigning. Although it is not possible to determine with any certainty what motivated her, the circumstances strongly suggest that, in outlining her concerns to Kenneth Lay, she was only seeking to distance herself from the wrongdoings at Enron. People often have mixed motives, but her action would not count as whistleblowing if it turned out that her aim was not public disclosure, but only self-protection.

Probably the most important issue about whistleblowing is that it relates to some form of wrongdoing. In all the cases mentioned so far, be they Karen Silkwood's exposure of unsafe practices in a nuclear facility or Daniel Ellsberg's concerns about Vietnam, some form of wrongdoing—typically corruption—was at the heart of the act. In looking at this notion of wrongdoing in relation to whistleblowing, there are some associated issues that need further examination. The first is the distinction between actual wrongdoing and the belief that some wrongdoing has occurred.

In well-documented cases of whistleblowing, it is very clear that some form of wrongdoing has occurred, and the role of the whistleblower has been to make the information public. However, in many other cases, this is not so. Accordingly, the distinction between the wrongdoing actually having occurred, on the one hand, and on the other, the whistleblower having simply formed a view based upon inference and limited knowledge, is vital. Because there are varying degrees of evidence that some wrongdoing has occurred, there is always the possibility that the individual has reached the wrong conclusion and that the deliberate decision to disclose is erroneous. As will be discussed later in this chapter, one of the characteristic features of whistle-blowers is their strong belief in their cause; but strong beliefs are not necessarily to be equated with *true* beliefs. Accordingly, it is important to distinguish between whistleblowing in the primary sense of public disclosure of an *actual* wrongdoing, and whistleblowing in the secondary sense of public *allegations* of wrongdoing, when the allegations are not proven and may in fact be false.

Another key element in the whistleblowing process is that it is purposive, in that the whistleblower places the information upon the public record with the clear intent that some remedial action will be taken. Whistleblowers are not disinterested observers of wrongdoing but seek to correct the wrongs that they see occurring. In most histories of whistleblowing, the individuals raise the matters with their superiors in the hope that the wrong will be rectified, but it is not. Disillusioned with the management's response, they explore other avenues and ultimately opt for public disclosure.

The final element of the analysis of whistleblowing is that the person making the disclosure has to be under a real or potential threat of some form of reprisal. As Gerald Vinten noted,

> In a survey of 87 whistleblowers from both the civil service and private industry in the US, it was found that all but one experienced retaliation, with those employed longer experiencing more. Harassment came from peers as well as superiors, and most of those in private industry and half of those in the civil service lost their jobs. A similar result emerged from a 6-year US study of 64 whistleblowers, ethical resisters who spoke out because they had witnessed a serious violation of legal or ethical standards.[125]

The element of the action taking place in a hostile environment is essential to the notion of whistleblowing. Indeed, if the person taking the action does not feel that it is going to trigger some form of reprisal, then, whether or not it eventuates, it could reasonably be said that the person is not whistleblowing. Rather, he or she is involved in a more or less routine complaints process. At what stage in the process the whistleblower comes to realize that there is going to be some form of threatened or actual reprisal, or at least intervention to nullify the disclosure, is not critical; what is important is that the whistleblowing continues in the face of the threatened or real reprisals, and other improper interventions.

Here it is important to make a number of points. First, as indicated before, the actual wrongdoing being disclosed is not necessarily an act of wrongdoing—though it often is. Second, there is a moral obligation on the part of the employee to disclose the wrongdoing. This requirement follows from the argument presented in Chapter 6 on collective responsibility in organizational contexts. Any member of an organization has a moral obligation—an obligation held jointly with the other members—to contribute to the elimination or reduction of serious wrongdoing within the organization, including by reporting such wrongdoing when it occurs. Third, any intentional and unjustified interference with the discharging of this obligation to report constitutes an act of corruption by virtue of being an attempt to undermine a morally obligatory institutional process. This is obviously the case where the process of reporting has been formalized and there is an explicit requirement to report. But it is also the case where the process is informal and implicit. For in the latter case, the moral requirement to report exists, even if this moral obligation has not been expressed in a law or regulation or policy statement.

The main elements of whistleblowing can be summarized as follows. The whistleblower is a member of an organization, and he or she deliberately places information about nontrivial wrongdoing on the public record, doing so for the purpose of having the wrongdoing stopped, and in the expectation that he or she may suffer some form of unwarranted interference and/or real or threatened reprisal.[126]

Let us turn now to the nature of the wrongdoing being disclosed. We have suggested that such wrongdoing is often an act of corruption. Abuse of office was involved in both of the examples previously described. Daniel Ellsberg believed that U.S. administrations had lied to the American people about the Vietnam War. Jim Mellors, along with many other Australians, believed that the procedures for federal politicians to obtain reimbursement for travel expenses were being abused. Furthermore, Clive Ponting in Britain believed that the Thatcher government had lied to the British people over the sinking of the *General Belgrano* for the purpose of gaining some political advantage. And as noted before, the actions of the organizations in taking reprisals against the whistleblowers are also examples of corrupt behavior.

If we were to attempt to list the activities that trigger whistleblowing, we would come up with at least the following ones: any illegality or infringement of the law; fraudulent conduct; abuse of office; mismanagement or maladministration; gross or substantial waste of resources; endangering public health, safety, or the environment; dishonest or partial performance of duties; breach of trust; and misuse of information (for example, insider trading).

We conclude that many, if not most, of the activities that trigger whistleblowing are forms of corruption. Accordingly, whistleblowing is typically an act of (so to speak) anti-corruption.

From the community perspective, it is no doubt comforting to know that in our midst there are individuals who are prepared to sacrifice their careers, wealth, and well-being to right the wrongs of corruption. On the other hand, the fact that some individuals have to make such a high level of sacrifice in order to protect the community from corruption is far from satisfactory. The need for courageous whistleblowers reflects a failure in normal processes of reporting wrongdoing. In a morally healthy organization, wrongdoing, including corruption, would be reported in-house, investigated, and dealt with. There would be no need for heroics.

Before proceeding any further, it might be helpful to consider how prevalent whistleblowing is. Terance Miethe and Joyce Rothschild[127] reviewed the relevant U.S. research in 1994 and concluded that the most prevalent reaction to observing misconduct is to remain silent. Although the average rate of whistleblowing (when misconduct was observed) in the studies reviewed was 42 percent, the vast majority involved disclosures to persons within the organization. Across all the studies reviewed, an average of only 21 percent of the whistleblowers reported misconduct to an official outside the company. In a more recent American study, some 1,300 public sector employees were surveyed in regard to whistleblowing. These results, combined with an analysis of the findings from several other published studies, led the researchers to estimate that approximately one-third of American employees have observed conduct that they consider to be unethical or illegal in their workplace. Of these, more than half said nothing about the observed malpractice.[128] Having examined what whistleblowing is and what its relationship is to corruption, it is useful to review some of the ideas about its causes. In very broad terms, these ideas are grouped into four categories: individual and psychological factors, situational factors, organizational characteristics, and cultural factors.

It is tempting to ascribe whistleblowing to personal factors. Illustrative of this tendency is a quote from a speech by the former Australian Federal Ombudsman Ron McLeod:

> At times, whistleblowers do not help the process by resorting to personal abuse when a problem may be systemic rather than personal. They may make threats, which unfortunately all too often lead to threats being made in response. They can be protective against any insult or offence to themselves, but make wild and sweepingly offensive statements about others. They demand proof at a higher level than they are prepared to offer. They can seem narrowly focused on a particular issue, or even obsessed by it. But then they expand the field of discussion, whether they're winning or losing on the initial point. They can be impractical and politically or socially naive; they fail too often to recognise that a small win is a win nonetheless and not just the first concession in what they believe will be a continuing process.[129]

To be fair to the ombudsman, he then proceeds to outline the organizational dimensions of whistleblowing, but the views expressed illustrate the tendency to look for personality-based explanations for the behavior. However, Miethe and Rothschild have observed the following:

> . . . contrary to popular images of whistleblowers, objective requirements of specific roles or jobs that employees find themselves in, coupled with employee's perceptions of the ethics, openness, and democracy of their employing organisation, have much more influence over the propensity to blow the whistle than do psychological or dispositional characteristics.[130]

A more productive theoretical direction is to examine situational factors. There is some evidence that the more serious the wrongdoing, the greater the likelihood of whistleblowing.[131] Miceli and Near looked at the role hierarchical position played in whistleblowing, finding that more senior people were somewhat less likely than their junior counterparts to disclose wrongdoing, but when they did, it had greater credibility.[132] Finally, anonymity in the whistleblowing action appears to encourage disclosure but to detract from its credibility.

Turning to the issue of organizational factors, Miethe and Rothschild note that research indicates that these are important determinants of whistleblowing.[133] Some types of organizations, like the police and the military, have legal restrictions upon the disclosure of information that actively discourages whistleblowing. Also, many organizations engage in active socialization of recruits with a view to discouraging any "rocking of the boat." Enron was such an organization, recruiting from universities so that new staff had little exposure to other organizational cultures; locating its staff in Houston away from potential professional peers; and regularly culling staff through its biannual "rank and yank" policies. All of these activities made it far less likely that employees would feel comfortable engaging in whistleblowing.

In stark contrast to Enron is the organization that encourages reporting of wrongdoing, and if required, whistleblowing in the pure sense of the term, that is, public disclosure in the face of reprisal. Such organizations adopt policies that countenance whistleblowing, through legislation (in the case of public sector organizations), policy statements from management, creation of hotlines, or other mechanisms; and they take overt action to protect whistleblowers. These mechanisms will be described in far greater detail later in this chapter, but it needs to be noted that there is little research evidence to determine the impact that these sorts of mechanisms are having.[134]

Finally, it needs to be noted that there are potent cultural images associated with whistleblowing. Although some whistleblowers have been elevated to hero status—like Karen Silkwood and Frank Serpico—most experience the opprobrium of being treated as a "snitch," "grass," or "dobber." Some researchers have noted that the strongest condemnation occurs when the whistleblowing is perceived to be motivated by spite, greed, or self-interest.

The broader cultural dimension has prompted a body of literature that overtly encourages individuals to engage in whistleblowing when they observe organizational misconduct. Illustrative of this body of work is the exhortation by Myron and Penina Glazer to promote what they term "ethical resistance":

> The efforts to destroy ethical resisters have not silenced them. On the contrary, there are encouraging signs of society's readiness to support those of its members who are willing, even at personal risk, to defend its long-term health and interests. In confronting corruption, lawlessness, and threats to the common good, whistleblowers and their allies provide models for all of us and offer hope for a future where industry and government are accountable for the consequences of their actions.[135]

Community groups have evolved with the explicit purpose of providing support and advice for those people contemplating whistleblowing. In Australia, an organization called *Whistleblowers Anonymous* has formed to bring together those who believe that they have suffered as a result of their whistleblowing activities. This dimension of community self-help has produced a body of work that serves to guide potential whistleblowers through the process. Velasquez gives whistleblowers some practical guidance by posing the following questions:

1. How comprehensive is the worker's knowledge of the situation? Is the worker's information accurate and substantial?
2. What, exactly, are the unethical practices involved? Why are these unethical? What public values do these practices harm?
3. How substantial and irreversible are the effects of these practices? Are there any compensating public benefits that justify the practices?
4. What is the employee's obligation to publicise such practices by working within the organisation or by going outside? What probable effects will either alternative have on the company's practices? On society? On the firm? On other organisations? On the employee? [136]

We have noted the obligations to report wrongdoing, and we have described the virtues of whistleblowing, and indeed we have provided practical advice in relation to it. However, whistleblowing can have costs, as well as benefits, to an organization. Whistleblowers may have got it wrong and may therefore unfairly tarnish the reputations of individuals and organizations. Again, whistleblowing may be motivated by a desire to bring a competitor down or to exact revenge on the organization that one is a member of. More generally, a culture of unreasonable reporting of mistakes and minor misdemeanors can develop; this outcome can undermine trust and ultimately be dysfunctional.

Balanced policies in relation to whistleblowing take all these matters into consideration. Such policies would reflect the appreciation of the damage that a successful whistleblower can do to the credibility of an organization and would involve taking some steps towards recognizing the value of dealing openly with criticism, both in avoiding damaging publicity and in rectifying the problems that have been identified. As will be discussed later, there are many ways in which organizations can respond to whistleblowing, ranging from a minimal undertaking to examine claims internally, right through to acknowledging the right of individuals to expose wrongdoing and to protect them from any adverse consequences. It is not surprising that in democratic societies, it is the public sector that has adopted the most rigorous approach to dealing with whistleblowing, although the sincerity of the commitment to the process can sometimes be questioned.

It is a helpful exercise to hypothesize how, if we had the opportunity to design the perfect system for dealing with whistleblowing, we would design it. The first of the building blocks would be a firm statement of ethical values supporting broadly held community values like privacy, honesty, accountability, protection of the environment, and respect for minority views and lifestyles. Looking specifically at whistleblowing, the statement of ethical values would include the following:

- A commitment to openness;
- The welcoming of constructive criticism; and
- A respect for the views of all the staff of the organization.

The ideal system for dealing with whistleblowing would then need to determine what forms of corruption or illegality might warrant whistleblowing. An illustrative menu would include the following:

- Any illegality or infringement of the law;
- Fraudulent or corrupt conduct;
- Substantial misconduct, mismanagement, or maladministration;
- Gross or substantial waste of resources;
- Endangering public health or safety and the environment;
- Dishonest or partial performance of duties;
- Breach of trust; and
- Misuse of information.

The next building block would be a comprehensive set of procedures for the receipt of complaints at an accessible point in the organization, with mechanisms in place to ensure that the complaint is treated with strict confidentiality. The ideal whistleblower scheme would allow for anonymous complaints. The processes should provide for investigation and adjudication of complaints by skilled and disinterested parties. As mentioned earlier, many whistleblowers act in the genuine belief that some wrongdoing has occurred, but they have reached that point because of some lack of knowledge or misunderstanding. On the other hand, some complaints are vexatious or frivolous. A credible adjudication process would weed out all unwarranted complaints.[137]

Another building block would be a set of procedures for passing on the findings of the investigation process to some authority capable of rectifying the problem identified. In many cases, those procedures would be internal, but it is obvious that in some circumstances, this authority may have to be external to the organization.

Another element of the procedures should be a guarantee that the complainant is not going to be disciplined for any breach of internal confidentiality processes merely because the complaint was made. This guarantee raises the very difficult question of whether the organization is going to countenance the unsatisfied complainant's going to the media. In practice, there are many different approaches, ranging from a total prohibition on going outside the organizational context, to a pragmatic acceptance that if the whistleblower is still aggrieved after the internal phase of the process, then going to the media may be inevitable and should not be punished.

The final element in the ideal whistleblower scheme would be formal procedures for the protection of the whistleblower from reprisals. The sorts of reprisals need to be spelled out and would include dismissal, disadvantage to career, intimidation, harassment, discrimination, personal injury, damage to reputation, and financial loss. As well as defining the nature of the reprisals that are proscribed, the ideal whistleblower scheme would have processes for the receipt and the investigation of complaints about reprisals. Following logically from this would be penalties for those taking retributive action. A comprehensive scheme would include processes for staff members accused of reprisals to be able to defend themselves, although taken to its extremes, such processes run the risk of miring the organization in claim and counterclaim.

Although we have offered an ideal whistleblower scheme, we need to be realistic and accept that organizations do not exist to look after whistleblowers; perhaps many ideal whistleblower schemes cannot be realized because of resource constraints and other priorities.

It is not surprising that the most elaborate whistleblower schemes are in the public sector. There are two reasons for this state of affairs. The first is that public sectors in democratic societies are highly sensitive to public opinion, and there is a very powerful incentive for establishing whistleblower schemes that enable some control over whistleblower complaints and, hopefully, keep them from becoming political scandals. Second, because public sectors are subsidiaries of legislatures, it is practicable to pass legislation that can go beyond the public sector employees and put in place legal protections for the broader community. This, of course, is not to suggest that private sector organizations are incapable of establishing and maintaining effective whistleblower schemes. However, it needs to be acknowledged that the authority of private sector organizations does not extend beyond their powers as employers.

As noted earlier, there is very little research on how well whistleblower schemes are working. There must be a strong suspicion that many such schemes are created for reasons that have more to do with being seen to deal with the issue rather than a deep commitment to encouraging individuals to come forward with their concerns and protecting them from any consequences. One whistleblower scheme that has been criticized as ineffectual is the scheme that applies to the Australian Public Service by virtue of section 16 of the Australian Public Service Act 1999. Recently, a parliamentary committee[138] observed that the scheme had the following deficiencies:

- The scheme applied only to half of the federal public sector;
- Only public servants can raise issues, not members of the public;
- The nature of the matters that are covered by the scheme is vague;
- Reports can be received only by the CEO and public service commissioner—the latter having no power to take remedial action; and
- The protection from reprisal is limited to those from within the agency relevant to the complaint.

The committee found the whistleblower scheme to be inadequate but noted that all the parties to the scheme were quite satisfied with it. The Australian public service commissioner has publicly reported that the scheme was working well. In the financial year 2001–2002, he received twelve complaints, of which nine were found to fall outside the parameters of the scheme—all of this in a public sector of over 110,000 employees.[139]

This example highlights the vulnerability of whistleblower schemes to being undermined by legalism and bureaucratic sandbagging. Another salutary lesson can be learned from the experience in New South Wales. The New South Wales Protected Disclosures Act 1994 (which is far more comprehensive than its federal counterpart) had been in operation for over two years when the Independent Commission Against Corruption surveyed public sector employees on their attitude to the scheme enshrined in the legislation. In brief, the findings were as follows:

- Of the respondents, 54 percent were unaware of either the internal or the external reporting channels;
- Of the respondents, 25 percent did not believe that the legislation had the power to protect them from negative consequences were they to make a report on corruption; and
- Although the overwhelming majority of employees were in favor of reporting corruption, one-third doubted that their organization would respond appropriately to a report.

The results of that survey indicate that even with elaborate statutory schemes to protect whistleblowers, there remains a significant degree of skepticism about their efficacy.

CONCLUSION

This chapter has examined the nature of whistleblowing, its causes, and some features of institutional systems for protecting whistleblowers and handling their complaints. Clearly, the activity of whistleblowing is inextricably linked to corruption; corruption typically provides the occasion and justification for whistleblowing. Unfortunately, as a society, we continue to be reliant upon the integrity of a small minority of citizens to reveal some of the most serious abuses of power and other forms of corruption; normal reporting systems are not sufficient. Moreover, the elaborate schemes for dealing with whistle-blowing, so beloved of lawyers and bureaucrats, are unlikely to achieve their purpose independently of the existence of the courage and integrity of individual members of organizations. This state of affairs is surely testimony to the inadequacy of our various institutional cultures, be they business or public sector cultures; evidently, our institutional cultures are not sufficiently hostile to corruption. If they were, our sense of *collective* moral responsibility would be sufficient to galvanize normal reporting processes in organizations and thereby render the heroic whistleblower redundant.

chapter nine

The Rights of Suspects

Many of the moral rights of both suspects and victims are given expression in legal systems. Consider the right to a fair trial or the right to protection from life-threatening attacks in one's home. As such, these preexisting moral rights become also legal rights. Moreover, many of these moral rights are articulated in such documents as the Universal Declaration of Human Rights, the International Covenant on Civil and Political Rights, and the International Covenant on Economic, Social, and Cultural Rights. Not all of these human and other rights are centrally relevant to the issue of institutional corruption, and this chapter will examine those that are. But here it is once again important to lay stress on the nexus that exists between corruption and the infringement of moral rights.

There are a group of human rights that can be violated if there is such gross corruption that the institutional infrastructure of the community is affected. For example, Article 26 (1) of the Universal Declaration of Human Rights provides the following:

> Everyone has the right to education. Education shall be free, at least in the elementary and fundamental stages. Elementary education shall be compulsory. Technical and professional education shall be made generally available and higher education shall be equally accessible to all on the basis of merit.

Laurence Cockcroft from Transparency International describes the effect of corruption upon education in China in the following terms:

> Since 1986 China's Ministry of Supervision has been the main focus of its "clean government" campaigns. In 1990 and 1991 its officers received a total of 1.5 million reports of misconduct of which nearly half concerned bribery, corruption and the abuse of power for personal benefit. An analysis of coverage of these reports by Chinese newspapers indicates that the vast majority of these were concerned with payments for school entrance, medical attendance, and public security. In fact backhanders to be paid for entrance to infant or middle school fall between US$200 and US$500—clearly a very significant sum. This may help to explain why secondary school enrolment rates in China are not more than 60 per cent.[140]

For very many of the human rights that are set down in the Universal Declaration of Human Rights, evidence is readily available that basic human rights, like the right to participation in government (Article 21), the right to an adequate standard of living (Article 25), and the right to freedom of opinion and expression (Article 19) can be undermined by corruption.

In Chapter 4, on what is wrong with corruption, we identified rights violations as one of the most important morally unacceptable features of corruption. In that chapter, the focus was on, so to speak, the moral rights of victims and potential victims—the ones whose rights were violated as a consequence of corruption. In this chapter, we shift our attention to the rights of suspects, the persons suspected or alleged to have engaged in corrupt practices. What we are focusing upon is the specific rights of suspects in the context of the detection, investigation, and prosecution of corruption. The particular rights being examined are as follows:

- The right to silence;
- The right to privacy, including the rights of individuals in search and seizure, and in relation to surveillance;
- The rights of individuals in court; and
- The rights of individuals in relation to entrapment, including police in relation to integrity testing.

Before proceeding on a detailed analysis of these issues, it is useful to reflect on the expression given to these moral rights in a document such as the Universal Declaration of Human Rights:

> All are equal before the law and are entitled without any discrimination to equal protection of the law. All are entitled to equal protection against any discrimination in violation of this Declaration and against any incitement to such discrimination. (Article 7);
>
> Everyone is entitled in full equality to a fair, and public, hearing by an independent and impartial tribunal, in the determination of his rights and obligations and of any criminal charge against him. (Article 10);

Everyone charged with a penal offence has the right to be presumed innocent until proved guilty according to law in a public trial at which he has had all the guarantees necessary for his defence. (Article 11 (1)); and

No one shall be subjected to arbitrary interference with his privacy, family, home or correspondence, nor to attacks upon his honour and reputation. Everyone has the right to the protection of the law against such interference or attacks. (Article 12).

WHAT JUSTIFIES RIGHTS?

Before we proceed to offer a critical analysis of some of the specific just-mentioned rights of suspects, it is important to provide an account and justification of moral rights in general. This general justification would in turn provide justification for the specific rights discussed later.

Moral rights can be classed under two main categories, *institutional* and *natural.* Natural rights are ones possessed by virtue of being human and hence are independent of the vagaries of specific institutional and cultural contexts. Thus, the right to life and the right not to be tortured are natural (moral) rights. By contrast, institutional rights, like the right to vote for the candidate of one's choice or the right to own property, are rights that exist only in some institutional context, such as that of government or the system of private property. It does not make much sense to ascribe a right to private property in a society in which all property is communally owned.

Here it is important to stress that both natural and institutional rights are *moral* rights and not simply legal rights. For a long time, women and blacks did not have the legal right to vote. Naturally, during that time they had the moral (institutional) right to vote; it is just that the law did not respect their moral rights. Again, under the Taliban regime in Afghanistan women, unlike men, were deprived of even a basic education. This deprivation was a violation of a moral (institutional) right.

According to Alan Gewirth, two fundamental natural rights that all people have merely by virtue of being purposive human agents are the rights to freedom and well-being. He argues that every person has rights to freedom and well-being simply because every person requires freedom and well-being to act as a naturally purposive agent. Insofar as freedom and well-being are the necessary conditions for all purposive action—for without some minimal degree of freedom and well-being, people will not be able to act in the pursuit and fulfillment of their chosen purposes—all human beings have rights to their freedom and well-being. These rights are natural because they emanate from our common and shared natural property or quality of human purposiveness—a property that we have, not by virtue of some institution, but simply as a constitutive part of our basic human nature. The following is an outline of Gewirth's argument for the justification of the natural rights to freedom and well-being:

Stage One: The Establishment of Prudential Rights

1. I act for purposes I want to fulfill.
2. My freedom and well-being are necessary in enabling me to fulfill my chosen purposes.
3. Others ought not to interfere with my freedom and well-being.
4. I have a right to my freedom and well-being since my freedom and well-being are necessary goods for all my purposive actions.

Stage Two: The Transition from Prudential Rights to Moral Rights

5. I have this right simply by virtue of being a purposive agent.
6. By the principles of universalization and consistency, I must allow that all other purposive agents also have these rights, because if I claim them for myself but do not allow that other purposive agents also have them, then I must involve myself in self-contradiction.
7. I ought, therefore, not to interfere with the freedom and well-being of all other purposive agents, as they must not interfere with mine.
8. I must, therefore, respect the rights to freedom and well-being of all purposive agents, as they must respect mine.

The conclusion in premise (8) of this argument is essentially a statement of Gewirth's Principle of Generic Consistency (PGC). The argument[141] provides a justification of the natural rights to freedom and well-being. These rights to freedom and well-being can, in turn, be used to provide a justification of other rights, such as the ones outlined in the United Nations Declaration of Human Rights. Insofar as the presence of those latter rights can be shown to be necessary for one's freedom and well-being, then those rights have been *indirectly* justified in terms of the ultimate value of human purposiveness. The right to property, for example, will have been indirectly justified, if it can be shown that the absence of the right to own property is detrimental and harmful to one's freedom and well-being. A similar argument can be made in relation to the right to vote and various other rights that are taken for granted in most, if not all, democratic states.

Before turning to the analysis of some specific rights of suspects, there are some further points that need to be made in relation to rights in general. First, not all moral rights have the same importance or ought to be given the same moral weight. The right to life is a more important and weighty one than the right to privacy. Forced to choose between saving a life and infringing someone's privacy, one would save the life. Similarly, the right to freedom from torture (Article 5 of the Universal Declaration of Human Rights) is arguably more important than the right to a fair trial.

Second, sometimes the rights of suspects are in competition with the rights of victims. On the one hand, the individual or collective victim of fraud has a right to have his or her money returned. On the other hand, the suspect has a right to silence, notwithstanding the desire of investigators that he or she speaks. Balancing these competing rights is not a simple task. One principle that might be of assistance here is provided by Gewirth: the Degree for the Necessity of Action (DNA) principle. The DNA principle is an attempt to show how conflicting rights can be adjudicated. Essentially a consequentialist principle, the DNA states that one right should be allowed to override a second right if so doing results in overall harm minimization. Institutions of justice—the courts, the prosecutors, and the police—bear the burden of the responsibility for making these adjudications.

Let us now turn to some specific rights of suspects. In order to focus our discussion, we begin with a case study.

CASE STUDY 9.1   President Clinton

On February 12, 1999, the United States Senate found the president of the United States not guilty of the charges of perjury and obstruction of justice that had led to his impeachment.

The public figure, Bill Clinton, was surrounded by rumors of misconduct even before his presidency commenced. In early 1994, Paula Jones publicly accused President Clinton of sexually harassing her while he was the governor of Arkansas in May 1991. Soon after, she brought a suit before an Arkansas court alleging violation of civil rights. President Clinton's defense team sought to have that action dismissed or delayed until his presidency had finished. A district judge agreed with that proposition, but it was overturned by the Supreme Court in May 1997. However, the Supreme Court gave the district judge the discretion to delay the case, if President Clinton could demonstrate that proceeding with the case would obstruct the performance of his official duties. President Clinton was ordered to submit to questioning by Paula Jones's lawyers.

Most of that questioning of President Clinton was not about the Paula Jones case but was about his relationship with Monica Lewinsky, an attractive young White House intern. When asked directly whether he had ever had sex with Monica Lewinsky, President Clinton denied that he had.

Within days the media was running hard with the Monica Lewinsky story. *Newsweek,* which broke the story, had access to tapes of conversations that Monica Lewinsky had with Linda Tripp, and soon these were in the public arena as well. Monica Lewinsky was not aware that those conversations had been recorded.

Kenneth Starr, who was also investigating the Whitewater allegations, was appointed special prosecutor to determine whether President Clinton had violated any laws in relation to the Lewinsky denial.

Starr negotiated an immunity deal with Monica Lewinsky, and she appeared before a Grand Jury. In that appearance, she confirmed that inappropriate sexual activity had occurred but denied that any pressure was put upon her to remain silent. President Clinton also appeared, acknowledging that he had had inappropriate intimate contact with Monica Lewinsky.

Starr delivered his report in September 1998. His report included highly descriptive details of the sexual conduct that President Clinton first denied and then admitted. The report was placed on the Internet, and the whole world could access this material.

In his report, the special prosecutor argued strongly that President Clinton's testimony in the Paula Jones deposition and at the Lewinsky Grand Jury was perjury and that he had been involved in the obstruction of justice. The report listed eleven grounds for impeachment, the House of Representatives accepted two grounds, and, as noted earlier, the Senate found President Clinton not guilty.

The impeachment of President Clinton raises some important issues. Kenneth Starr's investigation focused on Clinton's sexual indiscretions with Monica Lewinsky, and there was a consequent media frenzy on this matter, especially after Starr's report was placed on the Internet. This treatment raises the issue of Clinton's moral right to privacy; specifically, was it violated? Of relevance here is Article 12 of the Universal Declaration of Human Rights (cited earlier).

A second issue concerns the behavior of Clinton himself. Here we have in mind not the morality or otherwise of his sexual activities, but rather his duty to act lawfully, and specifically his duty not to commit perjury nor to obstruct justice. If, as alleged by Kenneth Starr, President Clinton lied in the deposition, he had breached that duty. Eventually the Senate found this not to have been the case. Clearly, perjury is a serious matter, and all the more serious if it is committed by a head of state. Aside from any other consideration, perjury tends to undermine legal processes; it is a paradigmatic form of corruption.

At this point, an important question arises. If we assume, as we presumably must, that Clinton has a moral right to privacy, then the question arises as to whether Starr's investigation—or that by Paula Jones's lawyers—*violated* Clinton's right to privacy, notwithstanding that the investigation was purporting to investigate whether Clinton had committed perjury. If so, then the further question that arises is whether or not Clinton was entitled to protect himself, that is, to protect his right to privacy, including by means of making false statements. Note that the favored method of protecting both oneself and one's privacy is by invoking the right to silence (see later for a discussion), including by not testifying (pleading the Fifth Amendment). Evidently, Clinton chose not to avail himself of this form of protection.

There are certainly cases in which a person is entitled to protect himself or herself by making false statements in relation to a (morally and legally) improper investigation. Consider a German Jew's making a false statement to the Gestapo—or indeed to an ordinary German police officer—in relation to his or her Jewish identity. Naturally, the right that the Jew is seeking to protect is his or her right to life—a more fundamental right than the right to privacy. Nevertheless, the right to privacy is agreed everywhere to be a fundamental moral right; and the investigation by the German police—or at least the line of questioning—is an improper one. So the example is, at least potentially, analogous to the Starr investigation, if we assume that Clinton lied to protect his right to privacy. We are not claiming that the manner in which Starr conducted his investigation was improper, but it is not difficult to see why someone might hold this view.

In an article in the *New York Times* about the decision of Kenneth Starr to call President Clinton before a grand jury, Anthony Lewis commented as follows:

> No other American would have to undergo that second turn of the screw. Targets of prosecutors customarily invoke the Fifth Amendment; Justice Department rules discourage calling them before grand juries. But Mr Starr, determined to get something on him after four years of fruitless investigation, guessed correctly that the President would not refuse to testify.[142]

Anthony Lewis's judgment is that President Clinton was denied the customary protections of the criminal justice system. As is well known, legislatures frequently adopt statutes that depart from the normal models of protection for the rights of those suspected of wrongdoing. Much legislation for protecting national security significantly limits the rights (particularly privacy) of suspects, proceeds of crime statutes usually reverse the onus of proof, and many anti-corruption institutions have the authority to compel suspects to answer questions. Of course, this situation does not show that such statutes are morally—or even legally—justified. On the other hand, given that moral justifications are offered and widely accepted for at least some of these statutes, we can conclude that the fact that Clinton was denied customary protections does not decisively settle the matter.

Rather, the matter now turns on whether or not the kind of investigation that Starr was conducting was of a kind that would warrant denial of the customary protections of the criminal justice system. Arguably it was not, because no imprisonment of a leader of organized crime, discovery of a terrorist cell, or even exposure of a Watergate scandal was in prospect here.

As already noted, the Clinton case study raises the issue of the rights of suspects and does so in relation to at least two important moral rights, namely the right to silence and the right to privacy. To the analysis of these we now turn.

THE RIGHT TO SILENCE

An Australian commentator has said that

> Like everyone watching those Enron executives plead the Fifth Amendment recently, I thought: wouldn't it be great if these guys were found guilty and sent to a real prison? After all, their actions managed to ruin thousands of lives and to tear at the social fabric, even the national economy, in ways that even the most visionary liquor-store stick-up artist couldn't match.[143]

So exactly what rights were these Enron executives—Kenneth Lay, Jeffrey Skilling, and Andrew Fastow—exercising, and what are the implications for them, for the Enron shareholders, for the former Enron employees, and indeed for the community? In the circumstances of the case, it is very human to feel frustrated, as did this Australian commentator, that the proper processes of an authorized inquiry were being subverted by what appears to be some legal technicality.

The legal right to silence stemmed from the practice in England in the sixteenth century whereby constables were required to bring suspects before an examining justice for interrogation as soon as possible after arrest. Widespread abuses led to judicial distrust of the investigative techniques of examining justices, and the common law came to include the right to silence. Some years after the establishment of the "New Police" in 1829, investigative and judicial functions were separated, and the police were given the exclusive role of questioning suspects. In 1848, the King's Bench issued Judges' Rules, according to which suspects should be issued a caution to the effect that they were entitled to remain silent. Now the right is recognized universally in common law jurisdictions.

In the United States, that right to silence is enshrined in the Fifth Amendment to the Bill of Rights. This amendment was added to the Federal Constitution in 1791 and provides that "no person shall be compelled in any criminal case to be a witness against himself." There are comparable guarantees in state constitutions.[144] In the Enron case, we saw a procession of key figures in the scandal "pleading the Fifth" before a congressional hearing. Even though the right to silence has been in existence for many years, there is still an active debate as to its validity.[145] Some of the arguments in favor of the right to silence are as follows.

The moral right to silence is supposedly based on a narrower, more basic moral right, namely, the right not to self-incriminate. So, for example, a suspect can refuse to be interviewed by police or refuse to be cross-examined in court, because in the course of such interviews or cross-examination, the suspect might incriminate himself or herself. This possibility raises the question of the basis of the moral right not to self-incriminate. One possible justification for the moral right not to self-incriminate in an adversarial system is to ensure fairness between adversaries. The prosecution representing the community is powerful and is attempting to incriminate the defendant. Given this consideration and given the principle that it is worse morally to convict the innocent than to allow the guilty to go free, it is important to provide the defendant with an array of safeguards, including not only the need to furnish proof of guilt beyond reasonable doubt, but also ensuring that the defendant can at least rely on one friend, namely himself or herself. He or she cannot be required to incriminate himself or herself. Certainly, the right to silence guarantees that the defendant can avoid doing so.

A somewhat different view is one that accords the right not to self-incriminate a more fundamental status. In this view, the right not to self-incriminate is a basic moral right that individuals would have under any system of justice, whether that system be adversarial, inquisitorial, or some other. This view is not inconsistent with the preceding view—rather, if acceptable, it complements it.

Here we need to make some distinctions. People might unintentionally incriminate themselves in the context of an interview or cross-examination. Indeed, it is often part of the purpose that interviewers or prosecutors have to get suspects or defendants to so incriminate themselves. Presumably, there is no right not to self-incriminate in this sense. Rather, if there is a right not to self-incriminate, then the right must be a right not to *intentionally* incriminate oneself. The intuitive idea at work here seems to be one related to the basic right to self-defense. Whatever wrongdoing a person has done—including murder—so the argument runs, he or she retains a basic right to defend his or her life and liberty. By analogy, the suggestion seems to be that a person has a basic right not to incriminate oneself in criminal cases in which it is one's liberty that is at issue.

Other arguments in favor of the right to silence do not assert that it is a basic moral right grounded in the right to self-defense; rather, they focus on the alleged untoward consequences of abandoning the legal right to silence.

One such argument relates to the capacity for the judicial system to draw adverse inferences from a defendant's refusing to answer questions. When the Enron senior executives were asked the question, Did you know that the company's reported profits were false?, they were placed in the position that to say no could—if indeed they did know—have involved them in contempt of Congress because it would have been a lie. To say yes would leave them open to criminal charges. By exercising their right to silence, they avoided either adverse outcome. Were it possible to draw inferences from that refusal to answer the question, then a court could have assumed that, given the circumstances of the case, they did indeed know. Therefore, the capacity to draw the inference would have had the same effect as denying them the right to silence—or at the very least, to increase pressure upon the accused to make some sort of admission.

A second argument is that if individuals were required to answer questions about their activities, then there would be an increased possibility of their perjuring themselves to avoid punishment. In the absence of a right to silence, accused persons would be faced with three equally unattractive options: self-incrimination, contempt of court by refusing to answer, or lying. Those who advocate the retention of the right to silence point to the futility of encouraging lying.

A third argument in favor of the right to silence is the "lazy prosecutor" argument. This argument turns upon the expectation that if prosecutors were allowed to compel accused individuals to answer questions, then they would not bother to go to the effort of looking at all the available evidence and interviewing witnesses. This issue was raised in *Miranda vs. Arizona*,[146] in which the Supreme Court stressed the need for the prosecution to prove its case by its own endeavors, rather than resorting to the cruel expedient of compulsion of the suspect.

Arguments against the right to silence tend to focus on the alleged unacceptable consequences in terms of the difficulties it creates for investigators and prosecutors, and ultimately the moral costs to victims. In the case of the Enron executives, when the evidence needed for conviction is extraordinarily voluminous and complex, it would make the prosecution's task a lot easier if it could require the executives to answer questions about what actually occurred. In many corruption cases, the activity not only is complex but also is carried out in secrecy. It is often extremely difficult for the investigator to penetrate the veil of secrecy surrounding corruption, and the right to silence can be seen by the investigator and the prosecutor as making their tasks much more difficult than it ought to be. The end result is that victims' rights are not upheld; shareholders, for example, have been defrauded, but the fraudsters escape scot-free.

This argument presupposes the truth of an empirical claim, namely that the abolition of the right to silence would in fact assist the prosecution. Although this claim is intuitively plausible, it would need to be somehow empirically tested. In this connection, a review of this issue in Australia concluded that this was an unlikely outcome. Most suspects do not exercise their right to remain silent when questioned and in fact cooperate with investigators. Indeed, only 4 percent of suspects charged and tried in the Sydney District Court remained silent in police interviews, and the Review's examination of international data indicated similar results.[147]

A second argument against the right to silence is based on the need for the justice system to have optimal access to the facts of the matter in question so that it can discharge its duties to determine guilt or innocence and to dispense justice. In its strongest form, this argument assumes that courts require the best possible opportunity to get at the truth and that anything that stands in the way of that aim is going to detract from the criminal justice system. Using this argument, the suspect is in the best position to know the ultimate truth of any particular claim, and affording the right to silence might deny the investigator (or the court) access to the best source of evidence. An important consideration that has the effect of qualifying—though not negating—the force of this argument is the recognition that some evidence needs to be excluded because its admission would create the danger of unfair prejudice, cause confusion of the issues, be misleading, or lead to conclusions purely on the grounds of cumulation. The rules for the exclusion of evidence are formalized in the United States's Federal Rules of Evidence, and similar rules obtain in other jurisdictions.

As mentioned before, the issue of silence is still a matter for intense public debate. It is interesting to note that two United Kingdom sources assessing the debate over the last decade agree that while that there are strong arguments in favor of its abolition, those in favor of its retention are even more powerful.[148] The strongest arguments in favor of keeping the right to silence turn upon the right of self-defense. In Australia, a report by the New South Wales Law Reform Commission concluded similarly.[149]

Before leaving the issue of corruption and the right to silence, it is worth noting that different jurisdictions can take very different attitudes toward circumscribing that right. In Hong Kong, the Independent Commission Against Corruption has wide-ranging powers to compel individuals to answer questions, and the information they provide can be used in the case against them. The Independent Commission Against Corruption in New South Wales, Australia, also has circumscribed suspects' rights to silence. However, in the Australian case, the power to compel individuals to answer questions occurs in an open forum, and legal representation is allowed; but if the witness wishes, the evidence collected cannot be used as part of any subsequent criminal proceedings. In effect, the latter approach limits its punishment of offenders to the public exposure of their actions, and their right not to self-incriminate, although qualified, remains essentially intact.

THE RIGHT TO PRIVACY

As mentioned at the beginning of this chapter, Article 12 of the Universal Declaration of Human Rights states that privacy is a fundamental right. Privacy is a complex concept, and it is necessary to look at it more closely for the purposes of ascertaining the role it plays in the investigation and prosecution of corruption.

The issue of balance is very prominent when dealing with privacy. Suspects have a right to privacy in terms of how they are dealt with by the criminal justice system. An even more contentious issue is the right that individuals have to privacy when they are not suspected of any specific crime but are being affected by procedures that are established to prevent and detect corruption occurring. To fully explore the implications of these issues, it is necessary to look more closely at privacy as a right.

Privacy has a social dimension in that it exists only relative to other individuals. If you live alone on a desert island, privacy is not an issue, because there is no one else to see or listen to you. However, few of us live like that, and there is a multitude of others who do see and listen; therefore, the issue of privacy arises. Before going any further, we need to examine what we mean when we talk about privacy.

Denis Galligan, a British legal expert in the area of administrative law, has described the tension between the criminal justice system and individual privacy in the following way.[150] He describes privacy as a series of concentric circles with the individual at the center. We can flesh this out by describing the layers of the circle, as illustrated in the accompanying diagram. At its center would be the inner self-perceptions, sensations, beliefs, and emotions that go to make up the core of the individual. The next layer would be the physical dimension of the individual (including the person's genetic endowment or DNA). Moving further out, there are those personal relations that individuals have with others: family, emotional, and sexual relations. At the next level out are issues about personal autonomy, and the requirements to live in peace, and to pursue one's own aspirations. Further out from the core are issues of privacy that are conferred by ownership of material goods, documents, and data (noting that in many instances, these are held by third parties, like a credit card provider). Finally, furthest from the center are the privacy issues associated with our public roles. These would include matters like fulfilling our obligations as citizens through voting for representatives, whereby intrusion into the process would compromise our ability to fulfill this public role.

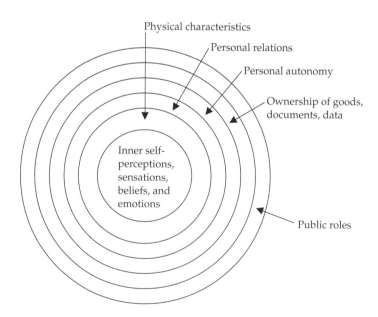

Now we could take issue with the details of Galligan's model, for example, to dispute that personal autonomy is further out than personal relations, or even that personal autonomy can be separated from personal relations and public roles. However, in doing so, one would not necessarily be rejecting the basic ideas behind Galligan's model. These are, first, that privacy is differentiated—there are different types of privacy. Second, privacy is not an absolute right—rather, it is a right that has to be balanced against other rights and interests, such as the community's interest in controlling crime. Third, some types of privacy have greater moral weight than others—so the further a privacy issue is from the center of Galligan's model, the less weight it has against competing factors; and conversely, the closer the privacy issue is to the center, the more weight should be given to those competing factors.

Implicit in this approach is that there should always be a presumption in favor of privacy. This means that in determining the balance between personal privacy, we should start from requiring that the proponents of intruding into privacy justify their case, rather than the individual's needing to justify the right to privacy. In the area of dealing with crimes of corruption, the sorts of justifications that would be essential would relate to the following:

- The seriousness of the crime;
- The degree of reasonable suspicion regarding the person whose privacy is being intruded upon;
- The expectation that the information gained would further the investigation; and
- The lack of alternatives that would not involve privacy intrusions.

Violation of the right to privacy can have serious consequences. In the case of President Clinton's impeachment, details of his personal activities were reported in virtually every media outlet in the world and this had enormous adverse effects on him, his wife, Monica Lewinsky, and even Linda Tripp. Using Galligan's model, consideration of the balance would indicate that Kenneth Starr's pursuit of President Clinton would be difficult to justify. Even if the charges had been proven, the investigation may well have been an improper one—because it violated Clinton's right to privacy. Accordingly, a real question arises as to whether or not Clinton's defensive actions—including possibly perjury—were in fact moral offenses in the circumstances.

Enforcement agencies have the physical, including technological, means and can obtain the necessary legal authority to undertake a variety of actions that intrude upon privacy. They can search premises, seize property and documents, tap telephone conversations, and install listening and video surveillance devices. However, most jurisdictions in liberal democratic countries have complex procedures for authorizing such intrusions that require an independent assessment of the justification for the intrusion, and also mechanisms for making the enforcement agency properly accountable for the protection and use of the information gained.

In the United States, the Fourth Amendment protects citizens from unreasonable searches and seizures, and a search warrant is required. Police are required to provide a neutral and detached judicial officer with a justification, and that officer has to apply the "totality-of-the-circumstances" rule so that the "whole picture" is examined. This rule was established in 1983 in *Illinois vs. Gates*[151] in the context of the Supreme Court's maintaining that a search warrant could be issued on hearsay evidence.

Let us assume that the investigating agency was asking the judicial officer for a warrant to seize the banking records of a suspect. The first thing the agency would need to demonstrate is that the offense is serious enough to justify the warrant. In the Enron case, that task would be easy. Second, it would need to demonstrate that the particular suspect could have committed an offense. The judicial officer would want to see some evidence (even hearsay) that the person was a senior executive or was in a position to be involved in the corruption. Third, the judicial officer may want to know how the information obtained would assist the investigation, and the agency would need to argue that it was likely that monies related to the Enron collapse flowed through that account. Finally, the judicial officer would ask whether there was any other way that the agency could access the information other than by seizing the suspect's personal bank records.

Because Galligan's model would indicate that accessing financial records is not a particularly serious intrusion, we would expect that in a case like this, the judicial officer would have no difficulty in approving the application. However, were the agency to seek authority to install a video camera and microphone in the bedroom of one of the suspects, on the expectation that that step would reveal conversations with other persons about the crime, we would expect a court to require a much higher level of proof, because the camera would also show the suspect undressing or even having sexual relations. That is, this form of surveillance is far more intrusive and, therefore, a much more serious infringement of a suspect's right to privacy. Finally, let us look at a hypothetical example in which the judicial officer would refuse a warrant. Were the agency to seek authority to install a bugging device in the suspect's confessional cubicle when talking to his or her confessor, it is almost certain that such a request would be refused because the information revealed would be close to the center of the accompanying diagrammatic representation.

Before leaving the issue of the right to privacy, it is important to note that we have only looked at the privacy rights of individuals suspected of corruption. Probably corruption, and more particularly fraud, are more effectively controlled by preventative action than they are by reactive response. Accordingly, there is substantial community benefit in adopting policies that involve the collection and the analysis by law enforcement personnel of data pertaining to whole populations of, say, taxpayers, none of whom have been identified as suspects. Such policies intrude upon privacy, albeit much less so than interviewing, surveillance, and the like. Thus, there may well be a conflict between effective law enforcement, on the one hand, and the privacy rights of citizens, on the other.

A salient example here is the Vendor Information Exchange System (VENDEX) established by the New York City Policy Procurement Board to deter corruption in contracting for public works and services. VENDEX works by creating a list of acceptable contractors, which is based upon a questionnaire that requires contractors wishing to nominate to divulge whether the business or any of the key employees has a criminal record. Although this is not the major reason as to why VENDEX has been criticized,[152] it highlights some serious privacy issues. Unlike the search warrant process described before, these contractors are not suspected of committing any offense, yet they are being compelled to answer questions that relate to their personal affairs.

In Australia in the mid-1980s, the federal government sought to enact legislation that would require all citizens to carry a photographic identity card, the *Australia Card*, which would need to be produced for a wide range of financial and government transactions. The government cited very large savings through the elimination of tax evasion and fraud in government programs. Notwithstanding the claimed benefits, there was an enormous public outcry that the government was intruding unjustifiably upon citizens' privacy, and the government shelved the project.

Both the VENDEX and the Australia Card projects were based upon the disputable proposition that corruption can be prevented if governments could collect and analyze personal information. Both projects raise serious issues about the right to privacy, not least because the justification offered for the intrusion is arguably speculative and is not based upon any particular corruption offense having been committed. In the case of the Australia Card, the program violated one of the principles of privacy protection stated in the Organization for Economic Cooperation and Development guidelines,[153] namely, that information collected for one purpose should not be used for another purpose.

These sorts of issues are going to become even more problematic as more records are kept electronically, as more financial transactions are undertaken over the Internet, and as the technical difficulties of storing and analyzing data are solved in the context of cheaper and more widespread use of technology. Also, the cases mentioned earlier concerned governments, but it should be recognized that private sector organizations hold and circulate vast amounts of personal data that could be accessed in the deployment of anti-corruption mechanisms, and accessed without the knowledge of citizens.

ENTRAPMENT

CASE STUDY 9.2   Abscam

"Abscam" was a political scandal involving the arrest of members of Congress on charges of accepting bribery. In an investigation begun in 1978, the Federal Bureau of Investigation created a dummy corporation called Abdul Enterprises, Ltd., and used FBI agents posing as Arab businessmen to contact various public officials for the purpose of offering bribes in return for political favors. The FBI videotaped such meetings involving public officials. The much-publicized tapes were central to successful indictments brought in 1980. One senator and four members of Congress were convicted of bribery and conspiracy. A fifth member of Congress was convicted on other minor charges.

One defendant, Representative Frank Thompson (D–New Jersey), used $24,000 in campaign funds for legal fees related to his Abscam trial in a practice that was then legal but that raised further ethical issues.

Public officials subsequently charged that FBI tactics amounted to entrapment of innocent individuals who would not otherwise have committed any crime. In 1982, the courts overturned the conviction on one member of Congress (Representative Richard Kelly, Florida).[154]

Investigators frequently use deception to assist in gaining convictions. There are many different sorts of deceptive techniques—using police officers not in uniform as decoys, tapping telephones, adopting the "good cop, bad cop" routine in interviews, or pretending that the evidence against a suspect is really a lot stronger than it is to encourage a confession. Of all the deceptive techniques, one of the most contentious is the sting operation as just described in the Abscam case.

John Kleinig has given four reasons as to why deceptive techniques used by investigators (usually police) are morally problematic:

- The possibility that the targeting of those on whom the techniques are going to be used may involve personal, political, or other partisan factors;
- The difficulty of drawing a line on the sort of deceptive tactics that can be used;
- The costs to individual officers of lying as a part of their job; and
- The cost to our social ethos and community values of elements of the criminal justice system using such techniques.[155]

However, the reason for the contentiousness of this sort of activity does not stem principally from its deceptive nature but rather from whether or not someone who is entrapped is really culpable.

As the Supreme Court said in *Sherman vs. United States*,[156] "to determine whether entrapment has been established, a line must be drawn between the unwary innocent and the trap for the unwary criminal." There have traditionally been two approaches for determining whether or not someone has been entrapped and therefore whether his or her rights have been violated. There are the subjective test and the objective test.[157]

The subjective test asks whether the suspect has a disposition to commit crimes of the kind in question. We might establish the existence of such a disposition on the basis of the suspect's past behavior, for example, past criminal convictions. Evidently, the point of this test is to ensure that the person entrapped has the requisite degree of culpability; the concern is that the police might have induced an intention or inclination to commit the crime that was otherwise absent.

The objective test asks whether or not the state has acted improperly by virtue of instigating the crime. This question resolves itself into two issues. The first issue is whether or not the contribution of the police to the creation of the opportunity to commit the crime is excessive. For example, suppose that an undercover police officer supplies a person with the raw materials and the equipment to manufacture heroin, and suppose that the raw materials and equipment are not available to the person from any other source(s). The second issue is whether or not the inducement offered to commit the crime was unreasonable (too strong) for example, offering someone a million dollars to engage in illicit sex.

A possible problem for the subjective test is that it does not rule out strong inducements. Police officers might abuse the system by offering inducements that are too strong, and yet conviction would follow if the suspects had strong dispositions to commit the crime. A related problem arises from the fact that a disposition to commit a crime is not equivalent to an intention to commit that crime. Suppose that someone has a disposition to commit a crime. However, knowing that the person has this disposition, he or she puts himself or herself in a context in which there is no opportunity to commit the crime. Consider a heroin addict who wants to avoid taking heroin and decides to live in a heroin-free area, or a pedophile who wants to avoid the crime of pedophilia by ensuring that he or she is never in the company of children. Now assume that a police officer presents the heroin addict with heroin or the pedophile with what the pedophile believes is an opportunity to engage in sex with a child. These examples show that the mere presence of a disposition is not sufficient for morally justified entrapment, so that the subjective test—at least as described before—would have to be recast.

A possible problem for the objective test is that it protects the guilty. Only people with weak dispositions and/or the absence of a prior intention to commit the crime are innocent. However, if strong inducements are used in cases of suspects with strong dispositions (the guilty), then the guilty will go free. On the other hand, it is far more preferable that the guilty go free than that the innocent are convicted. Thus, this objection is relatively weak. A stronger objection is that the objective test—insofar as it involves random testing—amounts to the government's engaging in integrity testing of its citizens. This practice is surely unacceptable; governments have no right to convict a citizen merely because the citizen fails to resist an inducement to commit a crime, even if it is an inducement that the citizen ought to have resisted. Moreover, the objective test is not a particularly effective test of virtue, because someone who lacked the disposition to commit that kind of crime, or indeed crimes in general, might nevertheless fail the objective test on a single occasion.

From a practical point of view, it would appear that the optimal set of preconditions for a morally defensible act of entrapment would be as follows:

- That there was a specific target set, and not just the random selection of a member of the public;
- That there was some objective evidence that the target was likely to commit a crime of this kind;
- That the target would have been likely to commit this kind of crime, even if the entrapment had not occurred;
- That there were opportunities to commit the crime, other than the opportunity provided by the state;
- That the incentive to commit the crime was not so high as to tempt the (previously) innocent; and
- That other investigation techniques would have failed.

Before leaving the issue of entrapment, it should be noted that the United States's law on this matter is different from that of other common law jurisdictions. In a recent Australian case, a police officer, with the authority of his superiors, committed the crime of importing heroin as a part of a "controlled operation," that is, the police organized a large-scale narcotics importation in an attempt to implicate some suspects in its purchase and distribution. The prosecution failed only because of the criminality of the police officer's actions. The High Court of Australia went to some lengths to emphasize that the case was not lost because of entrapment and that the courts of England, Canada, New Zealand, and Australia have all denied the existence of a substantive common law right of freedom from entrapment.[158] Of course, this fact does not mean that there are no ethical or moral implications of entrapment for police officers in these jurisdictions, only that entrapment is not available as a defense for those who have been entrapped.

POLICE INTEGRITY TESTING

Over the last three decades in the United States and Australia, there has been acceptance of the practice of integrity testing of police. Such integrity testing is not intrinsically different from the sorts of entrapment just discussed, but it does involve entrapment in a particular context, specifically in police internal affairs units or in external anti-corruption agencies, focusing on police officers in particular.

The reason why both the United States and Australia have become involved in integrity testing of police is that there has been a very public recognition of police corruption. In the United States, the Knapp Commission of Inquiry in New York City utilized integrity testing techniques to demonstrate the existence of widespread corruption.[159] In New South Wales, the Wood Royal Commission[160] used its powers as Royal Commission to use high technology equipment to entrap corrupt officers, using corrupt officers who had "rolled over" as the protagonists. In Queensland, another Australian state, the Fitzgerald inquiry[161] found systemic corruption in the police force. In both New South Wales and Queensland, specific police anti-corruption watchdog agencies were established to continue the work of the inquiries indefinitely. Integrity testing was introduced into the London Metropolitan Police in 1998.

In all these jurisdictions, police corruption has been identified as a problem. The fact that the police are employed, equipped, and authorized to enforce the law means that corruption in police forces is a major threat to society, not least to civil liberties. It is for this reason that integrity testing has been introduced.

The nature of the testing in the various jurisdictions is very similar. Typically, situations are created in which the targeted officer is faced with a choice of acting ethically and in accordance with police rules and regulations, or of breaking those rules for some personal benefit. A typical integrity test scenario would be the undercover internal affairs agent's handing over valuable property in circumstances in which the targeted officer has the opportunity of not reporting it and instead of stealing it. Another scenario is the undercover internal affairs agent's posing as a petty criminal who has been arrested, and then offering the targeted officer a bribe not to proceed with the case.

The major delineation in police integrity testing is whether it is targeted or random. In targeted integrity testing, the authority undertaking the program must form some reasonable suspicion that the officer is corrupt. Of the police services previously mentioned, only the NYPD has used random integrity testing. This was subject to a review by KPMG in 1996; the review found that the effectiveness of random integrity testing was not such as to justify its continuation.[162] A recent survey of practices in the eight Australian police forces found that two of them had introduced targeted integrity testing, two more were planning to introduce targeted integrity testing, and none used random integrity testing.[163]

It is clear that the reluctance to adopt random integrity testing is based upon ethical and legal grounds. As noted before, there are no legal impediments to integrity testing, although the United States law does circumscribe the sorts of action that can be taken. Turning to the ethical issues, police unions have reluctantly accepted targeted integrity testing but strongly resist random integrity testing. They argue that it is intrusive and unfair, and that it disempowers and deprofessionalizes their members. A significant problem with random testing is that it undermines the trust between management and employees that is so important for effective working relationships. Building trust is made even more difficult if there is the continual suspicion that some of the apparent day-to-day ethical choices that naturally arise could in fact be instances of deliberate random testing of integrity. On the other hand, as mentioned before, police do exercise considerable powers over citizens, and this fact alone may justify the infringement of what would otherwise be regarded as the moral rights of officers.

We conclude that integrity testing, especially targeted integrity testing, is potentially a useful tool for combating corruption in police services. However, we emphasize that it is not a magic bullet. Its role is presumably as an adjunct to other anti-corruption measures, such as developing a strong organizational ethical framework and an effective system for dealing with complaints against the police.

CONCLUSION

In this chapter, we have explored in detail a number of the moral rights of those suspected of institutional corruption. We have presented a number of case studies and have considered some of the possible violations of rights that took place as a consequence of the investigations and prosecutions of suspects. Here, as elsewhere, a moral balance needs to be struck between the rights of suspects, on the one hand, and the imperative to combat institutional corruption and to prosecute the corrupt. Perhaps that balance was not found in the case of Kenneth Starr's attempt to impeach President Clinton; the suspect's rights were not given sufficient weight. On the other hand, some might feel that the balance has not been found in cases such as the Enron scandal, for precisely the opposite reason; in this case, suspects' rights have been given too much weight.

chapter ten

Corruption
and Punishment

In this chapter, we will

- Consider the relation between corruption and punishment
- Discuss the standard theoretical justifications for punishment, for example, retributive, and deterrence
- Offer a detailed account of the restorative theory of justice
- Discuss the ethics of imprisonment as a form of punishment.

Many forms of institutional corruption, such as bribery and fraud, are also crimes. As such they attract punishment, including imprisonment. Of course, many forms of corruption are not crimes, and as such they do not necessarily attract punishment, or attract only minor forms of punishment. Our focus in this chapter is in large part on forms of institutional corruption that are also crimes and that therefore necessarily attract punishment. That is, our concern is with forms of corruption that are regarded by a society as very serious forms of moral wrongdoing.

Moreover, we focus for the most part in this chapter on a subclass of forms of corruption that are also crimes; our concern in this chapter is principally with white-collar crime. This narrow and selective focus is a matter of heuristics. In the first place, white-collar crime is the most salient crime category that in large part comprises acts of corruption; white-collar crimes are more often than not acts of corruption. In the second place, there is a reasonable body of empirical work in relation to white-collar crime and the punishment thereof, and this is simply not the case for other categories of corruption. It goes without saying that the narrow and selective focus in this particular chapter is entirely consistent with our view that the notion of institutional corruption is a very wide one, embracing a diverse array of types of corrupt action. In particular, there are many forms of corruption other than the economic variety.

It is sometimes claimed that, historically, there has been a greater tolerance of corruption—especially corruption that takes the form of white-collar crimes—than there was of crime in general and of street crimes in particular.[164] Perhaps assaults and robberies were more morally repugnant to the community than, say, fraud or bribery. Indeed, some forms of white-collar "crime" were formerly violations of civil or administrative law, rather than criminal law, for example, pollution or health and safety infringements. Accordingly, the punishment to be inflicted on transgressors was correspondingly more lenient. Moreover, it is sometimes claimed that white-collar criminals are very different from ordinary street criminals. In particular, it is suggested that unlike street criminals, white-collar criminals tend to be reasonably well-educated; belong to the middle or upper socioeconomic classes; be very concerned with maintaining an image of social respectability; not have an emotionally dysfunctional family background or history of substance abuse; and be rational rather than impulsive in their behavior.[165] This being the case, it is sometimes argued, the forms of punishment that are appropriate for white-collar criminals ought to be different from those imposed on street criminals. For example, the imposition of substantial fines is said to be likely to have greater deterrent effects on white-collar criminals than on street criminals.[166]

There is some evidence that attitudes toward white-collar criminals are changing; there is less public tolerance for white-collar crimes, and in particular for large-scale corporate crime.[167] Certainly, penalties for various forms of white-collar crime and corruption are increasing.[168] Moreover, there appear to be higher rates of conviction and increased recourse to prison terms for many categories of white-collar crime and corruption, such as fraud.[169]

Having said that, the incarceration rates for white-collar crime as a proportion of all offenses is very low. In Australia, data provided by the Australian Bureau of Statistics indicate that, as of June 2000, only 3.5 percent of prisoners are sentenced for "fraud and misappropriation"—the smallest of all categories listed.[170] Consequently, the analysis of the morality of punishment provided in this chapter, of necessity, is in large part concerned with the punishment of criminals as a generic category of wrongdoers; we cannot do otherwise, given that only a small subset of criminals is of the white-collar variety.

Furthermore, some recent work provides evidence that the sharp and straightforward contrast traditionally drawn between street criminals and white-collar criminals is open to serious doubt. For example, Weisburd and Waring[171] have recently argued that certain categories of white-collar offenders, for example, high-frequency, chronic, white-collar offenders, have many of the properties of street offenders, although there are some differences, such as the length of their careers and the age at which they desist. The careers of white-collar offenders are longer—they are often active well into their forties; by contrast, the careers of street criminals typically begin in their late teens and end by the age of thirty. At the very least, it is evident that the picture is a complex one, in relation to the profile and to the careers of both white-collar criminals and street criminals.

An important distinction in this regard pertains to the motivation for corruption. In Chapter 4, we distinguished between corruption in the service of *individual* self-interest and corruption in the service of narrow *collective* self-interest. In regard to the latter, the collective is typically an organization or solidaristic group, such as a family or the members of a closed organizational culture, for example, a network of corrupt police. One important species of corruption in the service of a narrow collective self-interest is corporate corruption. Corporate corruption, such as environmental pollution or the bribery of foreign companies, is obviously to be distinguished from individual corruption, such as embezzlement or selling confidential documents. The former is corruption in the service of the interests and goals of the organization to which one belongs; the latter is corruption in the service of one's personal interest or goals—the victim may well be the corporation to which the offender belongs. The matter is further complicated by the existence of corporate corruption in which the short-term success of the business organization is pursued, yet the organization is, nevertheless, essentially being used by executives to line their own pockets. Consider, for example, the Enron scandal in the United States or the recent HIH collapse in Australia. And there are further distinctions that could be made here, many of which have already been elaborated in earlier chapters. For example, there is the distinction between ordinary corruption motivated by self-interest, for example, financial gain, and noble cause corruption.

Arguably, corporate crimes committed in the interests of the business organization are rational in a way that street crimes and many other white-collar crimes are not. Perhaps such corporate crimes are "deliberate acts that weigh potential costs against economic gains . . . are situationally opportunistic . . . and [nonhabitual] because executives are not committed to a 'life of crime.'"[172] On the other hand, many street criminals and noncorporate white-collar offenders operate opportunistically, rather than habitually; and at least some corporate criminals act habitually. If we think of the rational criminal as someone who acts on the basis of the benefit to be had analyzed against the likelihood of being caught and the severity of the punishment if caught, then corporate criminals might be more rational than other criminals simply by virtue of the prevailing environment in which they are operating. For example, there is evidence that those who engage in crimes and/or acts of corruption on behalf of large corporations are likely to extract major financial benefits for themselves and their companies, and they are unlikely to be caught or severely punished. According to Simpson, "The body of empirical evidence suggests that it is profitable for firms to violate the law because the risk of discovery is low and the benefits of crime outweigh the relatively modest monetary costs of prosecution and guilty findings."[173]

Here it is worth noting that the habitual criminal who is also intelligent and careful may be more rational than the opportunistic one, because the habitual criminal may be an opportunity seeker in an environment in which there are plenty of opportunities to be sought out and a low probability of being caught and punished.

These various sets of distinctions between types of crime and corruption, and between motivations for crime and corruption, are important when it comes to the issue of punishing criminals and the corrupt. Crimes of passion or crimes committed by drug addicts in the service of their addiction are unlikely to be deterred by the threat of punishment. On the other hand, crimes motivated by financial gain on the basis of premeditated, rationalistic, cost/benefit analyses are likely to be deterred by the threat of punishment, but only if the punishment is severe and/or the probability of being caught is high. As far as "just deserts" are concerned, perhaps someone who performs a corrupt action for the sake of good ends should attract a lesser penalty than someone who performs the same corrupt action out of naked self-interest. Moreover, given that penalties ought to be meted out in part on the basis of considerations such as deterrence, perhaps—other things being equal—penalties for corporate corruption need to be greater than for individual corruption. If so, this might be because corruption in the service of organizational goals is typically much more difficult to eradicate than individual corruption of the same type and magnitude.

PUNISHMENT

The three central theoretical approaches to punishment are the following:[174]

- Retributive theory of punishment;
- Deterrence theory of punishment; and
- Rehabilitation theory.

The *retributive theory* begins with the assumption that some person or persons are morally responsible for a blameworthy act of moral wrongdoing. Thus, the persons are guilty of a moral—and often legal—offense, and accordingly they deserve to be punished. This account does not concern itself with consequences such as deterrence or rehabilitation; rather, the focus is on the wrongdoer(s) and the wrongfulness of the act considered in itself. Naturally, it is crucial that the alleged wrongdoer is in fact the person who performed the act and is indeed morally responsible for the act. In the paradigm case, the wrongdoer will have offended against some uncontroversial, central, moral principle that is enshrined in the criminal law, for example, murder, and the wrongdoer will have acted intentionally and with premeditation. Moreover, the person will not have had any moral excuse for the act of wrongdoing, for example, he or she was not coerced and was not in a drug-induced state such that the person was unable to control his or her behavior.

Retributivism assumes that we are autonomous moral agents who can make a reason-based decision to do good or evil, and to act on that decision. Retributivism appeals to the deep moral intuition that wrongdoers deserve to be punished: this is its strength. Its weakness lies in its apparent failure to take into account a range of other moral considerations, deterrence and rehabilitation in particular. An offender may deserve to be imprisoned, but what if imprisonment merely serves as an incubator of crime rather than a deterrence to it?

Naturally, the retributive theory might be cast in such a way that it can partially accommodate rehabilitation and/or deterrence considerations. For example, a particular rehabilitation program or effective deterrent might be consistent with what the offender deserves. Moreover, what an offender deserves might be more broadly conceived; recourse might be had to his or her personal history and circumstances. If so, it might turn out that the offender deserves to be rehabilitated and not merely punished for the offense itself. Furthermore, the costs to the community and the victim need to be factored in, and the retributivist could acknowledge this fact; after all, the community and the victim need to receive their just deserts as much as the offender does. An extended period of incarceration might be what the offender deserves, but what if imprisonment is prohibitively expensive to the community? Or what if imprisonment prevents the offender from paying much needed and deserved compensation to the victim?

A general issue that the retributive theory faces is to determine what punishment is in fact deserved—how to make the punishment fit the crime. Should white-collar criminals be made to suffer financial burdens such as fines, whereas murderers get the death penalty? What of muggers and other violent criminals who physically harm but do not kill their victims; should they be subjected to corporal punishment?

Consideration of the available punishments suggests that reliance on desert alone is insufficient; deterrence, for example, needs to be given some weight when it comes to punishment. The retributive theory is not so much false as it is insufficient; it captures an important dimension of the justification for punishment, but only one dimension.

The *deterrence theory* is a consequentialist one; it focuses on the potential future acts of wrongdoing. Here we need to distinguish between specific and general deterrence, and between objective and perceptual deterrence. Specific deterrence concerns the individual offender who is punished. The question to be asked is whether offender A will be deterred from committing future offenses if he or she is given a certain punishment for his or her current offense. General deterrence concerns the future writ large. Here the question to be asked is whether giving offender A a certain punishment for his or her current offense will deter *other* potential offenders from committing that offense. Clearly, a given punishment might have no effect, or even an adverse effect, on A, yet successfully deter others.

Objective deterrence concerns the relationship between actual punishments meted out and the levels of crime those punishments are intended to deter. For example, does imprisonment of white-collar offenders reduce the levels of white-collar crime? By contrast, perceptual deterrence concerns the relationship between a would-be offender's subjective judgments of probability and severity of punishment on the one hand, and his or her self-reported participation in crime on the other. The question here is whether the would-be offender's *beliefs* about the likelihood and severity of punishment act as a deterrent.

There is a good deal of controversy surrounding the success/failure of punishment as a deterrent. Some think that it has been successful in relation to at least certain categories of crime; others hold that it has been a failure across the board.[175]

Presumably, punishment is an effective deterrent in relation to certain kinds of crime and corruption, but only if it is thought by would-be offenders to be both highly probable and severe. If the punishment meted out is regarded as lenient, offenders might choose to put up with it as an acceptable cost in their cost/benefit analyses. On the other hand, if being caught and punished is thought to be extremely unlikely, then even severe punishments might not deter.

Unfortunately, many forms of crime and corruption, including many categories of fraud and bribery, do not meet these minimum conditions for the efficacy of deterrence. For example, there are simply not the resources to pursue all cases of even quite serious frauds in most contemporary societies. And even if there are resources to pursue some sort of investigation, they may well be inadequate given the power, resources, and legal expertise of some offenders, such as large corporations. For example, in relation to corporate crime, the antitrust budget of the U.S. Justice Department is one-twentieth of the advertising budget of the Proctor and Gamble Corporation.[176] Certainly the results of corporate anti-corruption bodies such as the Environmental Protection Authority (EPA) in the United States are often less than impressive. Between 1973 and 1978, EPA enforcement of industrial violations of the Clean Water Act in Region 11 (headquartered in New York City) resulted in approximately 43 percent of cases with the verdict "no action," 40 percent "warning letter," and only 4 percent "severe sanction."[177]

However, these problems are not so much problems for deterrence theory as such, as they are for the *implementation* of deterrence theory. Obviously, if deterrence is to work, then it will have to be adequately resourced. On the other hand, deterrence theory is problematic if in fact it *cannot* be adequately resourced, that is, if the resources are simply not available. Certainly, investigations leading to prosecutions in the case of complex, white-collar crimes are hugely expensive of time, money, and energy.

Moreover, deterrence theory has other problems. For one thing, punishments handed out to offenders may indeed have both a specific and a general deterrence effect. However, these punishments might be so punitive as to be unjust; the offenders might not be receiving their just deserts. Moreover, if deterrence is to work, this might involve not only severe punishment but also *immediate* punishment. Accordingly, due process rights of suspects may be compromised. These kinds of objections to deterrence theory are available to retributivists, in particular.

Furthermore, there is some evidence that deterrence theory does not work, even on its own terms—at least, when it comes to some categories of crime and corruption. For example, Katz has argued that armed robbers are often motivated by a desire to be feared and respected as persons who seek danger and excitement, and thus they are not fazed by the prospect of imprisonment or even death.[178] Perhaps many "corporate cowboys" and big-time fraudsters think of themselves in analogous ways. If so, punishment as an instrument of deterrence—even when the punishment in question is both probable and severe—may not deter.

As is the case with the retributivist theory, deterrence theory has identified a central and an important feature of punishment, namely, its role as a deterrent. However, like retributivist theory, deterrence theory captures only one dimension of punishment; it is insufficient. As we have seen, it fails to grasp the importance of retribution. But it also fails to grasp the importance of rehabilitation. In the last analysis, neither retribution nor deterrence is enough. As we have argued in earlier chapters, the successful combating of crime and corruption presupposes a moral community: a community of people who for the most part try to do what is morally right and to avoid doing what is morally wrong, because they desire or believe that they ought to do what is right and to avoid doing what is wrong. This being so, it becomes important to reintegrate as many wrongdoers back into the community as is possible; but reintegration relies on wrongdoers' having a change of character, or at least of motivational attitude; they need to abandon a life of crime and corruption in favor of a life of compliance with laws and social norms. But such long-term compliance requires more than deterrence; it also requires a belief on the part of offenders that social norms ought to be complied with and a corresponding desire to comply with them. In short, rehabilitation of the criminal and the corrupt is a necessary part of combating crime and corruption.

According to some of the proponents of *rehabilitation theory*, the retributivist conception is entirely erroneous; in particular, the notion of punishment being justified by guilt is supposedly misguided. The retributivist view presupposes that autonomous agents make rational decisions to do good or evil and that they then act on those decisions; moreover, it presupposes the notion of moral responsibility and therefore the reality of free will. However, such a view, so it is claimed, is inconsistent with the scientific conception of human beings and their behavior. Human beings, like physical objects, supposedly operate entirely in accordance with scientific laws of cause and effect; their actions are not free but are determined by causal laws. Accordingly, their behavior can be manipulated once those laws are known. Such views have been espoused by the likes of B. F. Skinner.[179] Naturally, one option open to the "scientific" conception is to use punishment as a deterrent in the context of the manipulation of the behavior of offenders. However, as we have seen, deterrence is insufficient. Accordingly, an alternative option becomes salient, namely, rehabilitation—albeit rehabilitation in accordance with the scientific method. In one influential conception, the practice of punishment should be abandoned in favor of a therapeutic response to crime.[180] This approach is most plausible in relation to certain categories of offenders, such as pedophiles, serial violent offenders, or those who offend because of their drug or alcohol addiction. It is the case that many such offenders really do seem not to be in control of themselves; rather, they seem to be under the control, so to speak, of their physiology, chemistry, or dysfunctional emotional history.

However, the rehabilitation theory, and certainly its therapeutic variant, is open to serious questioning.[181] In the first place, science has not delivered a complete, consistent, and well-confirmed theory of human behavior; we do not have a set of reliable causal laws that would enable us to successfully manipulate the behavior of the corrupt and the criminal. In the second place, even when the therapeutic response works, it relies on the freely made decision of the offender to cooperate; when an offender resists treatment, it is bound to fail. So even in the therapeutic model, moral responsibility reenters the picture. Lastly, therapy is clearly not what is required for many categories of offender.

Even if the therapeutic model has validity—albeit limited validity—its application to the small subset of criminals who commit corruption offenses raises some specific issues. For white-collar criminals, engendering a sense of moral questioning is made even more difficult by the value that our society places upon material wealth. When Gordon Gekko said that "greed is good" in the movie *Wall Street*, he was articulating a widely held rationalization of corruption, one that would surely undermine the attempts of any therapeutic intervention that aims to convince the white-collar criminal of the moral problems with corruption.

More generally, the rehabilitation approach is unidimensional; it fails to accept—as it must—the centrality of retribution and of deterrence to dealing with criminality and corruption. Rehabilitation must surely begin with some sense on the part of the offender that crime and corruption is morally problematic and is therefore not a way of life that the offender wants to continue with. At the same time, rehabilitation for many offenders is unlikely to take place without some element of deterrence; deterrence is a necessary, but not a sufficient, condition for rehabilitation.

In conclusion, the retributivist, deterrence, and rehabilitation theories each have something important to offer in relation to the question of punishment. Punishment should be deserved, it should deter, and it should contribute to, rather than undermine, rehabilitation. However, none of the three theories is adequate on its own. Accordingly, the way forward looks to be some sort of mixed account, one that combines each of three elements and that does so in such a way as to yield a coherent whole. At any rate, in the next section we turn to a consideration of so-called restorative justice theory. Restorative justice theory, at least in some versions, does in fact combine each of the three elements in question.

RESTORATIVE JUSTICE

The term "restorative justice" has come to mean many different things to different people—so much so that we fear that it is just ceasing to have any clear reference.[182] It is apparently being used to refer to an extraordinarily wide and diverse range of formal and informal interventions, including (1) victim/offender conferences in criminal justice contexts; (2) discretionary problem-solving policing initiatives in disputes between citizens; (3) conflict resolution workshops in organizational contexts; (4) team-building sessions in occupational settings; (5) marital advice and counseling sessions; (6) parental guidance and the admonishment of misbehaving children; and (7) apologizing for offensive or otherwise hurtful remarks in institutional and other settings.

The scope of the term *restorative justice* has widened to the point that it now has within its purview—at least potentially—any and all harmful, conflictual, or otherwise morally problematic actions, situations, or relationships. But even the term *justice*—let alone, *restorative justice*—cannot sensibly embrace the totality of what is harmful or otherwise morally problematic. Many moral problems are not principally matters of injustice. A drug addict may well be doing great harm to himself or herself, but the addict is not necessarily committing or been in receipt of any injustices. Interventions of various kinds may be necessary if a child is to undergo appropriate moral development; but such interventions are not necessarily in response to any injustice, and being developmental, ex hypothesi, they are not restorative or reeducative in any sense. Conflict may arise from a variety of causes other than injustice, including distrust, lack of sympathy, jealousy, and ambition. Finally, many acts of wrongdoing are not principally acts of injustice. Murder is profoundly wrong, but it is not essentially wrong by virtue of being unjust.

Naturally, many sorts of wrongdoing give rise to questions of justice. For example, it would be unjust for a murderer to go free. But many sorts of wrongdoing are not *essentially* issues of justice. Consider again the drug addict or the unreasonably jealous husband.

In light of the preceding, we have decided to restrict our use of the term *restorative justice* to contexts in which moral rights—as distinct from other sorts of wrongdoing or harm-causing—have been, or might potentially be, infringed and in which there is a need for redress or repair in relation to these infringements. Moreover, we are especially concerned with a subclass of those moral rights that the criminal justice system has been designed (however inadequately) to protect, namely, rights to protection from fraud, theft, bribery, falsification of evidence, abuse of power, and other criminal acts properly describable as acts of corruption. Other kinds of problems, including many conflict situations, are no doubt in various respects similar to cases in which moral rights have been infringed, and no doubt sometimes also susceptible of treatment by similar methods, but we doubt that this is typically or even very often the case. Nor should we be taken as necessarily rejecting the value or efficacy of any or all the methods that are used under the banner of restorative justice. There does seem to be a need in our society to explicitly confront moral problems and to revive a variety of formal and informal mechanisms for exposing and resolving them. At any rate, on pain of losing our grip on the topic of restorative justice, we have opted for our narrow definition.

The general concept of justice is complex, embracing notions of procedural justice (for example, fair trial) and distributive justice (for example, fair wages) as well as the notion of justice of greatest interest to us, namely, commutative justice, or justice in the sphere of punishment, rehabilitation, reintegration, and the like. As we have seen, in relation to punishment, there are an array of theories that are available, including retributive and deterrence theories. A further category of theory is in fact the explicitly called restorative justice theories. Restorative justice theorists emphasize the moral education of the wrongdoer and his or her reintegration into the community.

As we have already indicated, we do not believe that these general accounts are mutually exclusive. Indeed, in our view, elements of all three kinds of theory are required if a satisfactory theory of commutative justice is to result. Surely, consequences, including harm reduction, are important considerations; and deterrence—based on a credible threat of punishment—does in certain circumstances work. Consider the enforcement of speeding and drunk-driving laws. On the other hand, the evidence suggests that restorative justice programs in relation to juvenile offenders also work. Consider in this connection the so-called Wagga Wagga model of youth conferencing and its evaluation.[183] The youth conferencing process involves confronting a young offender with his or her victim in the presence of a number of the offender's and the victim's significant others, for example, members of the families of both parties. A discussion ensues, chaired by, in the case of the Wagga Wagga model, a police officer. The victim explains the impact that the offense has had on his or her life, expresses his or her feeling toward the offender, and so on. The offender also speaks and perhaps exhibits remorse. The situation is in large part confessional, in the sense to be explained later.

The success of these practical programs constitutes support for restorative justice as a theory. Moreover, reintegration might itself be a consequence to be aimed at. So restorative justice is not necessarily an alternative to all forms of consequentialism. Finally, some retributivist *sui generis* principles, such as that the guilty ought to be the ones to be punished or the ones to compensate victims, need to be maintained in many circumstances.[184] Indeed, as we will argue in detail later, retribution ought to be a component element in many restorative justice programs. In short, we are pluralists. Moreover, as pluralists we do not accept that any unitary theory, be it retributivist, deterrence, or restorative, can adequately accommodate the plurality of moral considerations in play. For example, in our view even sophisticated consequentialists do not in the final analysis succeed in reducing or otherwise accommodating retributivist considerations.[185] As pluralists, we do not disregard, attempt to explain away, or otherwise downplay moral consequences, the importance of deterrence, or the internal moral dynamics of reintegration, merely because we are also committed to punishment as desert. Nor do we see workable deterrence-based or restorative justice programs as being able to jettison retributivist principles.

Restorative justice in the United States, United Kingdom, and Australia, or at least its applications in criminal justice contexts, has been associated with developing and implementing institutional mechanisms such as youth conferencing, and in so doing, has in effect resurrected the institution of confession and (implicitly) the theoretical moral framework that underpins it.[186] These countries have, of course, developed other sorts of restorative justice programs that are not predominantly confessional in character, for example, programs in workplace conflict and team building. As such they require voluntary participation, open and frank discussion, and agreement on procedures and goals, and they presuppose some framework of shared moral principles.

Moreover, confession has been used in a wide variety of situations in which moral principles have been infringed, but not any moral rights. So the device of confession has been used in contexts above and beyond what we have been calling restorative justice contexts. Nevertheless, we believe that confession is a central element in many restorative justice programs and that the exploration of it may assist in the process of providing a philosophical foundation for, and taxonomy of, the varieties of restorative justice programs.

Here it is also important to point out that restorative justice in general, as well as many of its associated institutional mechanisms, is not something new and exotic. It has been part and parcel of systems of justice for thousands of years, in both Western and other cultures. For example, the institutional device of confession is a mechanism of restorative justice. Moreover, the practice of confession has existed in one form or another in most societies, including Christian societies in the West and the East, Japanese society, and New Zealand's Maori society.[187]

Confession ideally consists of (1) voluntary but painful confrontation of an individual with his or her moral failing; (2) truthful communication/expression of this moral failing to an/other person(s) such as a person's so-called significant others or the rest of the social group; (3) feelings of shame in respect to those moral failings; (4) emotional release from the burden of bottled-up guilt; (5) resolve or commitment on the part of the individual to refrain from wrongdoing and to try to make amends for past wrongdoing.

Confession presupposes (1) the existence of social norms that the individual has voluntarily infringed but that the individual accepts, or can be persuaded to accept; (2) that the moral worth of an individual is something that the individual believes and feels to be very important to himself or herself; and (3) that the moral approval of others is very important to the individual.

Finally, confession can result in behavioral change in the light of this moral watershed and moral reaffirmation by the moral community (and perhaps in some cases, reintegration of the wrongdoer back into the moral community to which he or she belongs).

Confession has proved to be a powerful device for moral transformation and reconciliation with victims in many different times, places, and contexts, including criminal justice contexts. However, it is a device that has important limitations and that can be misused. Accordingly, even if restorative justice and its associated institutional mechanisms are as successful as their proponents claim, there are some important qualifying and somewhat deflationary points that need to be made concerning confessional devices in particular.

First, confession can simply be deployed as a mechanism for social control by those who happen to be in charge of the processes. Historically, confession has often failed, been misused, and indeed at times has served grossly immoral purposes. Consider the Soviet communist show trials of the 1930s or the Chinese Peoples' Courts of the Cultural Revolution. Confession can simply be an exercise in social control for its own sake and can have as its main effect the destruction of the moral autonomy of the individual. Accordingly, the use of confessional devices cannot be given a general endorsement in either nonreligious and nonpolitical restorative justice settings, or elsewhere.

Second, and relatedly, restorative justice mechanisms should involve moral reflection and moral judgment making—we don't mean judgmentalism—directed to the truth; they ought not simply be the occasions for socially imposed, uncritical triggering of emotions—such as shame—

emotions that have been unhinged from cognitive states grounded in moral reality or even in moral reflection.

Third, restorative justice mechanisms might have problems in relation to crimes in which the victim does not exist or exists only in a diffuse form. For example, in the case of murder, the victim has ceased to exist; so in what sense can any important moral relationships be restored? Again, in the case of many crimes, such as fraud and corruption, the victim is a corporation or government organization or—in the case of tax fraud—the community as a whole. Accordingly, there is no specific human victim who can confront the offender, and there is no easily identifiable moral relationship that can be restored, other than perhaps tangential relationships, such as those with loved ones.

It might be replied that in the preceding sorts of cases, it is the moral relationship of the offender to the community at large that is at issue, and this can be restored by, for example, having community representatives in the case of many white-collar crimes such as tax evasion. Unfortunately, the presence of such representatives does not necessarily generate the requisite degree of moral emotion; and for good reason, they are only victims in an attenuated sense. On the other hand, insofar as compensation can be paid and the community is accepting of that payment as a morally adequate response, then reintegration may well be possible. However, such a process of reintegration is based on paying one's dues—hardly a notion exclusive to restorative justice.

RESTORATIVE JUSTICE AND RETRIBUTIVE JUSTICE

As has already been mentioned, among the proponents of restorative justice, there is a strong tendency to contrast restorative justice and retributivism, and to disparage the latter and strongly recommend the former. This recommendation is often based on the following two claims. First, it is claimed that retributivist, but not restorative, conceptions are punitive. Second, it is claimed that the restorative justice program, unlike the retributivist criminal justice system, emphasizes informal processes that place the moral relationship between the victim and the offender center stage. By contrast, the retributivist system involves a formal process of the application of abstract principles of justice by state functionaries to offenders: the victim has no part to play. Let us first respond to the latter claim.

We need first to remind ourselves of the fundamental role that the criminal justice system is at least *supposed* to have. The criminal justice system ought to buttress and enforce social norms. Social norms are a society's accepted moral principles. As such, social norms are fundamental to social life. Thus, social norms against random killing enable cooperative economic and family institutions. Moreover, social norms are in large part enshrined in the criminal law or its equivalents. Theft, assault, murder, rape, child molestation, fraud, and so on are actions that violate social norms in contemporary societies, and they are also criminal acts. Indeed, it is because they are held to be profoundly morally wrong that perpetrators of these acts are held criminally liable. Moreover, some of these actions are regarded as morally worse than others (for example, murder is morally worse than theft). Accordingly, the punishments meted out for murder are in general greater than for theft. In short, the criminal law is essentially a formalization, regimentation, and attempted objectification of society's most basic moral principles. Individuals can afford to disagree about, and indeed infringe with impunity, many moral principles—but not those moral principles enshrined in the criminal law. In effect, these moral principles are agreed by the society to be objectively valid. Moreover, these moral principles include not only prohibitions against specific forms of behavior but also moral principles in relation to moral responsibility and punishment: for example, the principle that moral responsibility consists in part of having an intention to commit a wrong or the principle that only those who are responsible for crimes should be punished and that the wrongdoer should be the one to pay compensation.

So criminal justice systems have developed complex sets of moral principles of the kind just described over long periods of time. Some of these principles are doubtless questionable or imperfectly applied. Moreover, there may well be a need to make greater use of informal processes and to give victims a greater role in both formal and informal processes. However, the point we want to stress here is that any system of justice—whether based on general principles of restorative justice or of retributivist justice—would also need to include its own complex set of *specific* principles, if it is to adequately and substantially replace the existing system. Having an array of processes is hardly sufficient. In short, the so-called restorative justice paradigm is in its theoretical and institutional infancy; or at least it is in such infancy if it sees itself as something more than simply a set of ancillary institutional processes to be grafted onto the existing system.

Let us turn to punishment. Restorative justice is often contrasted to retributive justice, on the grounds that the latter is held to be committed to punishment for its own sake, and the former to abandoning punishment in favor of shame, reconciliation, and forgiveness. We will argue that there is an ineliminable role for principles of retributive justice, including punishment, in the concept of restorative justice. We will further argue that the concept of shame is more closely related to punishment than might have been thought. Consequently, shame and punishment are not alternatives, but they go hand in hand within an acceptable restorative justice framework.

Let us first introduce some distinctions. First, there is the suffering in the form of painful feelings of shame experienced by an offender who undergoes a restorative justice process. Second, there is the restitution that an offender might be called upon to provide to his or her victim (for example, returning money that the offender has defrauded someone of). This is a burden imposed on the offenders; it is not simply the restoring of the victim's prior circumstances by some third party (for example, the taxpayer). Third, there is the compensation that might be paid by the offender to the victim to make up for the harm done (for example, the psychological suffering inflicted by the knowledge that one has been defrauded). Again, this is a burden imposed on the offender, and it is a burden above and beyond that comprising the restitution. Fourth, there is the punishment that might be imposed on the offender for his or her wrongdoing. By "punishment" it is not here meant simply restitution or compensation. For example, not only might a fraudster need to pay back the money that he or she in effect stole (restitution) and to make some further payment for the harm done to the victim (compensation), but also he or she might need to be punished for doing wrong.

Armed with this fourfold distinction, let us consider suffering in relation to confession. Confession necessarily involves suffering on the part of the confessor—it minimally involves the painful feelings of shame generated by his or her own as well as others' knowledge of the wrongdoing. So punishment, at least in the sense of painful feelings, is part and parcel of the restorative justice process, including the process that is manifested in confession. Part of the point of confession is to get wrongdoers to confront the fact of their wrongdoing, and that is necessarily a painful process.

Moreover, a wrongdoer accepts the community's principles of justice in relation to restitution, compensation, and punishment. Accordingly, a wrongdoer will typically accept the proposition that he or she—rather than some third party, such as the taxpayer—ought to provide restitution and compensation. Accordingly, restorative justice entails the imposition of burdens on the guilty above and beyond the suffering associated with shame. To this extent, it embraces a retributivist principle.

But what of punishment, as distinct from the suffering of shame, or the burdens of restitution and compensation? If punishment is an accepted moral principle in the community, then the wrongdoer will also accept that he or she should be punished. But this acceptance still leaves the question of whether punishment should in fact be inflicted. Here there are two questions that need to be kept separate: Should the guilty suffer and/or be made to redress the results of the wrongdoing? If the guilty should suffer, who should inflict the suffering? In general, suffering is a bad thing to be avoided and not to be inflicted on oneself or others. But we have already seen that the suffering of the guilty is justifiable—indeed mandatory—within a restorative justice framework, to the extent that it is involved in the shaming process and in restitution and compensation. But could there be a justification for some further infliction of suffering, namely, punishment for doing wrong? Suppose that an employer is hell-bent on making his worker suffer, say by continually using his position of authority to humiliate her. For her part, she is an innocent victim. A court case ensues, and he is found guilty. He is very wealthy and able to pay an amount to her by way of restitution and compensation. The employee's physical health returns, and she is no longer fearful of him, since she takes another job and the magistrate's threat to lock him up next time deters him from any further actions. However, he has gone unpunished, because the money he paid to her was of no great consequence to him, given his wealth. Nor does he accept that he has done anything wrong. As far as he is concerned, he would again cheerfully do exactly as he did, given the same circumstances. After all, it gave him a certain amount of pleasure to be able to dominate and inflict suffering on his employees. More specifically, if the man is to be reintegrated into the community, could this undertaking be done without some form of punishment? Here, Hegel and Reinhold Niebuhr are instructive.[188]

This kind of case serves to illustrate what might be called the "moral bond" between individuals. After all, morality is predominantly concerned with interpersonal relationships, including relationships to strangers as well as to the members of one's family and immediate community. Offenders breach these moral bonds. In a reintegrative theory, some form of punishment is necessary for the purposes of reintegration, and it is necessary for reintegration by virtue of the fact that the punishment (1) "washes away the stigma of the crime"[189] that is a barrier to restoration of moral bonds and (2) educates the moral judgment of the criminal so that he or she conforms to the requisite moral principles. In our example, it is hard to see how either of these two goals could be achieved in the absence of any punishment.

An important additional point to be made here is that, as Niebuhr puts it, the punishment should not belittle or degrade, but rather should inspire repentance and reintegration.[190] Accordingly, the punishment should accord with reasonable moral principles that the offender could come to accept as being reasonable and just; and ideally the offender should actually consent to the punishment—a quintessential Hegelian idea. This leads to the question as to what precise form such punishment should take. It could certainly be argued that imprisonment is not the best form of punishment for many, if not most, crimes or forms of corruption. Let us now turn, then, to the important issue of imprisonment.

IMPRISONMENT

The most obvious feature of prisons is that they restrict freedom; to be a prisoner is to have lost one's freedom. Let us then briefly consider the notion of freedom. There are different kinds of freedom. There is freedom of movement, freedom to buy and sell, freedom of association, freedom of thought and speech, and so on. Obviously, prison restricts some of these freedoms more than others. Freedom is intrinsically good; it is good in itself. But freedom is also a means to other goods. For example, the freedom to pursue a career is a means to making money and ultimately is a means to well-being.

We need to distinguish between negative and positive freedom. Negative freedom, or liberty, is freedom from interference. For example, if a person is locked up in jail, the person has lost elements of negative liberty. By contrast, positive freedom is not simply the absence of interference. Rather, it is a positive state in which one's desires are fulfilled or in which one realizes one's potential. Prison not only involves a loss of negative liberty—one no longer has, for example, freedom of movement—but also, in many cases, involves a diminution of positive liberty.

Prisons separate people from the outside world, force them into close proximity, and control much of their day-to-day existence. Irving Goffman has coined the term "total institutions" to describe such environments[191] where there is a social division between the world of the keepers and the world of the kept (prisoners). The keepers tend to regard the environment as theirs, while the kept are subject to it.

Goffman suggests that total institutions tend to create clients who permit themselves to be managed. A dependent frame of mind may be induced in a person by subjecting the person to "a series of abasements, degradations, humiliations and profanities of self."[192] The inmate is stripped of his preprison identity by having to give up his clothes and possessions, having to be deferential to the keepers, and having his privacy invaded in all sorts of ways. Goffman adds that for most imprisoned persons, mortification and curtailment of the self is very likely to involve acute psychological stress.[193]

A common feature of the total institution is a system of control that involves a set of "house rules" and that permits keepers to dispense minor privileges and relatively severe punishments. For the inmates, these privileges and punishments force them to play a small-child role with which they must psychologically cope. If a prisoner develops the kind of dependent personality described by Goffman, then he or she may no longer have the emotional resources and the will to develop his or her potential. If so, then there has been a loss of positive freedom, and this loss of positive freedom has resulted from a combination of the loss of negative liberty and the existence of a controlled environment.

Although prison restricts and undermines negative and positive freedoms—and bearing in mind that these freedoms are both intrinsically good, and good as the means to other human goods—none of these freedoms is an *absolute* good. Accordingly, there are times when freedom comes into conflict with other values and is justifiably overridden. More specifically, the freedom of an individual needs to be restricted under certain conditions, notably when the individual seeks to harm others, for example, by murdering or assaulting them, or by stealing from or defrauding them.

So it is obvious that even though imprisonment infringes the freedom of those imprisoned, it is nevertheless necessary in relation to *some* offenders and offenses. Our concern in this book is with the corrupt, rather than with criminals or wrongdoers more generally. We take it that imprisonment ought to be available only for serious criminal offenses. Accordingly, the issue reduces itself to whether and under what conditions prison is an appropriate form of punishment for those forms of corruption that are also serious criminal offenses.

There is some evidence that prisons are themselves conducive to certain forms of corruption. If so, then this situation would be a consideration against the imprisonment of the corrupt, at least from the perspective of deterrence and rehabilitation. Needless to say, it would not be a decisive consideration. Close and Meier provide the following scenario.[194]

CASE STUDY 10.1   Officer Bob

A prison officer, the popular and well-thought-of "Officer Bob," is within weeks of retirement, at the end of a long and well-considered career as a custodial officer in the state's prison service. Another custodial officer, new to the service, has remarked that on occasion, Bob appears to blank out and that his manner with inmates is sometimes too familiar for this observer's tastes. Bob's workmates defend him, citing the recent death of Bob's wife, his imminent retirement, and other considerations attracting compassion. The new officer is informed, "He is still the best officer on the shift," and, fearful of attracting workmate resentment, he says nothing further against Bob.

Later, the new officer is on duty in Prison Block G at 10:00 P.M., the time when prisoners are returned to their cells and locked in for the night. He is checking the utility closet in G block, ensuring that the block's cleaning supplies have been put away, when he glances through the window.

There is a clear view through the window of the utility closet to H Block, which is opposite—its layout is a mirror image of G block—and the new officer observes Officer Bob standing in the H Block utility closet in close proximity to a prisoner. Brown, the H Block prisoner, bears the reputation of being a homosexual and an inmate who engages in drug-dealing within the prison. Bob is observed to reach into his pocket and withdraw a small brown-paper package, which he gives to the inmate. Both men are smiling, and Brown accepts the package and in return embraces Bob and kisses him full on the mouth before departing.

As he stands in indecision at the window of the utility closet, the new officer is astonished to see Officer Bob and the prisoner Brown reenter the H Block utility closet at a time that is well past lockdown. They produce drug apparatus, and both appear to engage in inhaling a white substance from a vial. They then extinguish the lights in the closet and sink to the floor, below the level of sight from G Block. Shocked, the new officer backs out of the G Block utility closet, to unexpectedly confront his supervisor, Lieutenant Davis, who, remarking his shocked expression, inquires if anything is amiss.

The new officer, aware that Bob is seriously, perhaps even criminally, compromised by his actions, nevertheless hesitates. Had his eyes deceived him? If he repeated what he saw to a person in authority, would he be believed? What action should he next take?

McCarthy suggests that prison staff may engage in trafficking with inmates, that is to say, carrying contraband in or out of prison on an inmate's behalf, for a range of reasons.[195] These reasons may include prison officers' supplementing their coercive capacity to maintain a condition of calm within the institution through entering into exchange relationships with inmates. According to Sykes,[196]

> The custodians [guards] are under strong pressure to compromise with their captives for it is a paradox that they can insure their dominance only by allowing it to be corrupted. Only by tolerating violations of minor rules and regulations can the guard secure compliance in the major areas of the custodial regime.

McCarthy writes the following:[197]

> Corruption through friendship evolves from the close contact that prisoners and guards share in their daily interaction. In many cases, they get to know each other as individuals, and friendships may develop. These friendships may, in turn, affect how staff members use their authority. Corruption through reciprocity occurs as an indirect consequence of the exchange relations that develop between inmates and staff: "You do something for me, I'll do something for you."

That something may well be a financial reward or a prison officer's sexual gratification by an inmate.

Notwithstanding the possible corrupting impact of a prison environment, it would still not follow that prison isn't a just and reasonable form of punishment for *some* criminals who engage in corrupt actions. Certainly, from the perspective of retributivism, an argument can be made for imprisonment that is not defeated by the fact—if it is a fact—of pervasive corruption in certain prisons; perhaps the corrupt deserve to live in a corrupt environment. Moreover, consequentialists can make the point that while they are imprisoned, the corrupt cannot defraud, bribe, and otherwise harm the innocent individuals and the wider society. On the other hand, it is very difficult to see prison as an ideal environment for the rehabilitation of the corrupt. Corruption is a defect of character, and moral character-building does not seem to be a particular feature of prison life, at least as we have described it.

Naturally, there are many differences among prisons. If a prison has a relatively uncorrupt environment, has a regime of discipline, and provides an array of educational and vocational options, then a prisoner may well benefit from being imprisoned; the goal of rehabilitation may well be furthered. We have simply sought to draw attention to some of the potential problems associated with imprisonment as a form of punishment for the corrupt.

One way forward at this point might be to consider the empirical evidence in relation to imprisonment of white-collar offenders. If imprisonment deters or otherwise influences white-collar offenders not to reoffend, then that would be a powerful argument in its favor. On the other hand, if prison could be shown to have a backfire effect—to increase the probability of offenders' reoffending—then obviously that would be a powerful argument against it.

Wiesburd and Waring have undertaken some empirical work in relation to white-collar offenders.[198] They conclude that "These results suggest that prison does not influence the likelihood of rearrest for those convicted of white collar crimes."[199] They go on: "Overall, these findings reinforce the conclusion that there is no specific deterrent or backfire effect from imprisonment for these [white-collar] offenders."[200]

We are not in a position to confirm or disconfirm these empirical claims, let alone broader claims in relation to the deterrent effects of imprisonment on the criminally corrupt as a general category. However, if true, this evidence suggests that neither the strong advocates nor the strong opponents of prison as a deterrent for the criminally corrupt have got it right. Apparently, prison does not deter, but neither does it reinforce corrupt behavior. Accordingly, the arguments for and against imprisonment might need to proceed on the basis of considerations other than deterrence and its opposite, reinforcement of criminal and corrupt character traits. More generally, this evidence suggests that nonpunitive measures, such as commitment to social norms, participation in organizational cultures that are hostile to corruption, exposure to negative attitudes of significant others to corrupt and criminal behavior, opportunities for self-advancement by lawful, noncorrupt pathways, and the like might be more powerful inhibitors of criminality and corruption than the threat of punitive measures such as imprisonment.

CONCLUSION

In this chapter, we have discussed a variety of aspects of the relation between corruption and punishment, including various normative theories of punishment, for example, retributive and deterrence theories. We conclude that a suitably adjusted restorative justice model is the most appropriate overall theory. However, we stress that, by our lights, such a model is pluralist in character; it contains retributivist, deterrent, and purely restorative elements. We have also considered some specific methods of punishment, notably imprisonment. We conclude that there is much empirical work to be done to determine what specific forms of punishment should be imposed for specific categories of offense and offender. However, we have argued that prisons constitute an environment that is itself conducive to corruption in a variety of ways. Accordingly, its extensive use in relation to white-collar crimes, in particular, is correspondingly difficult to justify.

It is fitting that this chapter on corruption and punishment is the concluding one in this book, because punishment—and hopefully reintegration into the community—are the logical end points of corruption, if not in fact, then at least in theory.

In this book, we have offered a conceptual analysis of corruption and a variety of taxonomies of corruption, for example, political and economic corruption. We have addressed the question, What is corruption? We have identified a number of general conditions—and many specific ones, as well—that are conducive to corruption, for example, power imbalances, lack of transparency, and conflicts of interest. Moreover, we have done so in relation to a variety of different contexts, for example, Colombia in the days of Pablo Escobar, the Enron corporation, the U.S. administration at the time of Watergate, and so on. We have addressed the question, What are the causes of corruption? In light of our view that corruption is at bottom a moral issue and not merely a legal one, we have looked at the arguments for and against corruption, including rationalizations for corruption. We have addressed the question, What is wrong with corruption? In the second part of the book our focus shifted from corruption to combating corruption, to anti-corruption.

If corruption is a moral issue, then anti-corruption measures must start with moral responsibility. We addressed the question, Who is morally responsible for corruption? and—perhaps more important—Who is responsible for combating corruption? Here we placed the notion of *collective* moral responsibility center stage. If anti-corruption measures are in part about moral attitudes, they are also in large part about institutional design. So we addressed the question, What sorts of anti-corruption systems ought to be instituted? We concluded in favor of what we termed *holistic anti-corruption systems*. Finally, we turned to the question of the corrupt, or those suspected of engaging in corruption. We addressed two very central questions: What are the rights of suspects? What forms of punishment ought to be imposed on those guilty of corruption? As befits a book written in the philosophical tradition of Aristotle, Locke, Hume, Kant, and John Stuart Mill—the tradition of moral and political thought that underpins contemporary liberal democracies—we concluded, in effect, that the moral rights of suspects—taken together with the moral rights of victims—ought to constitute the core of our system of justice, but also that it is better to try to reintegrate the corrupt back into society than to cast them out.

Notes

1. See Zoe Pearson "An International Human Rights Approach to Corruption" in Peter Larmour and Nick Wolanin (Eds.) *Corruption and Anti-Corruption* (Canberra: Asia-Pacific Press, 2001).

2. This distinction between institutional corruption and personal corruption is not the same distinction as that sometimes made between institutional and individual corruption. See, for example, Dennis F. Thompson *Ethics in Congress: From Individual to Institutional Corruption* (Washington, D.C.: Brookings Institute, 1995) pp.30–31.

3. This kind of definition has ancient origins. See Barry Hindess for a recent discussion in his "Good Government and Corruption" in Larmour and Wolanin (Eds.) *Corruption and Anti-Corruption* op.cit.

4. Thompson op.cit. (p.31) argues that institutional corruption—at least in the case of political corruption—involves a political gain (as opposed to a private gain), an impropriety in the provision of a service (as opposed to an undeserved service) and a link between the gain and the service that is an institutional tendency. We do not dispute that when these three conditions obtain, there is institutional corruption. However, by our lights, the existence of all three of these conditions is not necessary for institutional corruption. Contra Thompson, we suggest that there can be a single, one-off corruption of an institutional process. Moreover, we do not accept that in the case of institutional corruption the gain for which a service is provided (the motive) is necessarily a political, as opposed to a private, gain. The institutional process can be undermined (corrupted) in cases in which there is a tendency for the service to be provided for private gain; so why not regard these as cases of institutional corruption? This view of the matter

comports with definitions of corruption, such as ours, that do not require there to be any particular motive in order for an institutional process to be corrupted. Thus, in our definition of corruption, neither of these motives (private gain or political gain) is a necessary condition for institutional corruption.

5. For one of the most influential statements of the abuse of public office for private gain definitions, see Joseph Nye "Corruption and Political Development: A Cost-benefit Analysis" *American Political Science Review* vol.61 no.2 1967 pp.417–427. See also A. J. Heidenheimer and M. Johnston (Eds.) *Political Corruption* (N.J.: Transactions Publishers, 2002) Part 1.

6. See Susan Rose-Ackerman *Corruption and Government* (Cambridge: Cambridge University Press, 1999) for this kind of view. See Hindess op.cit. for a critique.

7. Thompson op.cit. offers a sophisticated account of political corruption, and seems at some points to be suggesting that all corruption is political corruption, or at least corruption of public offices. See Thompson op.cit. p.29. This seems to us to be an unduly restrictive notion of corruption.

8. Spheres of activity are defined in terms of the type of activity, including the ends that are internal to that activity—and therefore in part definitive of it. See Seumas Miller *Social Action: A Teleological Account* (Cambridge: Cambridge University Press, 2001) Chapter 5.

9. See Seumas Miller "Corruption and Anti-Corruption in Policing" *Professional Ethics* vol.6 nos.3&4 1998 pp.83–106, and Seumas Miller and John Blackler *Ethical Issues in Policing: Contemporary Problems and Perspectives* (Aldershot: Ashgate, 2004) Chapter 5.

10. See Miller *Social Action* op.cit. Chapters 3 and 4.

11. Nancy Wilson Ross *Hinduism, Buddhism, Zen* (London: Faber and Faber, 1968) p.80.

12. Such a person has a disposition to perform corrupt actions but does so only when the opportunity arises; he or she is not prepared to create or seek out such opportunities. Note that there is a difference between the corruptors and the corrupted in that the latter do not necessarily intend or foresee—and nor ought they—the corrupting effect the actions in question are having on themselves.

13. The contrary strand is often associated with Hobbes. See Thomas Hobbes *Leviathan* (any edition).

14. Note the point we made before, namely that institutional corruption, insofar as it involves—as it must—the corruption of institutional role occupants, then it brings with it personal corruption, i.e., the corruption of moral character.

15. See Pasuk Phongpaichit and Sungsidh Piriyarangsan *Corruption and Democracy in Thailand* (Chiang Mai: Silkworm Books, 1994 (1996 Edition)) Chapter 3.

16. See Simon Strong *Whitewash: Pablo Escobar and the Cocaine Wars* (London: Pan Books, 1996).

17. John T. Noonan *Bribes* (New York: Macmillan, 1984) p.xi.

18. See Jeremy Pope (Ed.) *National Integrity Systems: The TI Source Book* (Berlin: Transparency International, 1997); Robert Klitgaard *Controlling Corruption* (Los Angeles: University of California Press, 1988).

19. See Seumas Miller *Social Action: A Teleological Account* (Cambridge: Cambridge University Press, 2001) Chapter 4.

20. See Michael Boylan *Basic Ethics* (Upper Saddle River, New Jersey: Prentice Hall, 1999).

21. See Mark Bowden *Killing Pablo* (London: Atlantic Books, 2001).

22. Ibid. p.234.

23. Ibid. p.361.

24. Ibid. p.29.

25. Ibid. p.127.

26. Ibid. p.91.

27. According to Mark Bowden, there is strong evidence from a variety of sources to link Search Bloc to Los Pepes; see Bowden op.cit. p.348.

28. Bowden op.cit. p.223.

29. See Jeremy Pope (Ed.) *National Integrity Systems: The TI Source Book* (Berlin: Transparency International, 1997); Robert Klitgaard *Controlling Corruption* (Los Angeles: University of California Press, 1988).

30. Trevor Sykes *The Bold Riders* (Sydney: Allen and Unwin, 1984) pp.1–2.

31. Peter C. Fusaro and Ross M. Miller *What Went Wrong at Enron* (Hoboken, N.J.: John Wiley and Sons, 2002) p.46.

32. Peter Behr and April Witt "Visionary's Dream Led to Risky Business" *Washington Post*, July 28, 2002, p.7.

33. Ibid.

34. Loren Fox *Enron: The Rise and Fall* (Hoboken, New Jersey: John Wiley and Sons, Inc., 2003) p.14.

35. Behr and Witt op.cit. p.8.

36. Fusaro and Miller op.cit. p.174.

37. Robert Jackall *Moral Mazes* (New York: Oxford University Press, 1998).

38. Athol Moffit *A Quarter to Midnight: The Australian Crisis—Organised Crime and the Decline of the Institutions of State* (Sydney: Angus and Robertson, 1985) p.210.

39. See, for example, Gavan McCormack *The Emptiness of Japanese Affluence* (Sydney: Allen and Unwin, 1996) p.32f.

40. Phongpaichit op.cit. p.110.

41. United States General Accounting Office 2002 "Identity Fraud: Prevalence and Links to Illegal Alien Activities." Online at http://www.consumer.gov/idtheft/reports/gao-d02830t.pdf. Accessed February 8, 2003.

42. Peter Grabosky, Russell Smith, and Gillian Dempsey *Electronic Theft: Unlawful Acquisition in Cyberspace* (Cambridge: Cambridge University Press, 2001) p.9.

43. Centre for Applied Philosophy and Public Ethics 2001 *eCorruption: eCrime Vulnerabilities in the NSW Public Sector*. Summary of a research project undertaken by CAPPE available on the New South Wales Independent Commission Against Corruption website: http://www.icac.nsw.gov.au/pub/public/pub2_48cp.cfm. Accessed February 8, 2003.

44. By "instrumentally desirable" we mean the kind of practical prudence attributable to an instrumentally rational agent intending to act corruptly in an environment in which corruption is either illegal or, if not illegal, at least generally considered unethical. In such an environment, it would be a desirable requirement of instrumental rational agency that the agent intending to engage in corrupt activity should take the required measures to keep the agency of his or her corrupt actions invisible or concealed, for not to do so could prove self-defeating and therefore instrumentally irrational.

45. The *self-regarding gain* need not be merely a *self-directed* gain accruing to the corrupt agent himself or herself. Thus the perceived gain from the corrupt activities of some of Nixon's associates in the Watergate affair was self-regarding, in the sense that it benefited the Republican Party of which they were members, but was not self-directed in the sense that it benefited or was intended to benefit those associates personally.

46. Naturally, invisibility would still enable a person to perpetrate acts of wrongdoing and not be caught and punished by the victim.

47. The "standard view" is provided by Michael Davies in his *Encyclopedia of Applied Ethics* (San Diego: Academic Press, 1998, Volume 1, A–D) p.590.

48. Davies ibid.

49. Dave Lindorff "Chief Fudge-the-Books Officer" *Salon.com,* February 20, 2002, p.2.

50. Michael Drummond "Class Action Warrior" *Salon.com*, January 28, 2002, p.6.

51. Alan Gewirth "Professional Ethics: The Separatist Thesis" *Ethics* 96: pp.282–300, 1986, p.295.

52. For an extensive and detailed discussion of this issue, see Edward Spence "The Ethics of Clinical Trials: To Inform or Not Inform? That Is the Question" *Professional Ethics: A Multidisciplinary Journal,* vol. 6, nos. 3 and 4, Fall/Winter 1998.

53. The content of this section appeared in an earlier form in Spence "Ethics of Clinical Trials" op.cit.

54. The case has been compiled using the following online sources: Ch. 5, "The Keating Five" at http://www.azcentral.com/specials/special39/articles/1003mccainbooks.html, and "Keating Five Scandal" at http://www.polisci.ccsu.edu/trieb/curr-tim.htm. All sources accessed on August 8, 2003.

55. Dennis F. Thompson *Ethics in Congress: From Individual to Institutional Corruption* (Washington, D.C.: Brookings Institute, 1995) p.37f.

56. Ibid. pp.42–43.

57. Davies "Conflict of Interest" op.cit. p.593.

58. "Teli" is the plural of "telos," which is the ancient Greek word for point or purpose.

59. For a detailed account of this teleological account of social institutions, see Seumas Miller *Social Action: A Teleological Account* (Cambridge: Cambridge University Press, 2001) Chapter 6.

60. This case was compiled using the following online sources: "The Scandal That Brought Down Richard Nixon," at http://www.watergate.info; "Watergate the

25th Anniversary" at http://www.chron.com/content/interactive/special/watergate/watergate1.html; "Watergate" at http://www.washingtonpost.com/wp-srv/national/longterm/watergate/front.htm. All sources accessed on August 8, 2003.

61. Susan Rose-Ackerman *Corruption and Government* (Cambridge: Cambridge University Press, 1999) p.2.

62. Francis Fukuyama *Trust: The Social Virtues and the Creation of Prosperity* (London: Penguins Books, 1996).

63. See Seymour M. Lipset and Gabriel S. Lenz, in *Culture Matters*, pp.119–120.

64. Ibid. pp.119–120.

65. Mark Bowden *Killing Pablo*, p.223. Corruption as such consists in harmful consequences to institutions. However, such corruption can have additional harmful consequences, e.g., to personal relations. We do not always explicitly distinguish between the harm that is constitutive of corruption and the harm that is not.

66. Terry Greene Sterling, "Arthur Andersen and the Baptists" (*Salon.Com*, http://www.salon.com/tech/feature/2002/02/07/arthur_andersen/index.html, p.2).

67. Ibid.

68. Bowden op.cit. p.350.

69. Bowden op.cit. p.38.

70. Mlada Bukovansky "Corruption Is Bad: Normative Dimensions of the Anti-corruption Movement" Working Paper 2002/5 (Canberra: Department of International Relations, RSSS, ANU, 2002) p.18.

71. Rose-Ackerman op.cit. p.38.

72. Ibid. p.88.

73. The discussion in this section relies heavily on Seumas Miller "Corruption and Anti-Corruption in the Profession of Policing" *Professional Ethics* vol.6 nos. 3 and 4 1998 pp.83–107.

74. Howard Cohen "Overstepping Police Authority" *Criminal Justice Ethics* Summer/Fall 1987 p.57.

75. See Edwin Delattre *Character and Cops* (2nd ed.) (Washington, D.C.: AEI Press, 1994) Chapter 11 for a discussion of such extraordinary situations, and the need—as he sees it—for consultation with senior experienced police officers.

76. See Justice James Wood *Final Report: Royal Commission into Corruption in the New South Wales Police Service* (Sydney: NSW Government, 1998).

77. See Seumas Miller "On Conventions" *Australasian Journal of Philosophy* vol.70 no.2 1992 pp.435–445.

78. See Seumas Miller *Social Action: A Teleological Account* (Cambridge: Cambridge University Press, 2001) Chapters 4 (on social norms) and 6 (on social institutions, including social groups).

79. An earlier version of much of the rest of this section appeared in Seumas Miller "Social Norms, Corruption and Trans-cultural Interaction" *Theoria* vol.92 1998 pp.57–77.

80. Since the Lockheed scandal there have been legislative changes in many countries, including the United States and Australia, making bribing foreign officials an offense. This outcome has flowed from an OECD convention strongly supported by Transparency International, an influential NGO committed to combating corruption.

81. References for this case study are: "Adler Faces Possible Jail Term" *Sydney Morning Herald* December 4, 2002; "HIH Regulator Deceived" *The Australian* January 24, 2003; "HIH Cover-up Claimed" *The Australian* January 17, 2003; "APRA Admits HIH Failings" *The Australian* January 17, 2003; A. Thirsk "Adler Back on the Stand" *ABC Radio National* October 12, 2002; R. Mealey "HIH Culture of Excess" *ABC Radio National* August 10, 2002; F. Varess "The Buck Will Stop at the Board? An Examination of Directors' (and Other) Duties in the Light of the HIH Collapse" *Commercial Law Quarterly* March–May 2002, pp.12–31.

82. James B. Stewart *Den of Thieves* (New York: Simon and Schuster, 1992) p.20.

83. Trevor Sykes *The Bold Riders* (Sydney: Allen and Unwin, 1994) pp.1–2.

84. Much of the content of this section and the final section of this chapter is taken from an earlier version published in Seumas Miller "Corporate Crime, the Excesses of the '80s and Collective Responsibility" *Australian Journal of Corporate Law* vol.5 no.2 1995 pp.39–51.

85. Roman Tomasic and Stephen Bottomley *Directing the Top 500* (Sydney: Allen and Unwin, 1993) p.6.

86. Including Stewart op.cit. and Sykes op.cit.

87. Ian Ayres and John Braithwaite *Responsive Regulation* (Oxford: Oxford University Press, 1992).

88. John Green " 'Fuzzy Law': A Better Way to Stop 'Snouts in the Trough' " *Company and Securities Law Journal* June 1991.

89. Brent Fisse and John Braithwaite *Corporations, Crime and Accountability* (Cambridge: Cambridge University Press, 1994).

90. Tomasic and Bottomley op.cit. p.174.

91. Paul Finn "The Liability of Third Parties for Knowing Receipt or Assistance" in Donovan Waters (Ed.) *Equities, Fiduciaries and Trusts* (Toronto: Carswell, 1993).

92. Much of the content of this section was drawn from earlier versions published in Seumas Miller "Collective Responsibility" *Public Affairs Quarterly* vol.15 no.1 2001 pp.65–82 and *Social Action: A Teleological Account* (Cambridge University Press, 2001) Chapter 8.

93. See Donald Davidson "Freedom to Act" in Ted Honderich (Ed.) *Essays on Freedom of Action* (London: Routledge and Kegan Paul, 1973) and John R. Searle *Intentionality* (Cambridge University Press, 1983) Chapter 3.

94. See John Martin Fischer (Ed.) *Moral Responsibility* (London: Cornell University Press, 1986) p.14f. For attempts to analyze free action, and related notions of autonomy, by recourse to higher order attitudes, see Harry G. Frankfurt "Three Concepts of Free Action" in Fischer and Gerald Dworkin (Ed.) *The Theory and Practice of Autonomy* (Cambridge University Press, 1988). For accounts of one's responsibility for one's character see Ferdinand Schoeman (Ed.) *Responsibility, Character and the Emotions* (Cambridge University Press, 1987).

95. A further distinction in this area is that made between retrospective and prospective responsibility. Retrospective responsibility is responsibility for actions that have already been performed, as opposed to responsibility for future actions (prospective responsibility).

96. Obviously moral responsibility is sometimes retrospective and sometimes prospective.

97. See Miller *Social Action* op.cit. Chapter 2.

98. Ibid. Chapter 5.

99. This mode of analysis is also available to handle examples in which an institutional entity has a representative who makes an individual decision, but it is an individual decision that has the joint backing of the members of the institutional entity, e.g., an industrial union's representative in relation to wage negotiations with a company. It can also handle examples such as the firing squad in which only one real bullet is used, and it is not known which member is firing the real bullet and which merely blanks. The soldier with the real bullet is (albeit unknown to him) *individually* responsible for shooting the person dead. However, the members of the firing squad are *jointly* responsible for its being the case that the person has been shot dead.

100. Miller op.cit. Chapter 5.

101. Ibid.

102. Peter French *Collective and Corporate Responsibility* (New York: Columbia University Press, 1984).

103. See for example Dennis F. Thompson "The Moral Responsibility of Many Hands" in his *Political Ethics and Public Office* (Cambridge, Mass.: Harvard University Press, 1987).

104. *Bold Riders* op.cit. p.8.

105. *McCormick vs. United States* 1991 (Supreme Court), and *Evans vs. United States* 1992 (Supreme Court).

106. *McNally vs. United States* 1987 (Supreme Court).

107. See Peter Behr and April Witt (*Washington Post Staff Writers*) "Visionary's Dream Led to Risky Business" *Washington Post,* July 28, 2002.

108. Our account of the LJM SPEs refers primarily to the account given of those deals in Peter C. Fusaro and Ross M. Miller *What Went Wrong with Enron* (Hoboken, N.J.: John Wiley and Sons, 2002) pp.132–135.

109. Australian Public Service Commission APS Values http://www.apsc.gov.au/values/index.html. Accessed January 4, 2003.

110. United States Office of Government Ethics http://www.usoge.gov/pages/laws_regs_fedreg_stats/lrfs_files/exeorders/eo12731.html. Accessed January 4, 2003.

111. Motorola website (http://www.motorola.com/code/code.html). Accessed January 3, 2003.

112. This framework is made up of a variety of statutes (Ethics in Government Act 1978, Ethics Reform Act 1989); Executive Orders made by the president (Numbers 10939, 1961; 11222, 1964; 12764, 1989; 12731, 1990; 12834, 1993); and

instructions from the United States Office of Government Ethics. The description of this system, as well as other statutory provisions mentioned in this chapter, are drawn from Robert North Roberts *Ethics in US Government: An Encyclopedia of Investigations, Scandals, Reforms and Legislation* (Westport, Conn.: Greenwood Press, 2001).

113. Executive Order 11222, May 8, 1965.

114. Frank Anechiarico and James B. Jacobs *The Pursuit of Absolute Integrity: How Corruption Control Makes Government Ineffective* (Chicago: University of Chicago Press, 1996).

115. A prominent campaigner for a broader view of corporate governance is John Elkington, whose 1997 book *Cannibals With Forks: The Triple Bottom Line of 21st Century Business* (Oxford: Capstone) is credited with starting this debate.

116. Australian Stock Exchange. Listing Rules, Appendix 4E. 2002. http://www.asx.com.au/about/13/ListingRules_AA3.shtm. Accessed July 3, 2002.

117. The procedure brought down to its very basic form is five steps:
    1. establishing the context, including identifying stakeholder interests and determining risk criteria;
    2. identifying all possible risks;
    3. analyzing risks on a cross-matrix of likelihood and consequence;
    4. evaluating and prioritizing risks; and
    5. treating the risks.
    This process is reiterative and should be undertaken with consultation and communicating at each stage and monitoring at each stage. This is drawn from the Standards Association of Australia. "1999 Australian/New Zealand Standard: Risk Management" (AS/NZS 4360:1999) Standards Association of Australia, Strathfield, NSW.

118. This policy deals with both fraud and corruption, but curiously defines corruption as a subset of fraud, which, arguably, has the effect of emphasizing the financial management aspects of fraud at the expense of the criminal dimension of corruption.

119. Australian National Audit Office. "2000 Survey of Fraud Control Arrangements in APS Agencies: Report No. 47" 1999–2000 (online) June 20, 2001. http://www.anao.gov.au/WebSite.nsf/Publications/4A256AE90015F69B4A25691400161DFB Accessed August 1, 2002.

120. In a federal system, there will, of course, be an intervening level of government.

121. R. A. W. Rhodes "Different Roads to Unfamiliar Places: UK Experience in Comparative Perspective" *Australian Journal of Public Administration* 57: 19–31, 1998.

122. M. P. Miceli and J. P. Near 1985 "Organizational Dissidence: The Case of Whistleblowing" *Journal of Business Ethics* 4 pp.1–16.

123. M. Duffy "By the Sign of the Crooked E" *Time* January 19, 2002.

124. D. Ackman "Sherron Watkins Had Whistle, But Blew It" *Forbes* February 14, 2002.

125. G. Vinten *Whistleblowing: Subversion or Corporate Citizenship?* (New York: St. Martin's Press, 1994) p.11.

126. A similar method of analysis came up with the following definition of whistle-blowing:

An act of whistleblowing occurs when:

1. an individual performs an action or series of actions intended to make information public;
2. the information is made as a matter of public record;
3. the information is about possible or actual, non-trivial wrongdoing in an organization;
4. the individual who performs the action is a member of the organization.

F. Elliston, J. Keenan, P. Lockhart, and van Schaick *Whistleblowing Research: Methodological and Moral Issues* (New York: Praeger, 1985) p.15.

127. T. D. Miethe and J. Rothschild "Whistleblowing and the Control of Organizational Misconduct" *Sociological Inquiry* 64 (3) 1994, pp.322–347.

128. J. Rothschild and T. D. Miethe "Whistle-Blower Disclosures and Management Retaliation." *Work and Occupations* 26 (1) 1999 pp.107–128.

129. R. McLeod *Blowing the Official Whistle.* Address by Ron McLeod AM, Commonwealth Ombudsman to Transparency International Whistleblowing Symposium, Sydney, August 2002.

130. T. D. Miethe and J. Rothschild "Disclosing Misconduct in Work Organizations: An Empirical Analysis of the Situational Factors That Foster Whistleblowing" *Research in the Sociology of Work* 8 1999 pp.211–227.

131. U.S. Merit Systems Protection Board *Whistleblowing and the Federal Employee* (Washington, D.C.: U.S. Merit Systems Protection Board, 1981).

132. M. P. Miceli and J. P. Near "Individual and Situational Correlates of Whistleblowing" *Personnel Psychology* 41 1988 pp.267–282.

133. Miethe and Rothschild 1994 p.335.

134. M. P. Miceli and J. P. Near *Blowing the Whistle: The Organizational and Legal Implications for Companies and Employees* (New York: Lexington, 1992) p.247.

135. M. Glazer and P. Glazer *The Whistleblowers: Exposing Corruption in Government and Industry* (New York: Basic Books, 1989).

136. M. E. Velasquez *Business Ethics: Concepts and Cases* (Englewood Cliffs, N.J.: Prentice-Hall, 1988) p.381.

137. In large organizations that receive vast numbers of complaints, such as police services, there might need to be a two-tiered structure for handling complaints. At the first tier, an adjudication might need to be made as to whether a complaint was worthy of investigation. Care would need to be taken, lest this gatekeeping role be abused, and complaints that should be investigated are not.

138. Australia. Parliament. Finance and Public Administration Legislation Committee *Public Interest Disclosure Bill 2001* (Canberra, 2002).

139. Australian Public Service Commission *State of the Service 2001–2002.* (Canberra, 2002) p.38.

140. L. Cockcroft *Corruption and Human Rights: A Crucial Link* Transparency International Working Paper, Transparency International, London and Berlin. 1998. Available online at http://www.transparency.org/working_papers/cockcroft/cockcroft.html. Accessed November 25, 2002.

141. For a detailed analysis and demonstration of the justification for the rights to freedom and well-being on the basis of the argument for the Principle of Generic Consistency, see Alan Gewirth's *Reason and Morality* (Chicago: University of Chicago Press, 1978), and Deryck Beyleveld *The Dialectical Necessity of Morality: An Analysis and Defense of Alan Gewirth's Argument to the Principle of Generic Consistency* (Chicago: University of Chicago Press, 1991).

142. Anthony Lewis "And Cauldron Bubble" *New York Times*, December 22, 1998, p.31.

143. J. Paterson "Masters of Shamelessness" *The Age*, April 20, 2002. Available online at http://www.theage.com.au/articles/2002/04/19/1019020707243.html. Accessed December 1, 2002.

144. *Bram vs. United States* 168 U.S. 532 (1897); *Wan vs. United States* 266 U.S. 1 (1924); *Miranda vs. Arizona* 384 U.S. 436 (1966); *Doyle vs. Ohio* 426 U.S. 610 (1976).

145. New South Wales Law Reform Commission *Report 95: The Right to Silence*. New South Wales Law Reform Commission, Sydney, 2000.

146. *Miranda vs. Arizona* 384 U.S. 436 (1966).

147. New South Wales Law Reform Commission *Report 95: The Right to Silence*. New South Wales Law Reform Commission, Sydney, 2000, p.38.

148. D. Morgan and G. Stephenson (Eds.) *Suspicion and Silence* (London: Blackstone Press, 1994); S. Aston *The Case for the Right to Silence* (2nd ed.) (Aldershot: Ashgate, 1998).

149. New South Wales Law Reform Commission 2000 *Report 95: The Right to Silence*. New South Wales Law Reform Commission, Sydney.

150. Galligan, D. J. *Due Process and Fair Procedure: A Study of Administrative Procedures* (Oxford: Clarendon Press, 1996).

151. *Illinois vs. Gates*, 462 U.S. 213 (1983).

152. F. Anechiarico and B. J. Jacobs *The Pursuit of Absolute Integrity: How Corruption Control Makes Government Ineffective* (Chicago: University of Chicago Press, 1996). The authors argue that VENDEX is essentially a government-controlled blacklist for contractors that discriminates against competent contractors, pp.126–132.

153. 1980 OECD Guidelines on the Protection of Privacy and Transborder Flows of Personal Data. Available online at http://www1.oecd.org/publications/e-book/9302011E.PDF. Accessed December 2, 2002.

154. Prentice-Hall Information Series (no date) *The Abscam Investigation of 1980*. Online at http://hcl.chass.ncsu.edu/garson/dye/docs/abscam.htm. Accessed December 2, 2002.

155. J. Kleinig *The Ethics of Policing* (New York: Cambridge University Press, 1996).

156. *Sherman vs. United States* 356 U.S. 369 (1958).

157. See Seumas Miller and John Blackler, *Ethical Issues in Policing: Contemporary Problems and Perspectives* (Aldershot: Ashgate, 2004) Chapter 4.

158. *Ridgeway vs. The Queen* (1995) 184 CLR 19.

159. W. J. Knapp, J. Monserrat, F. A. Sprizzo, and Thomas and C. Vance *The Knapp Commission Report on Police Corruption* (New York: George Bradziller, 1972).

160. Royal Commission into the New South Wales Police Service *Final Report* (Sydney: Royal Commission into the New South Wales Police Service, 1997).

161. G. Fitzgerald *Report of the Commission of Inquiry Pursuant to Orders in Council* (Brisbane: Goprint, 1989).

162. KPMG *Report to the New York City Commission to Combat Police Corruption: The New York City Police Department Random Integrity Testing Program* (New York: NYC Commission to Combat Police Corruption, 1996).

163. T. Prenzler and C. Ronken "Police Integrity Testing in Australia" *Criminal Justice* 1 (3) 2001 pp.319–342.

164. Sally S. Simpson *Corporate Crime, Law, and Social Control* (Cambridge: Cambridge University Press, 2002) pp.2–3.

165. But see Edwin Sutherland "White Collar Criminality" *American Sociological Review* 5 1940 pp.1–12.

166. See John Braithwaite "Challenging Just Deserts: Punishing White Collar Criminals" *Journal of Criminal Law and Criminology* 73 no.2 1982 pp.723–763.

167. Simpson op.cit. p.3.

168. Ibid. p.11.

169. Ibid. p.19.

170. Adam Graycar and Peter Grabosky *The Cambridge Handbook of Australian Criminology* (Cambridge: Cambridge University Press, 2002) p.49.

171. David Wiesburd and Elin Waring *White Collar Crime and Criminal Careers* (Cambridge: Cambridge University Press, 2001). See Chapters 3 and 4, especially.

172. Simpson op.cit. p.36.

173. Ibid. p.48.

174. For a useful introduction to theories of punishment, see C. L. Ten *Guilt and Punishment* (Oxford: Clarendon Press, 1987).

175. For a detailed account of much of the literature, see Simpson op.cit.

176. Ibid. p.47.

177. Ibid.

178. Jack Katz *Seductions of Crime* (New York: Basic Books, 1988).

179. B. F. Skinner *Beyond Freedom and Dignity* (London: Penguin, 1973).

180. K. Menninger, *The Crime of Punishment* (New York: Viking Press, 1967).

181. On this general issue, see Steve Curry "Future Developments in Ethics in Correction" *Report for the ACT Corrective Services* (Canberra, 2002) (unpublished).

182. A good deal of the content in this and the following section is drawn from Seumas Miller and John Blackler "Restorative Justice: Retribution, Confession and Shame" in Heather Strang and John Braithwaite (Eds.) *Restorative Justice: From Philosophy to Practice* (Aldershot: Ashgate, 2000) pp.77–93.

183. David Moore *A New Approach to Juvenile Justice: An Evaluation of Family Conferencing in Wagga Wagga* (Canberra: Report to the Criminology Research Council, 1995).

184. This is not a sui generis consequentialist principle, though consequentialists might think that they can derive it from their favored consequentialist principle in conjunction with certain contingent empirical facts.

185. John Braithwaite and Philip Pettit *Not Just Deserts: A Republican Theory of Criminal Justice* (Oxford: Clarendon Press, 1990).

186. John Braithwaite *Crime, Shame and Reintegration* (Melbourne: Oxford University Press, 1986).

187. M. Hepworth and B. S. Turner *Confession: Studies in Deviance and Religion* (London: Routledge and Kegan Paul, 1982).

188. G. W. F. Hegel *Philosophy of Right*, trans. T. Knox (Oxford University Press, 1942), and Reinhold Niebuhr "God's Justice and Mercy" in R. M. Brown (Ed.) *The Essential Reinhold Niebuhr* (New Haven: Yale University Press, 1986).

189. Niebuhr op.cit. p.29.

190. Ibid.

191. Irving Goffman *Asylums* (London: Penguin, 1961).

192. Ibid. p.14.

193. Ibid. p.48.

194. Daryl Close and Nicholas Meieir (Eds.) *Morality In Criminal Justice: An Introduction to Ethics* (Belmont, Calif.: Wadsworth, 1995) p.216. This is an edited and abridged version of the Close and Meieir scenario.

195. Bernard J. McCarthy "Patterns of Prison Corruption" *Corrections Today* December 1984.

196. Gary Sykes *The Society of Captives: A Study of Maximum Security Prison* (Princeton, NJ: Princeton University Press, 1958) p.58.

197. Bernard J. McCarthy "Keeping an Eye on the Keeper: Prison Corruption and Its Control" in Michael C. Braswell, Belinda R. McCarthy, and Bernard J. McCarthy (Eds.) *Justice, Crime and Ethics* (Cincinnati: Anderson, 1991) p.248.

198. Weisburd and Waring op.cit.

199. Ibid. p.103.

200. Ibid. p.109.

Index